THE 7 LOVELESS TRAITS

*Acquiring Knowledge, Understanding,
Clarity, and Breaking Free from Narcissism*

Leon R. Walker, Jr.

Empaths

Warm, reliable, present, attached, comforting, nurturing, virtuous, fabulous, gifted, talented, and blessed. You all embody traits that keep millions of people alive, well, and healthy. You are the branch and the olive. You saved my life. I was just hard-headed.

– Leon R. Walker, Jr.

Your grandmother and mother were probably empaths. I believe empaths of today were made, groomed, or even forced into their current role because of how the women before them were forced into an empath role by societal norms: men being called to war, chauvinistic men, or docile and subservient women. Then it became a trait that you all embodied. Soon after, it was your norm. Anything aside from that missing role of others, it felt very uncomfortable and unbelievable when others could not perform in that manner like you were able to.

Narcissists do not have that trait once they begin to suppress it early on in life, due to many circumstances, for it to never return. There are many paths, based on your childhood. Narcissism or the empath role are only two of many. People aren't aware of it, though, until their actions come to fruition. This is where and why you become confused when narcissists can't provide reciprocity and other healthy relationship mindsets and traits.

When you see women not being able to serve as an empath, chances are they were raised amongst mostly men, men that were dominant in the household, and the women didn't want to emulate their docile or abused mother or chose to disown their mother for various reasons. Those women developed a fear gene or trait to not be like their mom, yet more masculine like their dad. Empaths have to start becoming better managers of their loving and caring emotions and time spent with a narcissist. Equalizing, and then removing your gift. Not everyone deserves your gift. You master everything else, but over-extend yourself to *underwhelming* people. Don't ever doubt yourself while you're dealing with, being married to, or dating a Leon. Once you do, you lose! Narcissists specialize in creating doubt, because they are always doubting themselves, and no one knows. Doubt is a very hard pill to swallow for high-functioning narcissists. They enjoy fairytales— most people call them lies, but not a narcissist—fairytales are real to them. This is why they avoid being confronted by a lie they were caught in. As I created and then accepted the person who I built after my childhood, I overdid it. My mind had become conditioned to do wrong, to use, hurt, and mislead. Regardless of how aligned you are and how much you want to give to a Leon, make sure to always take precautionary measures. Even if you haven't been cautioned before, the time is now. Your gift of giving has to be reserved for someone that is in a receiving mindset. Someone of purity, someone that's appreciative of your gifts of not only giving but healing. Narcissists don't think they need any kind of healing. They see themselves as someone who can and is very capable of making you better, healing you, but only better in a toxic form to fit their needs, desires, greed, and lust. If you continue to waste your gift, it will not feel good to you anymore, because they have slowly removed your tonic trait!

Empaths can take care of many people,
but many people can't take care of one Empath.

Why We Need to Discuss the 7 Loveless Traits

Experts say that up to five percent of the population has NPD (Narcissistic Personality Disorder). That astonishing number alone means that *millions* of people are and have suffered from people like myself. Just imagine, from that five percent, how many people feel like or don't realize that they are incapable of love? From that, the number of people affected becomes insurmountable, and this is why we need to discuss how I and others lived and are currently living. I chose seven, based on how I acted and what I knew of myself.

These traits go unnoticed for many years, but when they are noticed, men and women remain suspended in disorientation, irregular mindsets, and declining health—some just barely holding on, being confused, lost, damaged, torn, and scorned—*except* Leons! It is extremely imperative and is now my duty to open up and be honest about these low-level traits—the ones that are so dangerous, unhealthy, hurtful, misleading, and are so ingrained in men and women, today. Therefore, knowledge is not only power, but enlightening and liberating. I'll begin with what I loved the most: money, sex, and favors.

Narcissists Love Three Things

If I made more money than she did, I had already looked at her as if she was beneath me. That was a major weakness and insecurity—the root of all evil!

Money: When you make more than your narcissistic partner, they always say, "We make this much." They have to have lots of money or access to it, and will run through it extremely fast. It's always about impressing other people. Impressing you starts in the beginning, but will slowly go away as they become used to you. Six figures and up will always be their goal. Anything less, and they'll act like they have more but you'll provide the offset. You'll keep them dressed nicely, in nice cars, and they'll use your credit, credentials, net worth, and network. If they don't have money now, they'll consistently talk about what they used to have, in an effort to make you think that they still have the ability to reach that amount once again. This braggadocios mindset remains heavy in the minds of ex-cons, drug dealers, and athletes. It's okay for them to claim your money, but you can't claim their money!

*Gem: If you ever want to know how they really feel about finances when they make more than you, claim their money as "ours" and just sit back and watch how they act and react.

Sex: They master all things sexual. We are extremely risky and will consistently put your life and health in some kind of danger. Sex and promiscuity are where their energy is focused, and not love, or caring, and this is one major way of building their supply—through deep seduction. The way you respond to them sexually feeds their ego. This becomes their comfort zone, their playing ground—and anything else you need, from an emotional aspect, will not be of any concern to them. The sex success aspect of one of their Loveless traits plays out mostly in women, ages twenty to about forty-eight. Middle-aged and older women want passion over just hot sex!

*Gem: If you want to know if they're selfish or selfless about sex, stop having "just sex" and ask them to make love to you.

Favors: Allowing you to do for and take care of them, draws you in. They want you to feel like they need you, but they don't. You're not only another supply, but you're also a supplier. Most want a mother figure but will never admit that. Your emotions will be played upon. You'll be made to believe that they aren't needy, but they are. This will cause you to want to do more and more for them. They'll deny your advances, just long enough to make you want to give more; and once you reach that level of giving more, you'll feel obligated to do for them—even more. Your favors will fall into a dark hole, with no end in sight. Their denial pushing you away is nothing more than hope—hoping you remain around long enough to finally sub-mit—and most do submit. You'll become extremely happy to finally be able to serve them, but at a risk and sacrifice. They become your responsibility. But you're not theirs. By you doing favors so much, it'll make you feel like you owe them, and that's exactly what they want. Some of you pay bills late just to make a narcissist happy and impress them. Your first risk!

Most times when they return favors, they're small ones, and it's usually after having great sex with you—a time when you don't require much of a gift!

*Gem: To find out if they will reciprocate a favor, ask them for a favor and money, all in the same breath—after sex or at any time. Usually if you ask for a favor after sex, they'll see themselves in you and then they'll become irritated, aggravated, and triggered, and normally will start an argument. This is an indirect "NO!"

Although I made about $120K a year in the Navy from 2007 to 2015, there was never a woman that was beneath me. In all actuality, the ones that made less than I did—which they all did, or some made just as much—were much better than I was and in many categories.

Leon—I'm not going to hurt you!

In order to hurt someone, I made myself believe that they were going to hurt me, sooner or later. Having that mindset took away all of my guilty conscience.

For the first time in my life, I let my guard down. "Leon, I'm not going to hurt you" were some of the first words that my third therapist softly spoke to me as I walked into her office in January of 2015. I can't remember ever hearing those words before (or maybe once before), and as I heard those words, I could remember feeling a small sigh of relief. But then, with the other woman that said that, I didn't let my guard down for her, like I did with my therapist—because I felt a sense of her trying to trick or fool me; she wasn't. I was the one infusing the tricks and foolery, either that day or prior to meeting up with her, so I thought others were going to do it to me. I wasn't going to take a chance, though.

My last therapist, in 2015, wasn't someone that I was physically attracted to. At that point, I was able to manage and regulate my lust for women. My other therapists, though—yes—I was physically attracted to her. After walking out of the elevator on the second floor of the Veterans Administration Hospital on Green Bay Avenue in Great Lakes—quivering, I walked about twenty nervous, painstaking steps—made a sharp left turn and stopped in front of her office. There she was, sitting at her desk, and leaning forward. And as she leaned forward, her cleavage caught my attention. I paused and quickly looked down to my left. A clipboard stared at me on a small table. "Room 215" stuck out in my peripheral vision and then I spotted the blue "Mental Health" sign right across from it. I stepped through her doorway, slightly chewing on a plastic stopper from Starbucks, walked into her office, and took a seat. Slowly gazing at her college degrees, neatly aligned on her beige wall, I quickly looked down to undress her, going into my fantasy world with her—like most women that I was physically attracted to. She didn't even know. Although maybe she did, because after sitting in her office for fifty minutes, not paying attention to anything she said, wandering off, and even occasionally looking at the dim lights on the ceiling—she asked me to leave. All women—their body, face, and lips—resonated with me first, regardless of how dysfunctional and mentally distorted I was. My mental health came last, if at all.

My point here is this. If your man or woman, or even your child, isn't ready to make some exchanges in life, the relationship, or within their broken and corrupt spirit, like mine, then therapy will not work. Having a clear mind and a mind that's receptive to constructive criticism—a mind removed from lust and a trial period that you want, need, and desire—is what it will take. Furthermore, when enrolling in therapy, there has to be a significant reason. Sadly, for most, losing your partner or even your family will not suffice. I was completely tired of Satan and living in that rotten flesh!

Contents

Dedication

I TAKE FULL RESPONSIBILITY—*PERIOD!*

Regardless of what happened or how it happened, my mind and brain are mine. I took it on, for both good and bad reasons. I used my disorder maliciously, at first. I was damaged, and so I damaged other people. It is mine. I may not want it, but it is mine. It may have come from other people but— it is MINE—I TAKE OWNERSHIP!

Through therapy, I finally realized that I didn't have to keep that mind—I had become greedy, selfish, self-centered, angry, and many more things, and just *didn't* want to let go of it because all of those traits felt really good to me. I never took heed of others' emotions, feelings, hopes, needs, and desires. Through that mindset, others hurt and experienced serious pain. They suffered and I didn't. I do suffer now, but it's well worth it, and extremely educational. My vision is clear, so instead of feeling and feeding my demons inside of me, I see them coming, before they plant themselves—*DISCERNMENT*—only through accepting God and seeking to do and be better in all aspects of life!

To all of the survivors, healers, and those who have taken their lives back, I applaud you. Those that have endless and countless hours, days, weeks, and years of pain, I admire your strength, fortitude, and will. This book with its enlightenment, teachings, and my lifetime of indiscretions, lies, deceit, bread-crumbing, ghosting, silent treatment, shunning, and theft—is for educational purposes and continued healing: I promise. Some people go a lifetime giving to thieves, because narcissists are thieves. We steal your time, heart, soul, character, morals, and integrity. You are esteemed, adored, and highly respected and highly regarded, because you continued to try and help someone that could not help themselves.

You are the real hero!

Introduction:
Pain and Vain

Through it all, my smile remained the same.

In the world today, there are more and more kids being born into poverty, with diabetes, ADD, ADHD, and many more things. Healthy eating habits and a healthy mindset have become boring to most of this generation. Being a product of dysfunctional environments, like I was, is still prevalent today. Be it the ghetto, where we see violence and womanizing as the norm, privileged kids turning against their parents, kids openly disrespecting their parents, coaches, and leadership, and many more things. I hear it far too often from gang members, in their rap songs.

– I have PTSD—Lord please forgive me, for I am about to sin, and spin—the block.

Gangs and rap labels are now a hotbed for developing or housing broken kids, and possibly even more and younger narcissists. Most are absent of love and empathy already, and most are without regret, but full of being selfish, egotistical, greedy, and lustful. The same things I embodied! The problem with diagnosing them is that they will not sit in therapy long enough. However, on the flip-side of that, with the military and corporate America offering a "mental health day" off—they just might remain in therapy long enough to become diagnosed. I can see the numbers in narcissism growing in the next five to ten years, far more than the estimated up to five percent of the population being diagnosed, now. The fast pace of the world makes them impatient, entitled, having no time for empathy, and developing a grandiose mindset—just to name a few characteristics.

Other lyrics that I hear: *This Lean in my cup makes me feel numb—I can't blame my actions on no one but my gun.*

I think violence or wanting to belong has become a badge of honor for some. Most may wonder why, after "spinning the block," they may begin to take on many more anger issues or even perpetuate anger itself, for themselves or those they have just shot, killed, or injured! Love, caring, passion, and compassion come second or third, if at all. Thrill-seeking acts, danger, and clout-chasing are high on the list for many. Empathy is extremely lacking and sympathy is at an all-time low. Having empathy or sympathy makes one vulnerable—however, being vulnerable is noble. Sadly, these young men and women will find this out much later in life, if ever. By that time, they've destroyed many people in their path and will ultimately end up dead or in jail. That notion has become a willing feat, too. Selfishness has become a comfort zone for many, and lots of people, mainly this generation, don't have a problem not extending a "Thank you, I love you, yes ma'am, no ma'am," and so on. If a father is tough on his kids, he's the bad guy. If a mom is tough on her kids—they stray. Young ladies tend to look for comfort in young men like herself, disobedient; or someone that she can use and abuse, like the disobedient young men; and vice-versa. They then bond from what she wants and not from how he should have been taught. The Path of Least Resistance (POLR) resonates with them more, but they expect more with giving less. Greed is in the forefront on many of their minds as well. Now, Take and Take has replaced Give and Take or Give to Receive. Cups do not runneth over!

Broken families seem harder and harder to prevent. Kids want to be treated like adults far too early, but expect to remain at home, doing nothing—well into their thirties!

My point here is this. I truly believe that some may take on the diagnosis of mental illness as a way of being tough and belonging, enjoying the fact that people see them as off or crazy. That's not what PTSD means, nor shall we see it that way. Narcissism, to me, will take on the same course, as a badge of honor for many. They say that 70% of men are narcissist and 30% of women are. If no one gets therapy, the number of untreated men and women will rise even higher and so will dysfunction, broken families, short or lack of marriages, cheating, lying, ghosting, gas-lighting, gray-rocking, shunning, mental abuse, verbal abuse, sexual abuse, spiritual abuse, financial abuse, love-bombing, and discarding. Social media is a wonderful thing; however, the media part of it has replaced real and honest people or things, with filters, views, followers, and so on. Young men enjoy more—playing games on computers and smoking weed. Young ladies enjoy the likes, views, and what people say and think about them, just as long as it is positive, and even if it's a lie. More and more women are starting to claim the "Alpha Female" mentality, too. Outer appearance means more and feels better than their internal moral compass and a great heart. The fairytale mindset, just like a narcissist!

We are closer to those that are further away
and further away from those that we should be closer to.
– Jay Shetty

Epigraph

– Like Noah, I had alcoholic tendencies. Like Abraham, I was a liar. Like Job, I doubted God. Like Samson, I was promiscuous. Like Moses, I have anxiety. Like David, I was a whore. Like Elijah, I was suicidal. Like Peter, I was ashamed to know Jesus; I was a weak and jealous disciple. Yet and still, God has always forgiven me and gave me chance after chance!

Love felt empty. I hated love, and loved hate. I developed a *true* feeling from emptiness, and a false feeling from being empty, but it all felt normal. Odd seemed even, and vindication resonated so well, for many reasons. Not relating, a lack of feelings and connections were all dispersed and understood so effortlessly, it was an alienation from pure life and self. I was always searching for an identity but always found empty values. I would seek solace, inspiration, but in doing so, I would consistently overrule pain, being failed by those I trusted and loved. Healing came secondary to hurting, hurting was my superpower. I was institutionalized, a prisoner, a slave of my own DNA, genetics, and people. My therapist told me: "Mr. Walker, you don't have the ability to make any sound judgments, based on your gut feelings, and this is one reason why you constantly flee!" I was forty-seven when she said this! I waited over 26 years before I sat down in therapy. Hearing the truth scared the hell out of me, and so I denied myself and others of healthy relationships with me, including my children!

Leon

I hated my true self, because I never knew him, he had the power to avoid me. All the good women saw him, but I didn't want to. Being good, doing right, just didn't feel good to me. I held onto my demons and honestly, they were a lot of fun but I regret allowing them into my mind and body. It didn't matter who I hurt or what I did, I was a demon too! Drama appealed to me, and anger gave me confidence. When I was angry, my ability to think of evil things to do to people was at its apex. During the apex, and since I gave negativity so much authority, my negative energy misconstrued the positive occurrences for my fragile and sinful ego, so it felt right to me. Sometimes, I enjoyed scaring women.

I wanted their hearts to race, just like mine. I wanted to see them wanting to help me and be close to my dysfunction, my filthy mind, and not walking away, especially those that were close to God. While they were close to God and I wasn't, I knew he allowed them to see me for what I was capable of, but I avoided that connection, attraction, and their selection of me. I gave myself years to play with God, knowing that he'll always welcome and bring me back, even after I broke a woman's heart. It wasn't my fault that I was sick, and she knew it. God protected me through you, so you didn't have a problem with loving Leon and you weren't going to give up on me! It was your duty! If you had the ability to treat me inappropriately, I enjoyed it until I couldn't take it anymore, and then—I wanted to hate and then try to love you, all at the same time. There was no love, but I needed that type of off-balance intensity; that's what I responded to! My feelings were always misplaced.

Nothing else would keep my attention: calmness, reasoning, *nothing*. Now, let's see whose demons are the worst—of course mine will be, and I knew that. I know you can't be any more despicable than I was, or hurtful. Not even close, so reeling you back in, after you were disrespectful and verbally abusive, that turned me on, to heights of pure ecstasy. That became a sense of emotional and enjoyable pain for me, particularly when you cried or asked me, "Why, Leon?" I had to be able to win and conquer you through your innate ability to remain, because you were dedicated to God, and loyal to him, while I wasn't. I knew that. Being quiet and hateful allowed me to drum up evil wishes and thoughts. Stay away from me, but come around when I am lustful, greedy, and needy, because I was all of that, and not just for one woman! I didn't deserve Leon, or a good woman, so I now know that God kept Leon and those wholesome women away from me. I was only able to procure them when I was fake, and when I lied, but I knew that it would be short-lived; still, I didn't care. Demons are hungry all the damned day!

I didn't deserve Leon but I knew he was there. I was jealous of him, so I did all that I could to outdo him, but it never happened. God created him and I allowed the devil to create the side that I remained with. Those of you that are like me, you will chase good, and when you attain a good woman or man, you will hurt them, for your own selfish reasons but love your toxic ways, because you can't relate to what's right. Your payback is coming. This is not a plea, or a threat, it's life! I know this all too well! Loving or liking unhealthy habits or people, you are slowly dying on the inside, while killing others—their dreams, hopes, and their spirits. I lived hour by hour, day by day, looking for any form of motivation to feed my demons. They kept me sick, evil, and off kilter. Be kind, free your spirit, and connect with Angels! You don't have to feed them, just realize that they're there, so simply be with them! It's much easier and it will not cost you, yet they will pay into you!

List of Other Books by the Author

Broken: Survival Instincts of a Child
Keeping Kids Safe from Porn
Loveship

Contact Information for Leon R. Walker, Jr.

For information about speaking engagements, appearances, and honest and truthful *help*, please contact:

Email: cmcwalker2015@gmail.com

Website: Leonrobertwalkerjr.com

Instagram: Leonrwalker

Facebook: Leon R. Walker Jr

Tiktok: Leon R. Walker Jr

LinkedIn: Leon R. Walker Jr

Google: Leon R. Walker Jr

YouTube: Leon R. Walker Jr

I am truly sorry that my motivation was outside of our home and our relationship. Everything about me is broken, except my demons!

– Leon R. Walker, Jr.

MENTAL HEALTH RECORD

CHRONOLOGICAL RECORD OF MEDICAL CARE

Location: Psychiatric Clinic, Pearl Harbor, Hawaii/Balboa Naval Hospital, San Diego, California.

Dates: October 1987 to December 1987.

Synopsis: Patient is 21 years old. Patient was observed and counseled by the ship's senior corpsman and referred to psychiatric treatment upon ship's arrival to Pearl Harbor, Hawaii. The ship's senior corpsman identified service member's experience with extreme trauma while onboard USS Stark, FFG-31, and his childhood.

Neurological: Oriented to time, place, and person.

Cognition: Alert. Needs work.

Psychiatric: **Patient has a long hx of trauma, neglect, abuse and a lack of care, or showing emotion.**

Mood: Irritable, angry, agitated, fearful, nightmares, afraid of darkness, cold sweats at night, compulsions, flashbacks, anxiety attacks, abnormal thinking, paranoia, intrusive thoughts, impulsivity, sleep disturbance, mood swings, racing thoughts. Notes: Visibly shaken. Patient walks into my office with either a frayed toothpick or a straw in his mouth. After further talks with patient about his childhood, I have determined that the toothpicks and straws in his mouth are due to his cousin's aggressive, open-mouth kissing of him at age five. Patient informed me that as a child, he chewed his shirt collars, wet the bed excessively and sleep-walked too.

In addition to the patient's other traumas, I was able to determine that the patient also suffers from oral fixation and avoidance issues.

Duration: Patient seen for three hours. His ship gets underway in a few days. Pt must follow-up for care, immediately upon arriving into the next port, San Diego. Intensive care is highly recommended. Patient has been reluctant to get help, as he sees it as a weakness. He now agrees to see additional psychiatric help upon arrival to San Diego, at the end of the ship's deployment. Service member showed signs of being "antsy" and I asked why. His response was alarming but honest: "Doc, it's been a long deployment and I need a drink."

Family: Patient shows signs of severe childhood abuse. Patient was molested by family members and his babysitter. First sexual abuse started in the first grade, and second incident began when he was eight. These incidents led to his addiction to porn, by age seven. His parents divorced when patient was eleven. Patient admits that made him feel unwanted and he didn't ever want to get married or have children. Patient is currently in a relationship but states that he doesn't know why or where it is going. Patient admits to struggling with commitment. Patient states that he shies away from love or even talking about love.

Patient also spoke about 2, S/I as a child and losing their home due to eviction. We ended our session, but follow-up and care are crucial to patient being successful in life and his relationships. I will follow up with his ship and Balboa hospital for treatment, and to further assess and coordinate with his new psychiatrist, along with setting his goals.

Assessment: Narcissistic Personality disorder, Insomnia.

Anticipated length of treatment: INDEFINITE.

Patient seen and counseled by: Dr. Jane Doe, MD.

Acknowledgements

"I had a monogamous heart—but a promiscuous mind."

I joined the Navy at seventeen years old and from that point moving forward, my uniform, smile, worldly knowledge, and the fact that I was serving this country, showed up on the surface. No one else. I had a girl in every port, and they were the first ones introduced to my greed and lust. I completely lost the way of my parents.

"Mommy, Daddy, I miss you both very much , and I am now very appreciative of the traits you gave me. I'm sorry for not using them sooner."

My mother and father died before I was able to tell them what happened to me. I was too far gone to reverse any of my egregious ways. I'm sorry...

To all of the good women that I hurt, screwed over, cheated on, lied to, left behind, and completely upended their worlds, I am truly sorry. I take full responsibility, regardless of what path I was on or put on. I knew at an early age that I wasn't this little monster that I portrayed myself to be, but a weak mind and being easily influenced, and then relying on a few physical and cunning mental attributes. I became abusive to not only myself but the women in my path. Those who came to me morally and characteristically fit. I could not relate, but I tried to. My attempts stemmed from a broken spirit, shattered dreams, and wishful thinking and hopes. I wanted to emulate how my parents were in their better times; I wanted to emulate my grandparents and aunts and uncles that had been married for years; but unfortunately as a child I was derailed and did not recover for a span of over forty years. It didn't have to be that way, nor did it have to go for that long period of time. I never knew of, nor did I have longevity or staying power in relationships. Since I refused to be honest, forthcoming, truthful, and real, I put thousands of unwarranted and unethical physical damages on my mind and body. The women I encountered as well. In 2013, life had done a number on me.

My Heart Attack!

My damage to women and others was external, from what I thought—not knowing the whole time I was dying internally, and so were they! Narcissists will blame their health issues on genetics, DNA, other people and other things, and not on how they treat people. They will or might change their eating habits but will not change their evil ways.

My chest was burning, it felt like heartburn. My heart was burning! My heart attack began while I was on base, at the gym, abruptly. This was right before I entered therapy with my third psychiatrist. I was in surgery for three hours, in the hospital for four days, and in therapy for four months. I wasn't able to run, just walk. I was taking nine pills per day, developed more intense anger issues, and lost my sex drive. I have a stent in my artery—which was 80 percent clogged. I had many choices to choose from in knowing why I had a heart attack. The year was 2014, August 13th. Most will listen to and believe what the cardiologists tells us, and rightfully so. But in an effort to reason with myself and God, I wanted to be fair about why I had a heart attack. People die from broken hearts, and I caused a lot of broken hearts. Thank God, from what I know, no one died because of my ways. Many were hurt, though. And since God kept me alive, this time, I told myself and believed that I was experiencing a broken heart also. It wasn't just from bad eating habits; it happened because I put so much pressure on my heart from sleepless nights, harboring bad spirits, soul ties, greed, and infidelity. Because I affected another woman's heart and mind, it was suddenly my time to feel what it was like to have a broken heart.

From those many sleepless nights, I was prescribed prazosin. I truly believed that my demons fought off the medicine because there wasn't any kind of effect. I would wake up in the middle of the night, just drenched—so much that I had to change my pillowcase, sheets, and blanket. I would lose fluids from those nightmares. It became embarrassing, but the next day, I would start all over with my antics. My health came secondary to healing. Narcissists push through life, and relationships. Destroying everything in sight, without a care in the world! If my health wasn't important, yours wasn't either.

My heart issues were totally unannounced and unexpected, just like the heart pain I gave those women. With a six-month decline in health, just like those women, I had to continue to be strong, go to work, hold my head up, wear a fake smile, and go through life like I was fine, when I wasn't. The women sure weren't, either; but I had to feel their pain, and I did. This is why I am still alive today writing my third book. Some may wonder why I respect women so much and why I have so much love for my mother. Well, it's because I've been on the side of a woman's hurt and it's no fun, and while growing up, I had always been around strong black women. Once I joined the Navy, I began to encounter strong white, Asian, Latin, Irish, Australian, Swedish, Aboriginal, Russian, and Native American women, too.

A Note from the Author

Narcissists have many masks. None are permanent, except the mask of pain!
– Leon R. Walker, Jr.

This book is written for both men and women, but since it is from my mind, and perspective, you will notice that I speak from a man's perspective, mostly. Women are the same exact way that I was, so you are not excluded from both the bad and good ways. Please bear with me while reading. Writing this book was tough on my soul, as I am still in my healing, awareness, and clarity process. I am healed enough to be able to grow, forgive, and teach everyone so they don't make the same mistakes I made. That's the purpose of this book. This journey has opened old wounds and traumas that I have covered up for years, decades even. Even though I tried to forget them and pretended that they did not exist, they were still very visible and present. Although my childhood is why I became this nasty, despicable, and lustful person, I still had a choice. It was still ultimately up to me to choose, and I chose to feed my unnatural needs, and sins, period.

I will be narrating this book to you all in *third person at times*, because that is what people with narcissistic traits, and narcissists, do; at least I did. I want this book to be an experience for you, for you to grow, learn, and not feel sorry for me—*at all. **God knows that I owe a debt, and I am here to pay God, and those that I hurt!*** I want to take you into the dark minds of narcissists and experience their thought patterns. ***There's no need to be afraid—you've done that long enough!***

> *Never fear. It is much better to receive a lesson here, as opposed to when it is too late and you are fighting to save your relationship, hurting, and crying or even saving your own life.*

You must understand that I was a very dangerous person at that time. I was a cancer to everyone I came in contact with, living the way that I did, without having God in me. The devil had become my best friend. I have to admit this, so that you know that I am speaking from a reprobate mind. I excluded myself from salvation on purpose; the lust was too powerful for me at the time, but it felt good to my corrupt soul.

I want you to hear the truth from deep down in my soul and spirit, and while reading my book, remember, I am in character. This is my way of giving you my truth—through every emotion, thought process, and poor excuse—from every inch of my body and every crevice of my soul.

More importantly, I am here to teach and inform you; I am here to help. I am transparent. I am open, and honest. I was one who lived as a narcissist for many years. It is imperative that I speak in this manner, so that you get the full scope of my lack of responsibility, mindset, and mental state as I grew up and developed a deep lust and greed for women. I had deep character and integrity flaws. My controlling ways, dysfunction, emotional detachment, and emotional dysregulation, as you will see, are all on display in *The 7 Loveless Traits*.

Please understand and walk with me. This is also therapy for me.

– Leon R. Walker, Jr., 2022

Prologue

On this day, May 18th, 1987, I started to handle death, easily. The death of a relationship and marriage became just as easy.

I have a story for you...

The men onboard USS Stark FFG-31 were crying, struggling, and bleeding! At age twenty-one I felt like I was going crazy. I had been in the United States Navy for almost four years and was really proud of myself. Things were going very well, and I was genuinely at peace with life until one fateful day when tragedy struck. The date was May 17, 1987—*I remember it like it was yesterday.* When we received the devastating news from our Captain, it was just thirty minutes shy of midnight. My ship was in the Persian Gulf at the time, on patrol. The heat was sweltering, upwards of 120 to 130 degrees.

The coasts of Iran and Iraq were lighting up and all we could do was watch from the ship.

> *The USS Stark FFG-31 has been hit by two missiles, gentlemen...our Captain informed us. Only one of the missiles exploded; however, some major damage was sustained.*

My fire team moved swiftly once we had received our orders. We had been called on to board the ship and provide assistance. USS Reid FFG-30 arrived in the vicinity of the damaged ship the very next day, May 18, 1987. We stayed there for twelve hours during which we recovered thirty-seven bodies.

They were all *murdered,* of course. From the look of the corpses, we could tell that a large number of the men had been burned alive. I picked up hands, fingers, toes, and other body parts soaked through with water. It was such a terrible scene. One really sick memory that I remember doing was *peeling* a young man from the deck. He looked to be about nineteen years old. As we pulled what was left of him from the deck, I could hear his skin ripping, tearing in every direction as if it was made of papier-mâché. All of us would have given anything to be anywhere else on that day, but this was what we signed up for, after all. We had to get all thirty-seven corpses into body bags. The atmosphere in that place was pregnant with sadness. Our heads were filled with so much doom and gloom that we could not even bring ourselves to cry; we were too numb, too paralyzed, to properly process what was going on. It felt like the devil was hovering several feet above us, a vulture feeding on our despair, on the pieces of our shattered souls strewn about. I felt feelings of *not understanding* or processing any types of emotion or hurt just leave my body in those twelve hours, and I didn't know why. I started talking to myself!

"Get it together, Leon, get it together."

"Deal with it, just deal with it."

As I spoke those words out loud, my friend just stared at me.

That day for twelve hours, I walked and sat among thirty-seven deceased men, as if it was just another day. I know from this experience, I was able to process death very easily. I never knew that I would process break-ups in my relationships the same way. It had become easy for me to kill…hopes and dreams! The death of a woman's goals and plans with me, and even her spirit.

After transferring the thirty-seven bodies to the USS *La Salle* AGF-3/LPD-3, my team and I were sent back to my ship, the USS *Reid* FFG-30, for rest and recovery. Hours later, we were screened by medical officials. I knew that I wasn't in my right mind, but I managed to push through. When my ship arrived in Hawaii for a few days of post-deployment rest and recovery, I was sent to see a psychiatrist, my first one, and there would be more. We were in Hawaii for about four days, so I was in and out of the hospital, and happy about that. Alcohol and women were more important to me. It was time to be with a Samoan woman. I didn't even know her, and it didn't matter! A one-night stand, yes, but I didn't care if she liked me or not. This began to feel really odd to me.

What did that ship and seeing those burned men do to me?

My numbness was at an all-time high, and I knew it. Upon our return to our homeport of San Diego, I started my therapy, seeing another psychiatrist a couple days a week for two weeks. The treatment came to an abrupt end when I found out I was neither healing nor making any form of progress. I was in deep denial—*How could there be anything wrong with me? My team and I just saved a ship.* I just walked away from my first psychiatrist!

We didn't save the ship, those brave men did. Thirty-seven men were murdered, I had become a search-and-rescue Sailor but I wanted to take credit. I made the decision to stop going to therapy. I did not want people to make fun of me, because deep down, I knew that something was wrong, that some deep trauma had been triggered that fateful day in the Persian Gulf, and in Hawaii. It was already too late. I left her right there on Waikiki Beach!

So, I couldn't care less became my favorite words to any woman that I met.

I remained in service in the Navy. Twenty-eight years passed; I had become a lot more successful, but the past still hurt. It hurt like a million knives digging into my back, and this pain I felt was transferred to almost everyone who came in contact with me. I hurt people in my path, and that started to feel good to me! I adopted a way to push women away and then pull them back in without any remorse, just like the pushing away had never happened. *DISCARD!*

Throughout my naval career, I had a lot of help and support from other people, but it was not enough; I needed more. So, in 2014, I started intensive therapy, which lasted twelve months. My attendance was sporadic, though. By this time, I had destroyed my marriage and had just destroyed another romantic relationship of six years. During the twelve-month-long therapy, my first psychotherapist was not effective because I did not spend much time with her, just like the psychiatrists in Hawaii and San Diego. And because of this severe lack of attention, and maturity, I was misdiagnosed by other medical professionals because I wasn't being honest. At this point, I knew that my spirit was broken. The question was to what extent? And how soon before the cracks would begin to show on the outside? How long before I broke down completely? I could not show that to anyone, not even a psychiatrist or a psychotherapist. I was right, they were wrong, and I was extremely successful—how could there be anything wrong with me? I thought that I needed medical professionals to tell me that I could have been overt, vindictive, grandiose, vulnerable, manipulative, seductive...among many more things. I continued living that way, drowning in the deep end of denial. I just needed someone to listen to me. Just like you know yourself, I knew myself, too. I understood perfectly what was going on, I only needed a professional to guide me through my tangled mess of a mind and to finally be honest. I was too proud.

I must be fair and warn you.

The stories you are about to read in this book are full of triggers. I understand I have to be upfront about these things for your sake; consider this a heads-up. Therefore, even though while reading this book, *The 7 Loveless Traits,* you will encounter different pains, ensuring you endure it all. Push through. There's healing on the other side of the ugliness, I promise. This book will help you see, heal, and become educated on the traits you have never noticed before now.

As a child, a lot of older people had a negative impact on me. I'm sure many of you have experienced this, probably with a teacher, or a parent. I have good news for you. You can and will recover just like I did. You must believe in your healing, even if there have been times when you believed in the devil and accepted his evil. I did that, too. And now, I am healed of all the trauma. You can do it too.

Do not let anyone drive you to thoughts of suicide, doubt, or make you lose confidence in yourself. They do not own or rule you. You also do not have to pretend everything is okay when it's not. Stop faking it, stop taking it, and start changing it!

I learned to control my anger, fix my dysfunctions, and overcome many addictions. This I achieved by recognizing and facing my triggers. More importantly, I talked about my issues and fought them head-on. The lessons you're about to learn here in *The 7 Loveless Traits* are straight from my heart. God has always given me the strength to talk about them to help people heal, and he has given you the strength, too.

This is the main reason I will remain open and honest while writing this book; I believe I must convey to you that, if I could recover, then so can you. You are covered, enlightened, and protected. I healed late because I refused to acknowledge my condition on time. But with this book, you have put yourself in the company of someone who has gone through the hardships and triumphed. You have an advantage.

Reading this book in school, at work, or next to your partner can help you out with so many things. It is sure to trigger a host of emotions, but this is ultimately a good thing as it will encourage you to reflect on your childhood and things that may have been passed down for generations. You will identify and understand why you act the way you do!

I do not recommend this book for anyone that is not ready to face their fears and make a change. There would be harsh reminders, mind shifts, and shockers, to say the least—all necessary points in the journey to find your peace.

Do not let the fact that this book is intense, scare you. If I had read something like this in my early twenties, I would have gotten the help I needed and healed sooner than I expected.

My Demonic Perpetrators

Ninety percent of your perpetrators
are someone you know or trust.

It has yet to be proven, but I have always felt like my perpe-
trators were my demonic spirits! I truly feel that, because
of them, I would ultimately become nothing more than
a nicely wrapped present, shiny and new on the outside
but rotten to the core, and I wasn't going to be—present!

One day, Karen looked in to my eyes—then said to me, "Leon, once a woman gets to know you, once she gets to know who you really are on the inside, she will wish she never met you. You leave a woman empty and hurt because you are also empty and hurt and vulnerable. You cannot give what you do not have. The only time I feel like I know you is when we're in bed or around friends and family; in those instances, your mask is on. No one can tell what is really going on inside. When we're alone, you act so cold—Leon—like you do not even like me. This is not working for me, Leon!"

So, I couldn't care less, girl!

I emotionally and physically starved women. My perpetrators were starved too but highly lustful. I had become them over the years. Although two were murdered later on, their flesh remained with me.

When She's Vulnerable

Once you let her hand and heart go—she'll be wide open
for another man and not you anymore. When a good man
or woman is pushed away, you actually release them from
your grasp. They'll begin to start their journey of heal-
ing, but may not realize it because of the current or past
pain. The first thing they gain during this process is their
vision—it's a slow-occurring depth perception. They'll
now start to see how ugly you were and are!

When a woman is *vulnerable*, she will make sure you take notice. This is her way of being fair. It is a heartfelt warning. There might be various reasons as to why she feels vulnerable; however, if you take care of why you make her vulnerable first, all other reasons will take care of themselves. Most of the time, the reason for her vulnerability stems from a *lack of attention on your part* and *not enough quality time* spent together with you.

These are two very crucial components you need to take notice of. When a woman is good to you, her *vulnerabilities* could stem from the *absence of her dad*, or *a lack of reciprocity from you* as far as displays of affection and attention are concerned. It is also possible that you remind her of her ex, or of certain things in her past. She'll push through though, to make sure it isn't her when the relationship isn't going well, so that when she does leave her regret level will be low.

Women dislike negative reminders; they feel it in their spirit. They want and need assurance. Most of the time, when a woman is good, her man takes her for granted. If you are unable to meet her halfway on every level and communicate in an honest and affective manner, she sees it as a form of disrespect and a lack of care. She understands that you have begun to devalue her. I made all women who came my way vulnerable, and when they left, I felt even more vulnerable and emptier inside. It is not a good feeling at all. But instead of fixing myself, I became VINDICTIVE.

Vindictive order of precedence:
Regretting the constructive criticism, becoming extremely hard to reach, intense anger, evil thoughts, rage, strict and uncompromising, revenge implemented, pain begins to engulf them, punishment, discard, smear campaign, ghosting, silent treatment.

The Shadow Traits of vindictive people:
Verbal abuse, physical harm, lies, making you jealous, disappearing acts, much less contact from them, disrespect, start blaming you, ignoring the kids, and empty cheating.

How vindictive people lure you back in:
Excessive phone calls, excessive text messages, extending quality time and ideas, listening more, eye contact, wanting hugs because they know this is what you want (not them), being overly nice, doing

lots of favors, being reasonable all of a sudden, fake compliments, sorrowful stories.

The "luring" is all "love bombing," of course, and it is not at all genuine. Vindictive people actually hate this. This is just a ploy to get the woman or man, back, to win no matter what, and then hit them with the explosive "hate bomb." Then all of a sudden, fake love becomes a thing of the past. I call this the "Terrorist Syndrome" and "Bullshit Bombing." You will surely feel like you were at war with someone you won't even know when they're done! You'll be a mess, too!

Real love isn't explosive and can't just be cut off or extended to fool people. It rings loud in your core and spirit, but only if it is real. It's soothing and calming. Know the difference, please!

Back then, I would be serious when she took me back, just for a little while. I would become more attentive, hugging and kissing, and treating her nicely. It was all an act. I knew it was only a matter of time before I went back to my old self. She had no clue, though. *The recycling of the discard phase.*

I realized that I didn't have the strength to deal with losing her. I left, and then I mourned. Women do the opposite: they mourn, and then leave, with a plan. She moves on to the man of her dreams. When she finds him (because she will), she will give him every part of her. If you ever see her again—and in most cases you will— she comes to see you with her new man, just so you can see what you are missing— and she will definitely look amazing. This is her *passive smear tactic*. Once she's educated on how you think and operate, and gaining her strength—she will start to mirror you. This is one of the first phases that narcissists hate. Once you mirror a narcissist, his/her mirror will break, and that's part of their karma. Believe it, please, because we will *never* tell you.

She wants you to see that she *was not* the problem, that it was you who refused to step up where another man did. She goes right for your ego! This would be a great blow to any man, that's for sure. Her spirituality takes over; she is not narcissistic at all during this, she has finally found herself and realized that I wasn't who I said I was. She gained her tools.

Equipment/Education/Transformation/Celebration

Men hardly ever prepare themselves for the impending absence of their partner. We never have an exit plan. This is when stalking begins, and you can bet, I did that too! Both my anger and happiness from revenge were short-lived. The anger always lasted the longest, though, and was much more fun. Sane people or those without a personality disorder do not understand this, and I get that. It's much better and healthier that you don't understand this. I was jealous of women that still had their parents and the parents that remained married for an eternity. As an "Avoidance" type of person, commitment was counterproductive for me!

This doesn't work for you, Karen? What do you mean? was my reply.

I did not take kindly to women who complained. This is another characteristic of the narcissist, the inability to take any form of correction or criticism. It hurts the soul.

I was twenty-four years old, stationed in San Diego, California. I couldn't care less about her emotions and pleas. I laughed it off, as I did often back then. She had no clue that I was hurting, deeply. I was suffering from *emotional dysregulation*

Non-Sexual ED:
Not Emotional or Erect in Standing Tall

Bad posture and unsure of themselves. Honest in their own dishonesty! When someone is emotionally dysregulated, they will tend to emotionally disturb—YOU—and—EVERYONE else! It's a tactic to mask and hide their insecurities. In addition to that, they act and react, and it's a selfish mindset—to keep you off-guard, off balance, confused—wanting you to believe in everything they say and do. They want you to see, respect, and follow their perspective and agenda.

False Sense of Reality

The act of *Emotionally Disturbing* people is well-known to them—it's a trait, that's mastered, and implemented in the "gas-lighting stage." You give them the benefit of the doubt, yet you remain and start to doubt yourself. Gas-lighting begins to allow the narcissist to believe everything they're saying. It's a slow rewiring of their brain and emotions from suppressing their true childhood feelings. They rewire into a *negative circuitry*; everything flows in the wrong direction, thus causing them to lie, deflect, escape, and avoid. When they're gone, so is your mind. In this stage, they feel comfortable, and have lots of heart and nerve, which is why they can act like everything is okay.

CHAPTER ONE

Emotional Dysregulation

I was vulnerable too, in more ways than one. I just needed her to take care of my sexual needs and to keep stroking my ego. Nothing else mattered. She was primed for another man. I did that to her. I told her I was going to cheat, and I did. When she left, I blamed her and had the nerve to not trust her. I was very unfair, selfish, and self-centered.

I was allowed to do it. She was not. It was that simple. Chauvinism was a major setback for me. How dare she leave me! She was in no way allowed to leave someone who was superior to her. She owed me *big time*. She was *anointed* and when she left, I was in trouble. A vain man is for himself only. Women experience "attraction shock" with a man who presents himself in a dignified and respectable manner only to follow up with sexting. He was *misrepresenting*. Once a woman goes along with that, she would instantly become my little toy and nothing else. I felt safer not expressing myself or my feelings. Some men are afraid to show their true emotions and I was one of them.

In my narcissism, my exterior was my greatest strength; I mastered many physical tricks and mental games to keep women around, in my world and not hers. They could look at me, admire me, lust after me, and I would do the same to and for them, but it would all remain superficial. There was no chance of ever opening up to them. I was a man afraid of his own feelings, scared of what I would find if I looked deep within myself, scared of the reactions if I shared that with others. I blame the fact that I never got to experience my mother's love, deeply, after age eleven. I loved excuses, especially if she believed me, and then wanted to nurture my lies and excuses—she didn't know!

For me, and possibly for a lot of other men, once a woman expresses her desire to know you physically and then stops at that, for the most part, that man will focus on those qualities of his and nothing else. Most are sexual qualities. Men are visual, not just to women, but to ourselves. If a woman is impressed by our physical features alone, then there is no need to be good or respectable with our values. In this case *the woman* would be with us but not be privy to meaningful conversations, emotional intimacy, any sense of reassurance or security, and holding me accountable.

We respond to women with the same energy they bring to us. If a woman demands to be treated courteously, then a man will do just that. And if she shows him that she only cares about his physique and fashion sense, then those are the only things she is bound to get. I go deeper into this topic in the book. I call this "present without being present."

The above statement reduces quality time spent in a relationship and with a woman. Every form of connection never rises above being shallow or superficial. This made me very narrow-minded, parochial, and insular. If a woman made no effort to know me beyond what I present to the rest of the world, then she had better brace herself for a ride through hell. Some of you might still be dealing with "attraction shock" now. I go deep into "attraction shock" in my second book, *Loveship.* I called it my "I.M.," which stands for Irresistible Minimum.

Irresistible Minimum

Focusing solely on the minimum, I determined that all I needed was a vehicle, an apartment, a good job, good health, and decent conversations every now and then, and I was bound to secure thousands of women, irrespective of any race or location. Being a sailor was a part of the problem. Overseas, the government rolled out the red carpet for military men and everywhere we went, we were guaranteed the company of beautiful women. All we had to do was show up, pay (or not, it really did not matter), drink, and leave. And then it was on to the next one. Looks are not as important overseas, and that is why you see not-so-attractive men with Asian, Australian, Latina, Canadian, and African women. It is not a knock on the women, or men, really. The women just want a better life and desire a good time, so they jump at any and every opportunity presented. For the most part, these are good women. I am still friends with some of them, people that I met overseas back in the 1980s. As young sailors, we were new faces with energy, sex drive, a smidgen of respect and integrity, showing them attention, and treating them right. They were able to live out a fantasy with us even if it was just for a couple hours or days. Since getting the company of a good woman was that easy, there was never any reason for me to step up.

CHAPTER TWO

A Woman in Every Port—
Don't Pray for Me

I was eighteen, and women were readily available, all over the world. This wasn't good for me at all. Military men with low self-esteem will spend valuable time with women overseas. The ones with high self-esteem, like my arrogant self, were not focused on anything more than physical contact with the women. I was just adding to my body count, which was high by that point. With the right woman or a good, respectable man as a mentor, this attitude can be turned around. The truth is, I had both, but sadly I took that type of leadership and care for granted. As we pulled into each port, there were solid men that spoke to us about that port and the women in it. Greg often pulled us together for a quick briefing. He was from down South, and Southern men were known for two things: being really hardworking and being extra religious. I teased him often but even though I'd never admit it to anyone, I really needed his prayers. I think we all did. "Greg, you brothas don't play about prayer, huh?"

"Boy, whatchu know 'bout ma-dear, nem? You Northern boys ain't ready fo big mama, nem!"

"Yea, I know, man, I know."

I saw men that prayed, as soft, too good for me to hang around. Southern people were also known for their delicious, home-cooked meals. It was their spiritual foundation. Greg fancied suits. He wore them any chance he got, drenched in Old Spice cologne, with three or four gold necklaces from Bahrain hanging from his neck. He always smelled like Kool cigarettes. And though you would never know this just by looking at him, Greg was close to the Lord. That was another thing I learnt during my time in the Navy: things are not always what they seem. Greg was a great mentor. I remember how he was always looking out for us, especially before we went on liberty. He would ask us to gather for prayers and then begin in his scruffy voice.

"Come on, Walker, get yo ass over here for prayer. Lord knows you the one that needs it most outta all o' us."

"*Mann*, come on, it's time to hit the streets!"

The entire time I would be thinking, "this country-ass dude."

As I walked over to the group, Greg would start praying. Immediately everyone was huddled up, but me. I would simply walk back to my spot against the wall, lean against it, look listlessly at the entire situation, tap my feet incessantly, and bite my bottom lip. Bored!

As he turned his head and stared at me, all I heard loudly was "...and lead us not into temptation, but deliver us from evil..."

My thoughts were "Nah, lead me *INTO* temptation and *DO NOT* deliver me from evil!" And every single time after the prayer was over, in less than an hour, I would locate the nearest brothel and immediately dive headfirst into all the debauchery. I had serious issues back in 1984.

I became a great listener, not because I was interested, but I wanted to know what you were missing so that I could master that and then master your mind and emotions through seductive manipulation.

Seductive Manipulation—Creates Vulnerability

Your feelings, emotions, and cravings will always be open to and for a seductive narcissist! They become your emotional regulator—but you give it to them! This is a huge ego booster that removes any thought of love but increases the lack of respect! I give to you physically, what you conveyed to me, as far as your needs—verbally. Your own honesty would be used against you, in a dishonest way. Through compliments, and you taking my advice, you feel like I truly care about you, but in all reality I don't. I only care about you falling for me and me rising from your letting go and submitting. In all of this, you are true, correct, and mature in how human beings are and how they are supposed to carry themselves; but I am not who you are, nor am I capable of being moral, or having what you have, which is a pure and genuine heart.

Women That Are Vulnerable

To heal and become stronger, you must attain the three P's. Also, remain engrossed in your reading, learning, research, and prayer about people like myself while staying away, *period.* Once you're educated and strong enough and ready to protect your heart and feelings, *then appear* in life and society. Prior to that, become a recluse, align yourself, and study the brain, personalities, and shadow traits. Be selfish until you have control of "selfness!"

My therapist said to me, *Mr. Walker, you need to stop dating for a while.*

In my mind and oddly enough, I thought that would be counterproductive. Only because I was selfish and not yet learning "selfness"—selfness enough to heal and protect other women from me, which would have been productive for all of the women that I would encounter.

Back to the Vulnerable Woman. Once you reappear in life and society, or we happen to have an occasional encounter, you'll see me differently and I will see you as different. A different look and mindset that I will not like, nor your status that you have grown into. I will not be able to appreciate, adjust to, or understand. Although I will make an attempt to regain the old you because the old you is what I am comfortable with, since it gave me power and control, you were able to take that back with your three P's: *Power in Prayer, Preparedness, and Progress!*

Now different, we are on different playing fields. On the playing field, you become active in your own right, leading instead of following, coaching, dominating in your winning spirit and attitude. People cheer for you, celebrate you and your winning record. At that point, I can only sit on the sidelines, looking, watching, and hurting. You are taking your trophy back—your life, your heart, and spirit—I can only be your student at this point, *now*. I can only just watch you and it hurts. I still haven't changed either, but you'll know. I then become respectful but still not truthful or trustworthy. *Stay away!*

At First, I Am the Mechanic of Your Mechanisms

If it feels too good for you in the beginning, it's only because you're vulnerable, and the good feeling is too soon for you to be *that* open with me, yet you are. There's no truth in the beginning for someone that has my personality disorder. You'll act and react from your bruised and starved emotions, which now rule and control you. So, I'm not in control but you think so. I sense this *and* your lack of boundaries and governance, hence why I can become the governor of your engine and all parts associated! I control the idle, the limits, and internal combustion. Without me and my oil, you seize up; with my oil, you run smoothly, too much oil, and you sputter and can't operate efficiently.

This is not to be or sound arrogant. It is derived deeply from the mind of a narcissist and how I used to think. Later in the book, I discuss therapy and rehab, which therapy to go to, and an ability to move on or deal with and cope with a Leon!

Vulnerability stems from developmental problems, personal incapacities, disadvantaged social status, inadequacy of interpersonal networks and supports, and degraded neighborhoods and environments. I have met people with these traits, and even those without these traits.

Some or most, depending on their quest, have needs or desires in life, be it recovering from a dilapidated childhood or wanting to emulate their successful parents or just following a tradition with reference to family values, goals, and expectations—what they all had in coming was extremely high levels of education, a driven mindset, being inspirational and aspirational—yet and still they all lacked knowledge and had fallen victim to a *Leon!*

Once I met these successful people, and you begin to think I have all of the aforementioned statuses that *you* may not have, your confidence and self-esteem start to decline and this is where you start to not only *believe in a Leon* but you also start to feel like *you need me. Except those women that were just like me.* Like minds suppress or hide their vulnerabilities, and this is why the true meaning of *victim* develops on others.

Even If I Say "Don't Pray for Me"

> *I've told women to not pray for me, because I was on my way out. Either next week or next month, and I didn't want to feel bad about your prayers—because I knew that I was going to forsake your prayers and God—I just could not tell you.*

Do it—pray for me! It shows that you are the bigger person, which I will never like, and this is another reason why it should be done aside from being real, honest, and doubling down on your discernment in your quest to rise above a Leon. You too shall forgive and pray for the wicked. Defeat me by what I don't like or want!

> My therapist told me, *Leon, today we will talk and learn about forgiveness.*
>
> *Doc, I never wanted to forgive anyone or for them to forgive me, I don't know anything about forgiveness. I'd much rather they forget that I hurt them or act like what I did, didn't happen. I never wanted anyone to pray for me, it felt like they were pulling me away from evil, or trying to, and I didn't like that. I never knew how, never wanted to get down on my knees and pray for anyone. I knew that people praying for me thought that I had to return the favor. I would just rather remain evil, show them my*

lack of care or concern about prayer, so that they changed their mind about praying for me.

Well, Leon—your homework this evening will be to write letters to family members, okay?

Begrudgingly, I tried my best to oblige. I walked out of her office, with smoke blowing from my ears and nostrils. I didn't write the letters, but her thought of doing so had anchored itself in my mind. It felt better just giving my family members the silent treatment. I still had a lot of work to do. She did make me think about how I was anchored in and with evil and anger, and it was just time to heave around on that anchor, take it in, and set sail on a new journey. Dysfunction felt so good to my soul. Anytime I felt my spirit, my conscience, start to force me to come to terms with the kind of life I was living, I shut it down instantly. I had no time for self-reflection. Quite frankly, I think I would have exploded from all the guilt. Deep down, I knew this was far from the best way to live my life, but I was helpless, caught in a tangled mess of my own making.

Everything I did was to gratify my flesh. Never mind that it was the part of me that would not live on after death. My flesh would become food for worms and microorganisms while my essence would live on. And yet, that essence, the beauty of my mother's covering, was the part of myself I paid very little mind. This mindset would follow me for the next nine years, when I became a Navy recruiter in Cleveland, Ohio where I would sleep with many women and also destroy my marriage. I'll tell you this much: everything about narcissists, be it mental or physical, goes right back to our childhood. We are a product of those early years in ways we cannot even begin to comprehend. When I was a young teenager, as wild as it sounds, I attracted the attention of a lot of older women. They always complimented me on my body and my looks, and because I was so young, all the sweet words went to my head; it only encouraged me to continue to work on my exterior alone and pay no attention to things that really mattered, like my character and values. This happens to women, too.

I became very superficial!

When dealing with narcissists, you would be amazed at how many faces they can present to the world and the efficiency and accuracy with which they can switch between all of them. They ascertain a lot of opportunities to practice their craft every day with unsuspecting people. Narcissists can have many faces or aspects to their psyche. The bizarre thing is that they believe in each character and treat it as separate from the others. You all call them "masks"; I called mine "when I needed them!"

They can easily verbally or physically abuse you, walk away, and blame it on the other character while delving into a lack of character, care, or concern at that moment. Strategically, the different characters will always return on special days, events, and times that are associated with you and your emotions. This is known as "anchoring."

Anchoring with Breadcrumbs

The unseen drug—novocaine—I am numb and high and will just make you high but not numb. I want you to feel it but I can't handle feeling any emotions. The trauma bond starts when you notice any of my red flags...and you stay! You're numb to the pain that comes from me—I'm numb and absent of love and the pain that I give to you!

In anchoring, I expect you to eat with me, dance with me, laugh with me, protect me, and have sex with me, all while I am hurting—this creates "your trauma bond"—but only for you. I expect you to ignore my red flags and deal with me according to how I repair myself, but I won't. You have hope and hope is tied into *your* faith, not mine. You're dutiful! Yes, it is disrespectful to you, but you pay more attention to how I make your body feel. That supersedes everything you have accomplished in life. Although I am a broken man, you admire how I pay attention to your vulnerable feelings and emotions; no one else has done this to and for you. I give you a little of Leon and it feels amazing for me to let you use your magical, empathetic powers on me. It's psychological—mentally releasing dopamine, and you feel this challenge. It becomes a slow drip all over your body—it remains with you all day, at work, at home, and even while you're away from me. The dopamine saturates your spine and goes throughout your nervous system. I'm used to being dysfunctional, but you're not. You look into my eyes, looking for pain, and you see it. Then, with each waking moment, each day, month, and year—you continue to look into my eyes—taking that drug into your soul—searching for an improved product, a growing man, all because you helped me and you want to see and feel that assist! You're my coach, my confidant, my nurturer, my planner and healer. We're now healing and planning together—which creates an even deeper bond for you. I understand you, I listen to you, but the imbalance comes in when I don't feel you like you feel me. You'll fight even harder for me to connect with you, to keep me. This becomes a high for you that you chase and chase and chase, while I run, making you exhaust every effort to pull me back in. You want that drug, you need that drug, and so I breadcrumb you and you continue to chase the high! You can have and deserve a full loaf of healthy, wheat bread, but you now settle for unhealthy, leftover, breadcrumbs.

You're STUCK to the possibility of seeing my potential come to fruition. Combine anchoring with trauma bonding and most women, and some men, feel and become stuck and trapped. You'll begin to experience mental health issues; your cognitive skills begin to become displaced and eroded; and instead of working on "you," you would much rather work on keeping or helping a Leon—and HIS POTENTIAL!

Trauma, as you see it, is what I went through, what I experienced, or how I'm dealing with it. Your hastily search for saving a situation in its dire circumstances puts you in a state of crisis and emergencies, always. You lose your vision, so neglect of others never cross your mind. You hold onto every thought, or even the possibility—especially the possibility of another person taking over your project and enjoying the fruits of your labor. You're a hard worker and will only be outdone by me, and no one else. That seems so insane to you that you would rather risk going insane than to let Leon slip way. That's failure to you! It begins to deepen, and the bond—which is like a strong, dark, gorilla glue—starts to seal itself around your once-beautiful aura. No one can see your aura anymore, but you can feel it—so things still seem to be bright and right to you, regardless of who's telling you "things aren't right and you look dull!" The only other deep, emotional feeling you want or need is from that toxic person. Anything or anyone other than that, will be a wasted high, and you refuse to want to be released from the novocaine. Not only do you lose your ability to think rationally, but you lose your vision and become consumed with a Leon. Your family, friends, or co-workers can't make you see straight at all. The person dropping the anchor in your spirit will always be removed from any level of empathy. Anchoring is done on purpose. It allows for the abundance of "supply." A Leon is numb, but all others are just "HIGH!"

Anchoring the sweet sounds of songs you all have shared, places visited, types of food you all ate together, the smell of a certain cologne that Leon wore, weigh heavy on your mind.

I lived this life for years. I avoided feelings, hurt, pain, the truth, and commitment, with a smirk on my face, believe it or not. I had my own Novocain, but mine was a lug, tightly securing any and all hurt, keeping it inside and close. Overcome the Novocain, so you can process the pain and not deflect, project, or go insane!

Nightmares

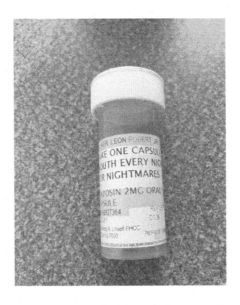

Narcissists are reprimanded for not being vulnerable. For me, the uncontrollable nightmares were just the beginning. My teeth would grind and grind and grind.

Aside from waking up, soaking wet, I would always dream about demons. They were white and furry, and also black and furry. I never had a choice in when they came or how they looked when they came. I never saw their faces, because they were always hunched over. They would just appear. Their backs were huge, and widespread. The demons would wiggle slowly, breathing deeply, swaying from side to side and just remain there, two to three feet away. Taunting me. My eyes were wide open and all I could do was look at their scruffy fur. They were never face-to-face with me. My mouth was sealed tight, and my teeth were clenched! I would swallow dry spit, deep gulps. I was just waiting on them to stand tall and pounce! This is by far no comparison to what I took women through, but it was painful. It would only be fair now to ask that I receive what those women received. During these episodes, I would squirm, bite down even harder, and grab my sheets so tight that I could feel my nails dig into the palms of my hands through the sheets. I would tussle, sit up, stare straight ahead, and then lay back down, delusional and staring at the ceiling, sweat running down my forehead, chest, and stomach. I could feel my back stick to the sheets from the wetness. There was no time limit on the timeframe or when it happened, but it did, and when it did happen, the nightmares were severely intense. I never wanted to go back to sleep after the incidents. I didn't want the demons to come back. My heart rate would rise higher and higher, I could hear my heartbeat, the temples on each side of my head would pulse. It felt like my chest and head were going to explode. My entire head would pound! As I lay in my bed, my feet would turn inward, and my ankles would strain and stretch, while my arms remained securely to my side, pinned down and close to my body. There was no protection at all. I couldn't even speak—I was gagged! There was never any kind of smell, just wetness, all over my body and pressure holding me down. There was never a vision of anyone coming to help me. I was in bed with my ex, but I felt alone. It was strange to me how I could experience this intense moment, and right next to me, lay a beautiful woman that slept very peacefully.

One time, one of my ex's told me;

Leon, I watched you sleep last night, you're not okay!

I've stated some negative things about vulnerability; however, as the Bible states, admitting to being vulnerable will lead to a connection. Being vulnerable is a source of hope, empathy, accountability, and authenticity. Once a woman told me she was vulnerable, I would let her go. I ran, and turned my back. I wasn't ready for a connection, so as I walked away, I disconnected. And in disconnecting, I gave up my ability to connect to her. She was honest and her words of vulnerability were laced with truth, honesty, and God. I was doomed when I turned my back on her. She was a Christian. I lied to her. Once I did a fake repent, but it didn't matter, God knew better and so I was stripped of any kind of masculine power that may have been granted to me at one time. So, I stalked her but the devil's energy and guidance fell on deaf ears. My hurt and pain from walking away from her didn't subside until I submitted, gave in, and left her alone. She was God's child and there was nothing that I could do about it. Never turn your back, hurt, misuse, abuse, or neglect any of God's children. When you do, you'll be visited by a demon that only shows you their back!

Eschatological

The Vision of God. The substance of the end of times. She saw it. She extended a branch to me, with an olive, so that I could eat and nourish my soul and spirit!

> *I forgive you, Leon, she said to me.*
>
> *I became upset because of my ego, but realized that she was the better person, much stronger, gifted, talented, and beautiful than me. She freed me with those words and graced me with knowing how to release myself, and I will always admire her for that. The high road is closer to God!*

Those demons that I saw were myself, hunched over. She faced me, though, a man she once feared, and then made herself stronger! It was the end, but also the beginning. Narcissistic or not, that woman, or any woman that extends a narcissistic man or woman an olive branch, you can begin to love deeply!

CHAPTER THREE

Loveless Trait #1: Acts of Disservice

I was abused as a child and lost my mother too soon. Her drug addiction, coupled with my parents' divorce, did me in! I lost my way of how to treat a woman early on! Narcissists only serve those that can serve them. Once you are locked in to serving them, they will begin to *bread-crumb* you—mommy issues!

Note #1: If your man or woman is not in treatment or therapy, you have to consider how far back their trauma goes. His/her mother or father, and grandparents—well over 100 years! Chances are, none of their family members received any kind of help. They just paid the trauma forward. You are now battling against well over 100 to 200 years of oppression, suppression, aggression, trauma, drama, neglect, and abuse, and possibly many more things. With this lineage of generational transmissions, you *can't* reach your partner, and you definitely can't reach their ancestors—until they *reach* them! Always remember that, but their issues can be healed—they just have to want it, and then enroll in therapy, and implement their lessons and make "exchanges!" *Discarding* their past, *ghosting* their issues and addictions, and giving the devil the *silent treatment*.

Note#2: When someone values their own bluntness and brutal honesty over their loved one's feelings, it's a sign of emotional abuse. Brutal honesty can be very hurtful. Remember this, next time you think about being blunt!

In trying to be blunt, your mind would most likely go back to that moment in time when you were hurt, neglected, or wanting revenge, and because of how you're feeling in that moment, you lash out.

"Hi, my name is Leon, but you will eventually meet Doubleo, and he's going to be of *great disservice* to you, your life, and your world." People don't say those things, but they will *surely* show you and some don't even realize it. I was one of those people. Doubleo is my nickname, and as you can see, I went into third person when warning you. That's deflection, protection of myself and my broken spirit, not yours.

I am going to screw you over and break your heart. I don't have a heart, so I don't know how it feels to hurt on that level. My spirit does not hold anything remotely close to pure, it harbors pure evil. I will treat you like crap, possibly feel bad, most often not, and then apologize, and you would still allow me to start the cycle over, and before you know it, it would become your cycle, too. By the time you realize it, you will not be able to let go, you would hold onto me like a mother to her child. When a man misses his mother, he will miss everything about you on purpose, like relating to you and what you require. Those things will not be his purpose or his target; he'll aim low, every single time.

The Dangers of Role Playing!

I am not good for you! Pure is boring to me, I am addicted to hell! I enjoy getting mad so that I can say hurtful things to you. I will make sure you apologize to me for making me hurt your feelings.

Look at what you made me do!

It's not that I did everything right, I did everything wrong. Everything! Isn't it strange that a narcissist or those with narcissistic traits know their actions are going to be lies but they choose to not express that part?

We swear up and down that we're okay, and even that's a lie!

Acts of Disservice include:

- Being extremely unfair
- A lack of humanity and lacking humbleness
- Possessing nothing noble—thoughts, ideas, or service
- Ignoring your white flags. You surrender but they will not
- Ignoring your needs
- Possessing a domineering mindset
- Withholding sex
- Consistent lack of empathy
- Avoiding growth with you on purpose
- Lacks all around vision and wherewithal
- Bad parenting
- Doesn't compliment you
- Disengaged
- Low relationship energy
- Very uncaring in, doesn't want to understand how you feel
- Uninterested in your life or lifestyle
- Inconsistent
- Lacking reciprocity
- Lacking remorse
- Inattentive
- Numb
- Repeating bad behavior
- Gross neglect
- Suppresses your authority
- Bypassing your needs
- Short responses
- Downplays your accomplishments
- Goes back on their word

CHAPTER FOUR

Manipulating the Truth

*Give me you until you are not you anymore, until I have
consumed you down to the last fiber of your being, and
then I'm gone!*

I have expressed to women the phrase "I am no good for you" just to
see what they would say, and they would just laugh. In their mind,
I could not possibly be that honest. I was hoping they would laugh,
because it was funny (even though deep down, it really wasn't). I was
really hoping they would laugh later, instead of cry, because the truth
was that I really wasn't any good for any of them.

I hated seeing women cry more than anything. I hated it because
now, I have to try and struggle and find feelings for her that I didn't
have. Why should I console them or be a shoulder for them to cry
on when no one did it for me? "Call me when you're done crying," I
would say to them. *"I don't have time for this shit!"* Brutal honesty.
Seeing her cry turned me on also. See the struggle there? Depending
on how I felt when I made her cry, that determined my immediate or
not so immediate approach towards her.

If I approached her, it wasn't to console her, not at all. I would
then kiss her, and if she kissed me back, it triggered a sexual emotion.
The crying then became a distant thing, that quick! I had to find a
way to connect with her tears, through seduction. Anything other than
that, I'd sit there and watch her cry and become infuriated.

I would storm off the scene, leaving the woman to tend to her tears herself, and then I would go have a drink, flirt with other women, drive around the block, and listen to music that triggered me, or music that made me think about my parents and my past, and then come back. I had to make myself feel better about what I had just done. Having alcohol in my system made me a lot meaner and much less caring. My dad was the same way. I was always scared to death of him whenever he got drunk. I would get quiet and not want to be around him, and so I knew the lady would be terrified and absent too. Of course, I would blame it all on the drinks the next day, until the next weekend came, and I repeated my same cycle.

Note: If I try to kiss you and you turn your head, I'm out, I'll leave. That's the best thing you could possibly do for yourself. Don't ever kiss me after I make you cry, please don't! Why? Well because the disrespect, mental abuse, and verbal abuse will take on a whole life, and get much worse!

After that, I'll never respect your emotional side, I'll see it as your desire to be intimate only! I can't allow you to have any kind of power over shifting my emotions. I have to be able to do that to you! Reverse psychology, but mainly "Psychological Reciprocity." I used this in a twisted way. My answer had to be your answer, even if your answer might have been the right answer. You cried because of something else other than what I did—I needed to hear that as your answer. I needed to and had to have some kind of input, though—for my own clarity, even if it was a lie. Then sway the lie, totally in my direction. My thoughts and ideas had to sound so truthful! Your input or answers were discarded and miniscule.

"You know what I'm saying, Lisa?"

"I do, Leon"

I needed her to agree with me, and not just say… "sure." Her answer of "sure" would feel disrespectful to me. I needed input, one that suited my philosophy of any kind. I was always sure to never revisit that topic again. I had to leave off with a "winning" mentality!

Psychological Reciprocity is a technique I learned in Persuasive Selling class. This also taught me to ask open-ended questions. I was assertive in my actual truth, and behavior, which is actually what women desire, but once I started to come clean about my negativity, bad habits and traits, they could not take it. Yet and still, they saw my depth of knowledge, awareness, and ability to converse. Something women love, just as much—so most, if not all, would settle on my potential!

"Girlllll, he is intelligent, though!"

I knew my ability to respond intelligently gave them that *inner* tingle.

Who is that honest after all? Well, I was, but I could not convince them of that fact. My truth was a lie to them.

In my double mind, and only to myself, I would mumble some variation of "I warned you, girl!"

It always happened at the bar when they were a tad bit tipsy and horny. I knew women loved when a man told the truth. Alcohol is a depressant, and even though my honesty was brutal, they still ultimately appreciated it. My truth was something they were not getting from someone they liked or loved.

"You can like me for one night; just remember, I warned you, girl!"

"Well, at least you're being honest. I can appreciate that, Leon. Most men lie about serious stuff when they don't have to."

"Yea, true."

Internal mumbling was my escape.

Man, she didn't do anything wrong to you, don't do it, shit. Doubleo comes first, not her!

My honesty was for my gain and not to appeal to them as an honest man, because I wasn't. I was just honest enough for them to let their guard down and be uninhibited along with me.

The only thing open after 2:00 a.m. are legs!

On other occasions, what I said to them was not true in the slightest, but my truthful manipulation was refreshing to them and I knew it. They heard the truth, but didn't see the manipulation.

On many occasions before I started to act up, I would have already warned her. Getting ahead of my "soon to come out traits," this was my way of deflecting and avoiding explaining myself when it did happen. I wasn't concerned about the fallout or residual effects. I was just informing her of what she should expect, before it happened. It was my weird way of preparing her. I knew that the other things I had planned to do to and for her, would supersede the pain that I would eventually inflict. This worked on women who were yearning for many things, those that have been neglected and not celebrated or appreciated.

"Yea, Leon, you did tell me, but you were laughing. How could I have known you were being serious?"

"That's because I was embarrassed."

I was trying to encourage them to act in a manner that's normally desired even when a man is being or seems foolish. It didn't work and I did not care. Help me help you to help me.

"Leon, you're so silly."

With a smile and while looking in her eyes, I would reply, "But, Lisa, I'm serious." My fingers were crossed behind my back. My little demon kid never left me. People that possess Traits of Disservice already know what they can't provide to a person in a relationship. They'll hide it, though. As for me, and I'm sure other men and women are conflicted, too, it was just easy to remain on my toxic path because that was safe for my heart.

Who could love someone that hates themselves? Well, lots of people can if they don't know that you hate yourself. It's easy; they just don't have to find out. I felt that if my mother could leave me, any woman could.

My struggle was that I felt like a giver—like my mom, but no one deserved the ultimate prize from me. I gave, to receive much more. I made myself believe that I was a good person even though I was nowhere close to that. So, seeking women broken like myself was the path of least resistance. "I'll grow when I'm ready," I told myself. I had become extremely comfortable with that, but I damn near never got to the point of growing.

The following took place on my 2019 book tour, during a radio station interview in Chicago. It was on "The Real 'Chat Daddy' Show."

"So, Leon, how do you know when you have the right woman?"

"I've always had the right women. But with me, they had the wrong man."

Deflection: *If you catch me in a lie, I'll simply lie about the lie you said I lied about.*

CHAPTER FIVE

Attracting Familiar Broken Spirits

This is the opposite of twin flames, and I call this "Mirrored Hell." We would argue, fight, have sex, drink, and then start over. She matched my energy, and was my mirror image. To me, this is the best and most efficient way to repel a narcissist or someone with these traits.

I discuss where this trait came from, later in the book.

Toxic Souls

We victimize each other and neither one of us will ever show our vulnerability—but are the first ones to look for it in other people! We both bear rotten fruit, lack humble-ness, and are too prideful. Always fighting back!

People with and those that attract toxic souls have been damaged very deeply during their childhood, the incubation period in their lives. The only thing they have to offer other people is pure hell. This has become their comfort zone, and they begin to believe that they have no one to connect to aside from those that are just like them. The expectations are low on both sides. Stepping up and assuming responsibility is fearful.

Narcissistic people, and those with the trait, do not and cannot deal with people that are the opposite, those who are strong, covered, blessed, and anointed. We are exposed before we can break you. I could feel their repellent before I got started. I had to try anyway!

People that are alike match each other's negative energies and, in the end, neither person grows. All they are interested in is who can win the war of attrition, who will lose the most, and who will lose first. Narcissistic trait carriers and narcissistic people actually keep score in their mind.

A Shared Purpose

We're both on an undeserving, impossible to have, throne and act accordingly—like we're deserving. We lack patience and always think we have to win. The feeling soon becomes addicting, like a hard drug. These types of people transfer so much toxicity into and towards each other. It becomes their form of an accepted loveless language; spewing venom and hate now resonates with them more than love and respect do, more than anything. Beware of their forked tongue. The reason these people continue on this path is because over time, they have become very comfortable with the negativity. In a way, you can say they have developed negative blood cells that are damaged and have replaced their ability to realize, conceptualize, accept, or even want "positive generated" blood cells. They run away from anything positive or wholesome. Their internal circuitry is composed completely of a flow of negative energy, and this results in total dysfunction and a damaged and toxic soul in dire need of a complete rewiring. They have a shattered psyche.

Their Human Potential lies dormant, but their twisted grip on religion keeps them in the church where, they turn to predators.

Human Potential and the Spirit

Human Potential and the Spirit reflect perfection, success, creativity, self-realization, and divinity.

Unhealthy People that openly speak of their religion, do so because this is their only sphere of influence. They know that it's an attraction for many people. Some do it as a way of gaining popularity with other religious people. Their spiritual growth suffers because their practices are

*not in place, not genuine, and neither are they aligned
or honest. More so than anything, the commission stages
of attachments, addictions, lies, deceit, and vices have
remained in place far too long, because they forget about
the act of 'omission.'*

God gave us our original mind, unblemished and free of any com-
missioning that's set in place to hurt or harm our temple, yet when
you find yourself struggling, like I did for many years, it's no one
but Satan tugging you in the wrong direction away from envisioning
your human potential. When this happens, you become a Fallen Man
or Fallen Woman.

These people are really afraid to consult their own weaknesses.
Doing so is how I began my self-realization and awakening. It's a
practice that requires time and care as you eradicate one weakness at
a time. Immerse yourself deeply in the thought of the damage that's
been caused by your vices and addictions. We give them life, and
our weaknesses take our life, day by day, week by week, month by
month, and year by year. As you abolish each weakness, your heart
and mind lose the attraction, feeling, and desire to the weakness and
all impurities.

Regardless of how loving they want to be, or how loving you
are to them, these impure people will destroy every person and relationship they encounter. The fear of getting help has presented itself
as a mental block to them, and they hold onto that as a means of
protection. They come up with the flimsiest of excuses, anything to
save face, not knowing that they are slowly rotting away, missing
out on who they really are. God doesn't create rotten people; people
create rotten people!

My Current Practice

Nowadays, I (1) strive for human perfection, (2) seek success by
being creative, (3) defy the odds against all social norms, (4) stop
being average or mediocre, notwithstanding the status quo, (5) think

outside the box, (6) gain self-realization (the awakening where you now understand what you are capable of), (7) remain on the path of Divinity, and (8) deliver my truth without fear or hesitation. There will be some days of discomfort, where I feel so sick, I can feel it in my stomach, but I do not let that deter me, and neither should you.

Traits and Actions of People with Shared Purposes

Drug addictions, past and present, violence towards each other, lies and accepted lies, fear of leaving any toxic environment, withdrawing from family, being comfortable with stagnant delusional bonding together to make themselves feel right and to prove others wrong.

Removing the Toxic Soul Timeline

All hope is not lost for people like that. They are redeemable. I was. We must conduct maintenance on both the inner and outer moral compass, starting our day off right. Toxic souls can be recalibrated with proper care and instruction. It begins with being true to yourself and showing up every day, authentic and genuine. At this point, you would not need to seek out that special someone; they will be attracted to you in this state.

Remember, like begets like. It will be a struggle at first, but if you are truly in tune with your true North, with your inner magnetic pole, your mind and spirit have no choice but to follow. Practice good and healthy thoughts. Become slow to react, listen more, meditate, stretch, select better friends, change your household scents, find colors that excite you, and only listen to good, positive music. These are tone-setters, built, made, created, and aligned by you to create the kind of environment to make you better. Internal cleansing is crucial too. Refrain from ingesting poisons; fast food is not good for your body. Make sure you drink better tea and cleaner water. Do more of drinking your food. Go green. Eat kale. Get a clear mind, a clear vision, a clear picture, and you become a better person. Clear equals transparency. When you are transparent, everyone knows and sees you, even the ones you once attracted as a toxic person. They'll now go the other way, or "clearly" see you differently.

My Timeline

It took me years to understand and implement these thought processes. Venom felt better for me. My girlfriend back in the 1990s derailed me, but had I taken heed then, my journey would have started sooner. She was enlightened and looked for and needed a father figure. I could have done that, but I didn't pay attention to her needs, just the ones that suited me sexually. My narcissistic traits began to grow deeper and deeper. I caused her pain but could not handle it when it happened to me. She was really good for me; I just allowed the devil to have his way with me. Some people think it is an act of love to share pain and trauma. It turned her on when I was angry.

> *Leon, sex is always good with you, but when you're mad, it's just insane!*
>
> *I know, but that wasn't me, it was my demon!*

I meant that, too. I had to always deflect, be it to a demon or whomever. I didn't want any kind of emotional connection. I truly believed that it was my demon making love to her. This was truly a sick idea; however, it was my way of deflecting the fact that I knew that I could fall in love with a woman. That demon helped me retain a cold heart. Yes, it was sick to think that way! Reckless abandon, cold, harsh, hard, and damaging. The two toxic people or one that's leading the healthy person, claim not to want to hurt one another, but we both know that the hurt, when it happens, won't mean anything to either one of us. You serve me and I serve you. That way, we'll avoid the deep hurt as well as our desire to rely on and do harm to people that hurt the little kid within us.

The two of us will never cross the line to enable growth; we've become too comfortable with being hurt. When you hurt the kid in me, you also awaken the demon inside of him, the one you knew about. It is not my fault you chose to do this. This is all on you. I never did harm anyone physically; my abuse was more mental and verbal, which was a lot worse. It felt good to warn a woman about my inner little demon, because after the inflicting of pain occurred, I was not only in a free state of mind, but free of any fault. My good nature fought and struggled with this.

I would say "I'm sorry" as often as I could, but it usually came out without any hint of remorse. A terrible thing indeed.

Healed People Heal People

Hurt and severely damaged people have a skewed since of reality. What I learned about that, is that it was very hard to let go of that since I never thought that there was anything was wrong with me—I knew there was—it was just too damn hard to let go of my demons—*I was comfortable being in hell*! But I couldn't let anyone know. From that, I either made people sick, sick of me, or want to heal themselves. I was just fine with them leaving me or leaving me alone. Sadly, in my mind, they were the ones with all of the issues. Hurt people have blind-sides and blind spots that cause collisions, damage, collateral damage. All because we're being uninsured—not covered. Sound familiar? Always have heart/soul insurance.

I've had many experiences with *mirrored hell* types of women. She was never built to be a bride. We reflected each other's pain and addictions, and basked in it. Relationships are supposed to make you a better person, but around them I only got worse.

I felt really comfortable in their company, and they felt the same way. We were used to being treated unfairly and had also suppressed their feelings until they met me.

All of us unmasked our deepest desires and told each other our darkest secrets. This was a mistake in retrospect, a very dangerous thing to do. In this relationship of disservice, the first person to give into feelings and emotions would be the first one to act out in anger and violence. Seeing my mother get beaten up when I was a kid was a very harrowing experience. I decided I was never going to punch or hit a woman; however, if a woman hurt me, my only way to hurt her back, without physical harm or violence, was to cheat, sadly. It made perfect sense in my head at the time. That was when I knew I had a major problem. I was completely empty on the inside. The emptiness was so shallow and off-putting that it got to the point of me being able to sleep with one woman and lay next to the one I was dating barely an hour later.

With the mirrored woman, I did not have to do much aside from showing up, smiling, laughing, going on dates, and anything else we had in common. It was all superficial stuff, by the way. I didn't do drugs but I was comfortable sitting there watching her get high. I knew she was going to take care of me after. She had other guys, too, and probably laid next to them before or after me. I had to make myself believe this so that I didn't get jealous. I never asked her if she was seeing other people. Honestly, I really was not interested in the answer, because I knew deep down inside, regardless of how strong I thought I was, I couldn't handle her truth. That's the downside of being with someone just like you; a "mirrored hell" woman is just as dangerous as the man. You had better not get in too deep with them. Had she told me that she was seeing other people, I would have tried to sleep with her close friend, or someone else she loved. We acted the way we did because we were in some kind of twisted sync; my needy traits matched hers. We weren't changing anything about each other, just exchanging one pain and trauma for another.

If you have any "traits of disservice," you'll deplete people who come around you. Lying would come easily to you because you are only looking to receive and not give in return. With that mindset, you don't care if you get caught in a lie. People have many reasons and ways of extending a disservice. Mine just happened to be lust, deeply rooted in feeding my demons. Lust was all about self and not her, not her needs. For the most part, the women I dated were sexually satisfied and entertained but it wasn't anything more than that. If I catered to what they needed outside of sex, it was to get what I wanted in the bedroom or get a similar gesture in return. It was all about my needs and what I stood to gain.

Due to the fact that I had to deal with loss at such an early age, I had so many fears that I had suppressed. However, because these things are never really gone, they soon reared their ugly heads, never mind that I buried them deep in my psyche. Although I had great mentors growing up, we never talked about dysfunction, anger issues, integrity, character, or marriage. It was almost like we were merely playing a role in each other's lives. There was never any real interest in tackling deep issues and things that actually mattered, just like it was with my "mirrored hell woman."

I wasn't **groomed to be a groom,** and the women I dated, just like myself, were not **built to be brides**. I never discussed marriage with any of them, nor did they with me. We both knew that our sick and twisted journey would be short-lived. Marriage was a joke for both of us. We knew better.

As a naval recruiter, from 1992 to 1996 in Cleveland, I was a year removed from stalking my ex-girlfriend in San Diego and my dysfunctions were in full swing. I was getting sicker by the moment and dating many women without a care in the world. While we were at a bar and drinking, flirting, and womanizing, my brother mentioned to me one day:

Yo bro, I think there's something seriously wrong with you.
Have you thought about getting psychiatric treatment?

I of course laughed it off. How could there be anything wrong with me?

Man, I just won Recruiter of the Year, I'm number one,
potna— shiiiiiiit, I'm good dog!

Between the liquor, the loud music, and all of the beautiful women gathered around us complimenting me and my uniform, while in the bar, his words danced in my head. I was only five years removed from speaking to my first psychiatrists, at age twenty-one!

Get help Leon, yea, get help.
Nah, I'm good, I'm number one!"

I had to constantly remind myself that my mind wasn't slipping away, that I was okay—but I wasn't okay. Success kept me afloat, but being unsuccessful in all of my relationships drowned those women. A rather large amount of the women in the bar that night, and those we would encounter throughout the weekend, partying in Cleveland, were nothing but Leon's!

A mirrored hell type of woman whispered to me:

Leon, we both know the deal, so let's just continue this until we can't stand to hurt each other anymore!

I thought she was sick. She was—but I was too!

Through it all, in Cleveland, I got married in 1995. I wasn't ready, not even close, and I remember reading about my parent's divorce while retrieving the divorce decree of a young man I was trying to put into the Navy. Their divorce papers were still in the courthouse. I remember that it hurt like hell to read those words…*Dissolution of marriage awarded to Sylvia E. Walker.*

When I read my parents' divorce, the accusations about my dad dawned on me: *The defendant has been guilty of extreme cruelty.*

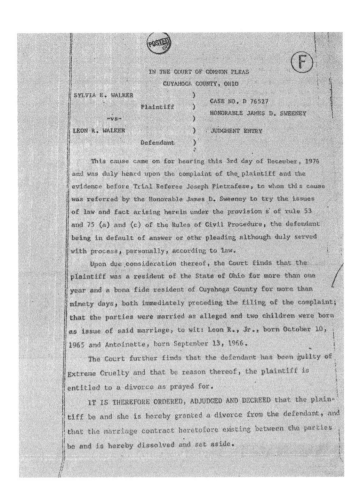

IN THE COURT OF COMMON PLEAS
CUYAHOGA COUNTY, OHIO

SYLVIA E. WALKER)
     Plaintiff)   CASE NO. D 76527
-vs-)   HONORABLE JAMES D. SWEENEY
LEON R. WALKER)   JUDGMENT ENTRY
    Defendant)

This cause came on for hearing this 3rd day of December, 1976
and was duly heard upon the complaint of the plaintiff and the
evidence before Trial Referee Joseph Pietrafese, to whom this cause
was referred by the Honorable James D. Sweeney to try the issues
of law and fact arising herein under the provisions of rule 53
and 75 (a) and (c) of the Rules of Civil Procedure, the defendant
being in default of answer or other pleading although duly served
with process, personally, according to law.

Upon due consideration thereof, the Court finds that the
plaintiff was a resident of the State of Ohio for more than one
year and a bona fide resident of Cuyahoga County for more than
ninety days, both immediately preceding the filing of the complaint;
that the parties were married as alleged and two children were born
as issue of said marriage, to wit: Leon R., Jr., born October 10,
1965 and Antoinette, born September 13, 1966.

The Court further finds that the defendant has been guilty of
Extreme Cruelty and that be reason thereof, the plaintiff is
entitled to a divorce as prayed for.

IT IS THEREFORE ORDERED, ADJUDGED AND DECREED that the plaintiff be and she is hereby granted a divorce from the defendant, and
that the marriage contract heretofore existing between the parties
be and is hereby dissolved and set aside.

Reading that hurt like hell. For one, I never saw my dad as cruel; and number two, through therapy I learned that I was also cruel. I was hoping that my kids never saw me in that light either—but they did. At age fifty-six, I am still dealing with how cruel I was to my kids.

What did my father do wrong? Was I just like him? Had I turned out like that? The answer of course was "yes," in many ways. I would mimic not only my father's ways but my parents' divorce—thirty years later! Aside from being a cheater, lying, misleading, not being a fair partner, and making the women think I was someone that I wasn't, I was very cruel in all of that. I had become the same person that my mother said my dad was in their divorce papers. That's why it hurt so bad: I saw it in writing!

I was served my divorce papers on the pier, Naval Base, Norfolk, the same day I was promoted to Master Chief. This was back in April 2006. My life was nothing but a series of high highs and the absolute lowest of lows.

CHAPTER SIX

Shadow Trait Number #1: Lust

Narcissists lust for flesh, control, dominance, attention,
your belief in them, sex, seduction, and your silence. The
devil is hard at work with them—he holds our hand and
he's our escort—right to hell! Don't taste me, as I am a
deadly sin—poison so good that you'll eat it, drink it, and
consume it in large quantities. Being demonic, the poison
wasn't poisonous to me. I carried it like a deadly serpent.
There is no mercy in lust!

– Leon R. Walker, Jr.

I could *taste* lust; it was sweet and savory. I could see it, just like a
fiend can taste and see their much-needed favorite drug. The antic-
ipation engulfs them. This is why they don't hear you or see you,
because you're not important in this moment. It's not the taste that
we so insanely seek and conquer, though; it's the euphoric feeling and
the thrill, set to enter our veins before and during. Not after! After
the thrill and euphoric feeling dies down, it's a long and hard fall, so
we start our quest all over again, regardless of who's hurt during the
intense quest. The repetition has to be ongoing and constantly fed.
Narcissistic people are drug addicts and hunters, too!

I was afraid to love, but not afraid to lust. I was a prisoner of lust!
My mouth would actually water at the sight of women. Sometimes, I
didn't even have to see them; sometimes all it took to get me slobbering

like a dog was catching a whiff of their perfume. It was that bad. Had I remained a virgin until my late twenties, my body count would never have entered the high numbers. Sadly, that reality was already ruined when I was eight.

Although lust was just a shadow trait, not hardwired to my personality, I discovered my first "act of disservice" by relating to the devil more than God or anything holy.

My Seven Deadly Sins

Gluttony - I was a sex pig.

Pride - Proud to be a slut.

Envy - Of those that were able to live right, or at least tried to.

Wrath - Anger, rage, and hatred of being me.

Greed - I wanted women of all races, complexions, and personalities.

Sloth – I avoided God, so that the devil could have my flesh. An idle mind is his workshop, after all.

Eight Ways of Giving

1. Spend money on others.
2. Spend time with others.
3. Volunteer.
4. Be emotionally available.
5. Perform acts of kindness.
6. Compliment someone.
7. Make someone laugh.
8. Tell your story.

Being afraid to love caused me to keep myself away from hurt. I knew that I was dodging hurt, because it was inevitable that I was going to cheat and would not be able to handle that pain coming from her when she found out that I did. I had to always be prepared to walk away, so I had to hurt her first, to keep her back on her heels, uneasy, and uninformed. I needed to be proactive and place myself in control of her feelings and emotions.

We were both missing and needing the same thing, but I had to make myself aware of the impending doom before she did somehow, even though we had similar mindsets on the whole issue. Being this way was extremely unfair, but I knew that a woman who thought and acted like me would be very evil and dangerous indeed. I was not a Boy Scout by any means, but I always made sure I was prepared for anything, and for this type of woman, I already had an airtight plan for entry and exit. For the women that are not like this, some men have just an entry plan, and we don't bother with an exit plan because she can easily become our teacher, not a partner we will become addicted to. Why? Well, because she's the motherly type, and only our mothers are more important than a woman that thinks and acts like us. This is why a woman just like us can't hurt us, unlike the woman that isn't. We honestly have more respect for the womanly woman. She knows us, we know her, and she can help build us, care for us, and we do have chemistry with her. We just never seem to be ready for a real woman. I know I wasn't.

Nurturing women will take us back, over and over again. But since she's real, genuine, solid, and trustworthy, she'll possess the ability to walk away and not be hurt over and over again. This is what we're really afraid of, because we always wait until it's too late to get our shit together. No man, narcissist or not, wants to be left by that kind of woman.

We can always find a woman who is pure and willing to ride it out, unlike the broken woman, who'll leave just as quickly as we will. We just enjoy always being halfway out instead of all the way in. We have serious commitment issues. Attractions and addictions to people and what they have or give you, can and will take over. They say opposites attract, and they do; however, they do "distract" and "subtract." Although at that moment when you meet someone for the first time, it may just be a casual encounter. Speaking of "casual encounters," people that do not talk much will talk when they first meet you, to draw you in. After that, the real person will show up.

Silent or Sneaky People Carry:

- Relationship laziness.
- Self-centered agenda.
- Hidden red flags.
- Lies.
- Personality disorders.
- Possible abuse issues.
- Fear of moving forward.
- Trust issues.
- A lack of ambition.
- Low energy towards you because they know that you know who they really are.

Traits of Disservice Numbers (TODN)

For me, it was injected into my soul on many levels. I was already fighting and losing the war of attrition as a kid. What are your life numbers in relation to the eight ways to give, and the seven deadly sins? They can and will cancel each other out. Mine were:

I possessed all of the seven deadly sins. And only one way of giving, which was to *make people laugh.*

What's your TODN?

Here's mine:

+1 in Way(s) to give, I was at a −7 in giving.

All seven sins. This equals to 7 and −7, with a +1.

I had a totally depleted soul and spirit.

Low Relationship Credibility Score

These people are attractive! They live and thrive through their external appearance. Verbal abuse is very easy for them. They have a forked and quick tongue. Low relationship energy, brag a lot, and love material things, too. Very seductive. Hard-headed, callous, angry, and greedy. They lack decorum, morals, and wherewithal. They're very good at triangulation, and lie easy. They lack remorse. Most can interchange their morals but remain more often without morals. Very cocky and arrogant, too.

During my thirty-two years of service to my country in the Navy, and also in the time since I began my healing journey, I've learned through study of my actions and inactions that when you come across someone like me who doesn't show *acts of service* but *acts of disservice*, you must help them and give from your good graces. Using your gift, like I do now, you must be obligated, accept, and be ready to cover them. Don't worry about fear, as that is natural in your new role of covering people, leading, and understanding your gift from God. Believe me, walking away from the devil was hard because of my greed and tarnished flesh, but I knew where I was headed, and it even looked beautiful to me.

Walk up the hill, to heal, on your heels—that's part of the struggle. You'll feel pushed back but just keep going! It won't be easy, but just remember that the people you hurt didn't have it easy either. Sometimes we attract the opposite sex to keep them alive with our gift.

In 1987, when the USS *Stark* FFG-31 was attacked by two missiles, I had to see my first psychiatrist, and he told me *Mr. Walker, successful people see their success before it even happens.*

From that day, I started seeing things, visualizing my future, creating thoughts, and envisioning different good scenarios for myself. I did this for my career first, and then for my relationships. I still wasn't ready to be in one, but at that point I had acquired the blueprint for relationship success but my motivation remained outside of the relationship, instead of inside of it. The vision for a successful relationship, like my psychiatrists said, was only faced, for many years—not engaged in, like my job. Sadly, I could surely sell it as a success in the beginning, though. I cried hard every time I got this vision because I understood just how true and possible it was. With a little effort, the reality could be in my grasp. I just had to be disciplined, obedient, and believe it. This is also what you need to do. But I didn't. I just talked a good game!

I will always say this: "What happens to you as an adult and how you perform when you get older, goes back to your childhood behaviors."

I never got help for my issues until I was forty-seven. Forty-seven! Can you imagine that? I had at least five loveless traits I understood and used regularly. Every last one of at least five. These were my primary languages. I knew them well, as most people do. It's not only about how we are raised but also how we are created. It comes from the interplay of nature and nurture. We lose or strengthen these traits based on how we're brought up and the path we select or are forced to be on.

At eleven years old, I lost three major things: love, a parent, and a home.

Now, seeing as though my first love language is Acts of Service, I enjoy being a giver. However, as an adult I would consistently revert to my childhood issues of anger, loss, and abuse. This clouded my ability to think clearly and perform in a healthy role, as I always wanted to get revenge on my molesters and oppressors, rendering myself unable to give unconditionally. Their faces were on her face. No matter how hard I tried, I could not unsee it. I struggled with this for years, and then eventually, I submitted to my demons of protection. My service to her was for her mind, soul, and vagina, and was just to manipulate, misguide, and keep her weak, and on her heels. I couldn't care less about love; in fact, love terrified me. Anytime I found out that someone loved me, I would become quiet, not wanting them to detect any lack of reciprocity on my part that they were no doubt expecting. It was like I was being defeated, and narcissistic men and women have to hurt you first or last, they do not like to lose and then wallow in defeat.

In January of 2015, I began to love myself. I was now serving and facing and not acting. According to the Bible, we should give according to our heart's desire and not reluctantly or under compulsion. Numerically, I was heartless.

CHAPTER SEVEN

Meeting a "Traits of Disservice" Narcissist

Some people are attracted to narcissists, so it is your duty to know and understand what you like and what you are against. You just might be their mirror and be able to exchange their energy; if not, you will be abused. I'll mention the "six-figure man" here because I used to be one and in today's society, women are all about that. It's a very shallow desire, because being a six-figure man, I was still useless as your man. I had money but no honey. Between 2006 and 2015, I made upwards of 120,000 dollars per year in the Navy. I wasn't shit, though.

When looking for a six-figure man, irrespective of whether or not you are in a relationship or plan to get into one, it's crucial that you take the following steps to make your relationship better by preparing you for the next person or ensuring you keep the one you have. Stop looking for a man's money. If you do it right, he'll give accordingly and you'll both be much better off. Stop with the demands, especially if you don't allow him to put demands on you.

Aside from talking about and seeking a person's physical attributes, and finances, you must:

- Gently bring up mental health. Women hardly ever ask this question.
- Listen to their conversation.
- Watch their patterns.
- Pay attention to body language.

- Absorb the mental stimulation.
- Acknowledge the good traits.
- Be willing to build and yield.
- Get to know his good side, the things he tells you about himself, and watch them play out.

We all know that everyone is flawed, so try not to hold that against him, especially since you know you are flawed, too, and would not want him to do that to you. Lots of times, when you meet a man for the first time, some of you come in guarded based on the last man. Women, at times, refuse to qualify men in the beginning; they look to disqualify him and then wonder why they aren't together. Stop being so physically and financially judgmental and do more mental judging based on his character and integrity finances.

The good men come with a financial numerical figure too:

- Commitment = 20K
- Passion = 20K
- Loyalty = 20K
- Ambition = 20K
- Drive = 20K
- Compassion = 20K

If you give men, women, and yourself a chance and really get to know who we really are, above is your real six-figure partner. Had they disqualified me like that, I would have been in and out of hundreds of relationships just trying to show the woman that I had more good qualities. I would keep trying to prove myself by doing away with my bad qualities, and learning to be more patient. Please pay attention to red and white flags. I mention "white flags" because men that hurt, for whatever reason, also want to surrender against the war in their head. Don't ever lower your standards but don't put them out of reach, either. Be fair. Men do deserve chances, and that's why I include the notion to not disqualify them early on. Don't be an assessor, a grader, or feel like you are better than them. If you are a psychologist or psychiatrist or even a social worker, be extremely careful when you ask questions. Your profession could possibly get in the way and this can make you come off as insufferable sometimes. Yes, it does help, but we want a woman at home and not a boss or therapist.

Bringing your work home and using it hourly, or daily, will run a man or woman into the ground. When speaking about mental health, it is crucial that you ask this in a fair and pleasant way. Mental health is and has always been a taboo topic. People shy away from it, hide their issues, medication, and actions. I had many problems with my mental health. For one, my PTSD was severe. It became my disability until I learned how to manage it when it started coming on. I am not violent, but I do get irritated easily when women repeat things and disrupt my comfort zone. I have triggers from past relationships. Both men and women are like this. Don't ever look down on people; give them a chance by first looking up to them; then if you do look down, it would be because you have done all that you could possibly do. After that, if you go back to a person that you now look down on, check yourself and realize that one of your sins is now your problem: Gluttony.

Remember your TODN, the numbers I mentioned earlier? You and your partner must grade your "sins." Add them up. Also do this for your "ways to give" and see what you come up with, and then start working from there. These numbers will tell you a lot about a person's soul, spirit, and both compasses, internal and external. This will also give you your life and relationship credit score. Because of my fear of love and having a good heart at the same time, I struggled. I know you may think that sounds crazy, but it's true. I had to make a decision as to which way to go: to be a genuine lover or an innocent looking monster? I chose to be a monster. It was safer.

I was so empty inside, yet I was extremely experienced. I used many things against women to hide my flaws and remain on top and in charge. If I was with you, and wasn't in charge, I found someone to be in charge of while being with you. I needed my fix. It was like a drug. I had to find a way to balance my attrition out. I was afraid to lose in any way to a woman.

The Dangers of Self-Serving

Extending "Acts of Disservice" will not always play out in your favor. One day you're going to meet someone with hell in their soul, just like you. Instead of the person being your "Mirrored Hell" they may shatter your world. I got a little lucky. Disservice isn't fun or healthy.

My dating sights were off. My vision was clouded, and I would delve deeper and deeper into promiscuity.

Here's a little anecdote for you. I'm sitting around in my apartment, bored and lonely. Clicking on the computer and logging in, my heart starts beating fast as my toes tap lightly on the carpet. My log-in credentials are always ready. I look for certain features in a woman. I have never cared about what is on her profile. We are all here for the same thing. Not trying to get it twisted. If her looks and body are average, then nothing else matters to me. I would find other things to turn me on later.

When you are lonely, you can only hold onto your morals for so long, and as soon as you let your guard down, the truth comes out and we both become uninhibited. Greed clouded my vision. The sites had become extremely dangerous. There's a difference between self-love and self-respect, and I had neither.

Cheryl. She was from overseas, the Middle East. She was a medical doctor working at a prominent hospital in Chicago. Her perfume smelled horrible. I did enjoy her coal-dark, thick, black hair, though. Women in the Middle East are not really valued in their country, and if they want a good education of some sort, they must escape. Titles have never really interested me. I wanted someone that wanted to have fun and she did, but for just a brief period. We had breakfast in Kenosha, Wisconsin, talked a little, and headed to her home. I was following her in her car and as we arrived, we pulled into her driveway, and then she opened up to me. In her accent, she began speaking as we hugged in front of her house. Cheryl kept looking around and it bothered me.

"Yo, why are you looking around and looking so nervous? Hug me tighter!"

"Listen, Leon, I enjoyed breakfast and I'm into you, but I must warn you. This isn't my house, I rent a room in the basement. I'm not only a doctor like I told you, but also a fugitive from my country. My husband abused me, so I left the Middle East, family and all, and I am being tracked to get murdered. If they catch me and take me back, I will be stoned to death. You must go now, okay?"

I heaved a deep sigh, taking in all she had just said. And then slowly, I let her go, looked around a bit before darting to my car.

"No problem, thank you for breakfast and for the warning!"

I still hadn't learned my lesson.

The site and needy women closed my vision and increased my desire for the easy catch. We were all on these sites for the same things: attention, being uplifted, casual encounters, and many more frivolities.

Lisa. She was from Chicago. She warned me about who she was, and that really enticed me. She had new ideas. I knew, as a child, that I liked different or weird women, and was even teased about it, but I didn't care. The Navy had already introduced me to much more than weird women. I have one friend who was addicted to midgets. During my time in the Navy, I met women that wanted to be bitten, hung upside down, wrestled, slapped very hard, along with a host of other intense and extreme things. Years later, when I finally met someone that genuinely spooked me, I wasn't ready.

She was very cute, wore all dark clothes, black lipstick, and was deeply into all things Goth, bondage, and S&M. It sounded very exciting. Her eyes were mesmerizing. We met up and after seeing her "sex tools" and listening to her instructions, I knew that she was out of my league. Lisa played other roles that she was into as well. We sat at Panera Bread, in the parking lot, ten miles north of Chicago and discussed her submissive role, life, black people, white people, you name it. She happened to be fond of black people.

"I like black men, Leon, because my parents don't. They're racist and for some reason, I have this deep, dark, desire and fetish to punish them through willfully giving myself to a black man."

At first, I felt good and important that a Goth woman wanted to meet with me and hang out. Now, I felt like I was being used. What a blow to my ego. At first, the submissive role she wanted to play sounded really good, being the narcissist that I was, but after she told me she wanted to be my slave, crawl up to me and serve me, I just couldn't do it. A few ideas stuck with me, though, except for the slave thing. I know all women enjoy dressing up, playing roles in the bedroom and all that, especially if their sex life is boring. Don't tell them directly. Suggest it.

Carey. She was from New York. We met up at Joe's Crab Shack in Illinois. Her hair was short and shaved on the sides. It made her look very attractive. According to her profile, she was polished, educated, and enjoyed walks in the park. Most of that shit wasn't true, and besides it was too slow for me. Why the hell would I be walking in a park with a woman during the prime of my life? Our food came. We ate and started talking about the Chicago Bulls. As soon as she got full and had her drink, the real Carey came out. She put her drink down, and leaned forward a little before clearing her throat.

"So, Leon, let me show you something."

"Cool, let's see."

She took off her sweater and I thought she was going to show me her titties. She then rolled up her sleeves, peeled back her collar and turned her head to the right.

"See these?"

She pointed to her wrist first.

"Uh, uh, yea, what's up?"

"Psych ward shit. You need to be careful who you date. I'm just going to be straight up with you, because you're cool. I think you're attractive, cool, and have a really cool story, but I'm just out here!"

"Huh?"

"Two attempts at suicide when I couldn't kick the meth habit is what you're looking at."

Carey had tried to slit her wrist and cut her own neck. There was one scar that ran across her entire neck, from ear to ear, and the other scars on her wrists were vertical, at least three inches, so I knew that she knew what she was doing.

"Oh, wow, sorry to hear that."

"It's okay, thanks for dinner. It was nice meeting you."

"Uh, okay, Carey. See you later!"

When you are of a disservice to people, expect the same in return. I was starting to get my karma, my reward, for being a narcissist.

My narcissistic traits were:

- Make you mad on purpose, go away, come back and make you happy.
- Ignore you when I know you like to talk.
- Don't give you too much attention.
- Hurt your feelings and watch you cry.
- Act like I don't care about you.
- Deflect.
- Avoid answering questions.
- Make you feel guilty when I'm the one guilty.
- Don't keep my word but make it up with things you like or like to do.
- Lead you on.
- Twist your words around.
- Refuse to apologize.

- Show you attention in front of other men, not women.
- Make you feel less than me.
- Give you very few compliments so that you feel ugly, when you're not.
- Very nonchalant acting.
- If you reject me, I have the ability to make myself better real quick, come back to you, weeks, or even months, much better to get revenge.
- "It's me, not you, I need time to get some things together." (Fake honesty.) "I do need to work on a lot, and not a little, but will string you along, and you'll wait for me. I'll return with the same excuses."

It seemed like I was meant to meet these women. I started to become more aware that I was looking for things just like them, maybe not so extreme, but it was my desire to live life on the edge and find someone that was emotionally detached yet still needed to be satisfied at almost any cost. I tried to make myself believe that I was okay, but I wasn't. It felt odd and against who I really was, the person I was searching for. Meeting these women also made me realize that being totally uninhibited wasn't sitting well with my spirit. I needed more restraint. As a cheater, I would always feel this way. Odd, but I didn't know what it was. Hearing Lisa say "I want to be your slave" hurt me. This submissive role seemed to be like a form of bondage, like Lisa was a sneaky dominatrix, because she was imposing her desires on me even though I could not bring myself to do it. I realized that I wasn't really into dominating a woman, I only wanted to use a woman's body in a way, to control her body and feed my rotten core and flesh, heightening my sins. The thought of it felt demeaning. She even asked me to spit on her and call her names. I took this as God's sign to me that I wasn't healed when I actually thought about the spitting scene. The thought only came to me as a way to show her that I was able and not scared, but I was terrified, and at the same time struggling with my morals. I knew that I could not spit on her, but this situation made me see that even though I never spit on women or Lisa, my forked tongue was, for years, spitting venom through my thoughts, words, and actions. I was deeply conflicted.

Dating sites are good if you find the right one. They tend to attract certain personalities for what and who people are looking for. I was clearly in the right one for my demons but the wrong one for my suppressed morals and integrity. If you are not healed, you'll go where negativity pulls you, you'll go where you feel wanted, needed, and in some cases, in charge. Taking the path of least resistance, there will not be much resistance from people that are hurt, want to hurt you, or have hurt themselves, from people who need attention, somewhere to hide, or a place to act out their race fantasies. We were all demonic.

You never want to meet a man like I was. I didn't want you but didn't want anyone else to have you either. I studied you and knew what your buttons were. They became my playthings. I gave you just enough to keep you on your heels and interested, regardless of how I treated you. I made the time I spent away from you be just long enough for you to be mad and start to get over it. I also knew when you were hungry for me, and then I'd pop up to fill your void. It felt so good to be in charge of their emotions but it killed me inside to suppress mine due to fear. I'll turn your life upside-down.

Seductive and Amorous Narcissists

I had to know your body better than you knew your own body. I had to know your menstrual cycle, and even when you're ovulating. When I nurse you back to feeling better, you'll return the favor and then take care of me. Your body had to be mine; it was my playground. I wanted to do to you what no man has ever done. When I'm done, another man's touch wouldn't feel the same and you'll think of me when you're with him. I know this for a fact. Once I find out you slept with someone else, I'll begin to starve you. Your experience with him can't compare to the one I gave you. I'm cocky in this way, so you can't hurt me, and I truly believe this. "Once I had my orgasm, sometimes before you, or after, my timing depended on how far I wanted to take your mind into thinking I cared—my sexual emotions went away. Sexual emotions were all I had, and I knew this. I knew nothing else, emotionally, except sexual passion!"

Slothful-Lazy & Needy-Disservice People

One thing for sure, my parents gave me and my siblings what we needed, and sometimes what we wanted. We were very grateful for what we had, which made it easier to understand and bear with our parents when we didn't have certain things. I was humble as a child, which was a very valuable lesson for me. Now, my kids aren't needy or greedy because of that life lesson. I've always had a hard time accepting compliments from women, and it was very hard accepting gifts.

I am self-motivated and self-serving. The self-serving became reverse psychology on myself, as it turned into greed and lust for a woman's body.

I used to pride myself on not taking money from women, but I was wrong in thinking that this was their most prized gift. It wasn't. I was taking their heart whether they gave it to me or not, and I would later pay dearly for it.

Have you ever seen a sloth? The animal itself is innocent but moves really slowly. This is why lazy people are also described as slothful, because of their mental and physical reluctance to do anything. They will drain you, as they are slow to move and react when you ask for their help. When it comes to people that embody the emotional languages of "Acts of Service," they are the worst people to meet. You'll constantly try to help them, bring them out of a funk, and inspire them but you can't. It's like flogging a dead horse.

They constantly need affirmation, money, help, and advice to get them moving, but they will not give you any affirmations or indeed anything else in return. They offer you things only when they feel like it just so they can stay in good graces with you, and even then, they will put in minimal effort, at best.

Their greed fills them up and makes them think and feel like they've accomplished something, and then they look at you like you should be happy with what they've done. They are very needy, and you'll find yourself always prying, trying to get anything out of them. They are very selfish and need to be complimented all the time. They feel ugly and act that way. They are what I like to call Passive Abusers. When they are done with you, they'll put you down, cut you off, ignore your calls, never return text messages, and generally avoid you. They never have any good ideas, money, or quality time to extend to you. The moment they fall into a crisis, they reach out quickly with a sob story.

"Hey, baby, I'm in the area and was thinking about you, would you like to have lunch?'

"Wow, what did I do to deserve this surprise call and visit?'

"You know I'm still feeling you, see you shortly."

They won't give you a chance to say "no, don't come by," or "no, I'm busy." Their agenda is hot right now.

During their plan to connect or reconnect, their concocted story will be loaded with tears, needs, begging, charm, kisses, cooking, and all of a sudden, care and bright ideas for you. This is their way of drawing you in, tugging at your heart strings, to make you emotional before they close the deal with the *impending doom*.

The impending doom will be a story about their kids, or explaining about how they're in therapy, at which time you'll be surprised to hear and happy for them and now you're emotional and begin to feel close to them again. They can sense this, and when they do, the story gets even juicier. They'll even complain to you about their ex, and the current person they're dating, comparing you to them and how much better you are than them. This seals the deal. You are now deep in your emotions and they know you're a serving type of person, a true giver.

"Baby, I need a small loan, can you help me?"

The best way to deal with these types of people is to first make up your mind that when they come by, ask to come by, call, or text, your first answer should be a resounding NO! You must always believe and *know* that when they reach out, it's always about them and not you. Pay attention to their voice, body language, and facial expressions when you tell them "No." Notice how anger immediately follows and how they make their exit quickly. Now, all of a sudden, they don't have time for you. Never regret saying "no" to them, as they have two or three more people lined up who they will practice their routine on until they get what they want.

If you don't believe this, while they are in front of you and after they ask you for a favor, ask them for one that's not related to what they asked of you—and again, watch their body language, facial expressions, and attitude. It'll change right before your eyes. They become very uncomfortable and can't hide it.

The Groomer and Energy Vampire!

They will always have a need or agenda, or both. It's usually both. They are very sweet in their approach, and also charming, and quite fake. They are impatient. You'll notice their presentation is powerful yet hasty. Your schedule or what you have going on at the moment doesn't matter. At this time, your life has to revolve around theirs. Their energy is extremely high during this time and the lies are constant, and with really juicy stories to back them up. Remember, it's all rehearsed. Don't be fooled by any of it.

CHAPTER EIGHT

Through Porn:
How Leon Saw Women and Why

I started watching porn at age seven. In my bedroom closet, I would spend hours there and no one knew!

If your man or woman is not romantic, they have some issues from their past, possibly porn addiction like me, or they were touched, raped, or molested, most likely by someone they trusted. There isn't much romance in porn, and even if there is some semblance of it, we skip right to the action. This is where the lack of romance, attention, and affection are lost along with patience and exploring. When my seven Loveless traits began, they were rooted in selfishness, greed, and lust.

I want to start off by showing you how my mind developed and what it did to me. My porn addiction opened my mind to how women are, what they want, what to do with them, and why they participated in porn. I know the world of porn is make-believe, but it affected me deeply. All women are not this way, please know this. They choose this profession for many reasons. Just like with prostitution, most times it comes from a place of desperation. I was just like them in that; we both yearned for something much deeper than a sexual desire. Even good parents would have a hard time keeping their children away from the type of things that I did and experienced. My parents were strong, solid, loving, and caring, but the lure of greed and lust presents a tough challenge for good parenting methods. Get a hold of your children early. The older I got, the more my condition worsened.

I go into great detail about this in my ebook, *Keeping Kids Safe from Porn.*

The year was 1972.

Home address was 14408 Alder Avenue, East Cleveland, Ohio. Location: my bedroom closet. I was seven years old. My parents had their own hell going on, their divorce was on the horizon, so I did what the hell I wanted to do. Chipping away at my small fingernails with my little teeth, I sat on the floor, leaning against the bottom bunk where my brother slept. I waited for my brother to fall asleep. Once he began to snore, I knew it was game time.

Yes, I whispered to myself as I clenched my little fists and brought them down to my side. My bedroom closet was dark, the door locked easily. I was equal parts nervous and excited whenever the thought of naked women entered my mind. As I slowly inched and crawled away from the bottom bunk, constantly looking back to see if my brother would wake up, my heart pounded in my chest with a vengeance. I carried a pillow and blanket along with me, slowly opening the door and propping them up against the low wall in the closet.

Plugging the eight-millimeter camera up, it began to hum and as the light flickered, the credits rolled. I was ready. I stuffed clean and dirty clothes at the bottom of my closet door— T-shirts, jeans, socks, whatever kept the light from glaring under the bottom of the door so it wouldn't awaken my brother. I sat down quietly, with my knees pressed firmly against my chest, my arms wrapped around them and leaning forward. I gently bit my bottom lip, stretched my arm out, and then pressed play. Crunched up, I was in the closet alone, with hours upon hours of private time. My brother couldn't hear the movies or see the small light flashing against the wall. He slept on the bottom bunk and his head was away from the closet, closer to the bedroom window. Due to my excessive bedwetting, I was sleeping on the floor, and therefore getting up in the middle of the night and crawling towards the closet was simple. My brother never woke up during any of my escapades. His snores had reached level ten, which muffled the noise coming from the projector and the sound of women moaning.

I watched so many movies that the camera started to overheat. The first movie I saw was an interracial one. Black men with white women, the white women were being extremely submissive. The women performed on cue, did what they were told and didn't object. The times of day that I watched porn fluctuated, depending on how tired I was or what time my parents went to sleep. Normally, I didn't care how much sleep I had gotten, as my mind was set on watching these women get dominated and used. I would smile so much and for so long, my cheeks would hurt. I would sit for so long that my legs would go numb. I didn't see anything wrong with it. School wasn't important to me then, because my family was slowly falling apart. Porn was my outlet, and I desperately needed an escape from the pain of living in a shattered home. I fell behind in class often. My focus and concentration were off.

This didn't bother me, though. Every night, I would return to the closet and the projector would roll and roll and roll.

Dear Mom and Dad,

When kids are closed off, quiet, unhappy, hurt, and even bullied, you'll be surprised at what makes them happy. They will lie, cry, and deny anything about their addictions just to remain happy, even if it hurts their parents.

Continue to love them and encourage them to open up to you.

Loving Women
My Attractions and Knowledge Gained

I grew up fast so I skipped love!

You're fooling yourself if you don't think that your teen son doesn't like older women, regardless of his age. The same goes for your daughter. My lust started at age five, so please pay attention to your children. Depending on how your son or daughter processes their lust or childhood abuse, they may become many things: an angry person, a rapist, child molester, verbally controlling and physically abusive in a relationship, a cheater, liar, or just very sexual. I became a verbally abusive, controlling whore.

The year was 1970 and I was in kindergarten. I remember Mrs. Watts swatting me for crawling around on the floor while looking under little girls' dresses. I didn't like her for that, plus she smelled like mothballs. My adult attraction started in the second grade; color didn't mean anything to me. Mrs. B was a tall white lady with blonde hair. She wore ruby-red lipstick, high heel shoes, and nice skirts. As she taught us, she walked around the classroom. I couldn't wait for her to walk by me. Her perfume would linger as she walked by. As she stood at the chalkboard, I only noticed her sculpted calves, and how her hair lay on her shoulders. She was married and I found myself a little jealous when her husband came to Chambers Elementary School to pick her up. I developed an attraction to a few of my female teachers. My attraction didn't start in kindergarten or the first grade, it was when second grade came around that all the urges came rushing. Although there was that one time in the first grade when Mrs. Triller rescued me. When I got to school that day, she saw the bruises on my face, neck, and forehead and she immediately tended to them. Her role was as a mother that day to a little, sexually assaulted boy. Both third-grade teachers had nice, fit bodies with long, black, silky hair, too. I didn't care whether it was a weave or not, their hair looked luxurious, and I would stare at them all day. Things were different at Kirk Junior High. In the seventh grade, Mrs. B was a smoker with dark lips and funeral home lipstick, not attractive at all. Mrs. Harding, however, was beautiful. She taught English and would always chew on orange slices. She also wore that ruby-red lipstick. Her hair was golden-brown, the color of my babysitter's who molested me. I was always in a zone, staring at her while in English class. I remember holding my head and slightly covering my eyes like I had a headache.

But as my eyes pierced through my hands, I would watch her slide those orange slices between her lips. Through all of my school years, I had gone through many emotions and attractions to older women. This came from the porn and the glory-hole we drilled in my parents' bedroom wall. The Friday night parties my parents threw were loaded with attractive, full-figured, grown women, and I would watch them through the hole all night! In high school, my biology teacher had a nice, manicured afro, and she wore darker-colored lipstick; her head and cheeks were fat, though. Mrs. L was light-skinned and wore her hair down; it was beautiful. She had a nice body, too. There was also this white teacher who had wide hips and long black hair. She wasn't pretty but her camel toe kept my attention.

Back to Alder Avenue

That eight-millimeter camera was rolling right along. I memorized the rewind and fast forward buttons. Fast forward was easy to find, as I didn't care about the hand holding, talking, cuddling, or removal of clothes in the movies. My lack of touch and communication began its course during this timeframe. This hurt me for years later on in life because I was dead set on just jumping right into bed with a woman without any foreplay. Due to the movies I saw, I had become very impatient and lacked the ability for proper touch, making eye contact, and exploring a woman's body. Due to this, I studied and categorized all women but much less the romance.

These stereotypes are all interchangeable and only from my experience, so don't be fooled, nor should you misjudge. The kissing part for me was easy. Sadly, it was my cousins who taught me how.

In the porn films, black women seemed more at ease, and wanted more than anything to make love. The white women were very wild and loud; they were not afraid to express every movement, feeling, and emotion. The case was different with black women and white men, though. I don't know if this was an act or if the women were just excited to be with a man of another race. I believe the latter, and that's how I approached women of other races for years to come. I didn't see Asian or Latina women in porn until I joined the Navy. The scenes with them were pretty much the same. All Asian women seemed like they were in pain, though, and were being tossed around and very submissive. Latinas looked like they were very comfortable, just like black women, but sensual and wild.

As you can see, the vision that entered my mind from those movies, transferred from the eight-millimeter to all grade levels in school.

CHAPTER NINE

Leon's Categories of Women

Caucasian Women

Some are kept around as homemakers or great business partners and they love oral and anal sex, oral above most things. They'll even ask questions like, "How do you want it? Sloppy, tight grip, loose grip?—Huh, this shit's easy!"

Lots are great wives, for sure.

They aim to please orally, at all times. White women also enjoy being spanked and admire the red to purple bruises left on their butts and breasts. They love having their hair pulled, too. Although as white women get older and gain weight, they feel less attractive to their spouses. Some men become too superficial. I know I did that as well, leaving behind the time we spent together, raising great kids, and being proud to reach a fiftieth wedding anniversary. Anniversaries aren't respected much anymore. White men discard white women, pay them off, and move on. But not all are like this. During the marriage, Caucasian women have spent years giving oral sex and receiving much less throughout the marriage. No disrespect to white women, but this is why lots of men suspect that all white women love giving head, or as they call it, a "BJ." It seems to me that they have been groomed to give and not receive.

Here are some conversations I've heard white women have after a few glasses of wine.

"Brad hasn't gone down on me in years, but he sure expects me on my fuckin' knees when he comes home!"

"Did you do it?"

"Fuck yeah. I mean, Leon…I enjoy it, but it'd be nice to have the favor returned, shit! My entire fucking life, it's been called a 68, and not a 69. I give him a BJ and he owes me one! That's like the first rule of sexual politics."

"Most black men would not dare ask a black woman to meet him at the door on her knees."

"Really, Leon?"

"Hell, nah!"

"How many women have you been with, Leon?" "

"Quite a few."

"Geez...and you say it without any reservation?"

"Yea, I know. I'm not proud of it, either."

"Well, school us."

"As far as Black women, they like to know ahead of time to make sure she pleases her man thoroughly. She wants her mind and body to connect. She's all about totally satisfying her man, a good man. Latinas put the kids away before papi gets home and make sure grandma is asleep as well. Just make sure you tell her how wonderful it feels. Her hair will already be in a ponytail too. Sadly, most times I look at white women and I think "orally talented." No disrespect to any other great traits you all possess, though. White women remain married and immerse themselves into taking care of the kids, if the kids are still around. The husband will move on and she'll remain home alone, find a hobby, and spend her money on body improvements or her new boy-toy."

"As far as white women are concerned...you're petty on point with that!"

I continue...

"Not sure why it's this way, but when white women retain their weight and become single, black men seek them out. If they were racist before, that changes once they receive attention from black men. Some white men do this too, but not a lot. When white women lose their husband, some just give up on life and sex. They'll then look for small groups of like-minded women. Some spend lots of time looking and searching for their spouse's new girlfriend or put money and time into the grandkids."

There are a great number of them that fantasize about black men. Most refrain from dating black men because their family will not approve or they'll lose an inheritance. Some don't care, though; they like who they like and will go against what their families believe in. Some are told and taught to never, ever mix their race. After finally acquiring the man of their dreams or satisfying their desires to be with a black man, their own families do not hesitate to disown them. This happens in the South, especially in West Virginia, but also in many other places.

Thin black men and some of regular height and weight proportion search for white women that are heavy-set or pushed to the side by the white men. The white women that have been discarded normally do not give much push back. They're not doormats, they have only been neglected, and this has led to them feeling unloved and unattractive. They refuse to be hurt in that way ever again. They take on the responsibility of taking care of a man that makes them feel good and appreciated again. Some white men want a nice "rack," an open mouth, and someone who acts as a master to white women. They believe in superiority and don't want a big butt, so some white women literally come over to the dark side with their weight, natural breasts, and big butts. White men that were raised around blacks enjoy a big butt and sometimes have a hard time dating white women with small butts.

At times I felt like black men were only liked in our hometown, but while serving in the Navy, I learned that black men are accepted, liked, loved, or even cherished in Australia, Japan, Thailand, Canada, and many more places. Later, I would learn that all men are liked and loved overseas as well. Many minority races are treated as rare commodities since they're not seen that often. It's obvious when Navy ships pull into foreign ports. New York loves Sailors, period.

In many places overseas, especially in Canada, Australia, and Haifa, Israel, I've had conversations with white women where I get the same response.

"So, what's so intriguing about black men, Amy?"

"I've heard the rumors about your endowment, sexual prowess and how passionate black men are. Hell, I haven't been kissed in years and I've fantasized about full lips for so long. What really turns me on is the skin, the contrast, you know? You guys are confident, can dance, move your body, and that's what I like. I did notice that you guys disappear a lot, though. Why is that, Leon?"

"Well, for me, I suppose, it's just hard telling the truth upfront about not wanting a relationship, but just looking for sex. Not all white women feel the way that I am speaking of. There are other things that they like. Some will never date a black man. We are not for everyone, if I do say so myself. The fact that they think we're all hustlers, drug dealers, gang members, angry, and aggressive are stereotypes that have lingered for years. Some white women are taught this early on, and once they find out that not all of us are like that, they have a problem listening to their family about black men. White women rarely leave the home. A lot of them find happiness in pen pals; they enjoy being flirted with and they will easily fall head over heels for a man that shows them attention when their husband leaves. Most of them are loyal, though. When they orgasm, they may go into convulsions. It's scary!"

Latinas

Latinas like it rough and are very passionate. They're into hair pulling, sweaty sex, sloppy and passionate kissing, being flipped around, hanging and dangling from the ceiling, being under the bed, and anywhere else. They're extremely verbal, so you better speak up.

When Latinas engage in sex, it's personal; they need to hear how much you like, love, or care about them. When you tell them what to do with their body, they do it with passion and motivation. They want handcuffs, ropes, and hot wax, too. Their men are very possessive and controlling, which makes them look for freedom from other men of any race. They believe deeply in oral sex, too, both giving and receiving. They are very fair in this exchange. Most Latinas possess a very wet vagina, too. Shaving their labia isn't a big deal since their hair down there is fine and silky! If it's not shaved bald, it'll surely be trimmed, and well- manicured in a sexy style. They're big on family as well. Latinas exude great levels of jealousy, have a fiery personality, and love hard and good. If you don't take charge in any situation, they sure will. Latinas are fine with being at home and taking great care of the family. They look for and create harmony in their relationships. Culturally, Latinas are taught to take care of their man, cater to him, and put him on a pedestal. Even if they are on their period, they will please their man orally. Massages are an integral part of their sexuality too. They look to ease the stress on their man. When they orgasm, their most inner love for you comes out. They grab your head, look into your eyes and demand that you tell them you love them, while gyrating their hips—just say it!

Asian Women

Sadly, they are involved in sex trafficking from a very early age. In the Philippines, back in the 1980s, women were imported from about 7,000 islands to service military men. They are not allowed to say "no" or disagree in any form. This will make a young man very arrogant, eager, and conceited. Their small bodies are a delicacy for all men. They are very easy to handle, light in weight, and subservient. An Asian woman's shallow vagina builds a man's confidence; it makes him feel well endowed, if he's not. Japanese women don't mind being stretched out as it gives them a euphoric feeling, one that they become addicted to. They enjoy facials, too. Filipino women, as well as women from Thailand, China, and Japan, age well. They are loyal but change when they come to the United States. In their country of origin, they are held to a low standard, and are used for sexual purposes, as well as housewives and workers. Their workload is equal and expected to be just like the man, but that's the only equal thing they possess. This is why they change when they come to the United States, where they have more freedom and are treated as women and not slaves. However, domineering men, and men with low self-esteem, or ones that aren't liked or respected by black or white women, choose Asian women. Asian women are very intelligent like other women, but they rely more on that skill-set when they are challenged only in a relationship, job, or life. Don't be fooled by their small size, because they are tough. They can be calculating, driven, and motivated to survive, thrive, and be successful. This is based on their lack of respect as young ladies when growing up. Most are kept in the background, and they never forget that. Asian women may seem arrogant, but remember that once they find or create an opportunity to better themselves, they jump on it. They do have a more docile and subservient culture and mindset. Korean women are more on the tough side, comparable to black women. It's as a result of their harsh living conditions, hustling mentality, and the fear imposed by senior leadership. When they orgasm, they normally let out a screeching cry, almost like a cry for help, or go into convulsions like white women, and their toes normally pop and their hands extend. Afterwards, they act like it wasn't a big deal. They truly enjoy it and while their bodies contort, they're not embarrassed about what just happened.

Black Women

If she's not satisfied the first two times, chances are you will not be called back. And if you try to come back without rectifying your issues or lackluster performance, then they'll hurt your feelings.

You just can't play around with Jamaican or Black women, sexually. It's not a game to them! Even if a man isn't well endowed, if she likes him, she'll make it work. But he at least has to be amazing, orally—that's the *only* caveat.

Some Black women suffer from a lack of body exploration, passionate love-making, and passionate kissing. Some Black men learn how to treat Black women early on. I didn't. I loved their full lips, though, so lips did receive lots of attention from me. Because of my selfish ways, most, if not all Black women who had sexual relations with me were starved as far as their erogenous zones were concerned. Some Black women refuse to kiss or allow a man to kiss them passionately because it's "too intimate" early on in the relationship.

Since I'm a kisser, this has caused problems in my relations with Black women. Therefore, if your man is a kisser, you'll definitely have to come to some form of understanding and agreement. Men yearn for attention and affection too. Black women that have experienced white men vaginally or orally become fixated on that. Gay women have given me some great pointers. Black women encounter well-endowed Black men in their early years—well, at least most of them do, and those well-endowed men, if not taught about the vagina and its components, will bypass oral stimulation and the Black woman's G-spot. This causes Black women to suffer more than most women, in my opinion. More Black women are starting to eat healthy for many reasons, such as to prevent diabetes, high cholesterol, and other ailments. They, like lots of other women, stay hydrated and enjoy tasty fruit, consuming less acid to ensure their vaginal juices have a very pleasurable taste. They love and cherish their Black men, but most of them expect healthy, respectful, and leading roles from Black men, just like their dads were for them. They don't want anyone else to have us, and once we date outside of our race, we become, in their mind, weak, trash, traitors, and many more things. Black women possess a high sex drive, and enjoy all things sexual. They are not easily satisfied and desire passionate sex, love-making, and some aggression. Not all are like this, though. It depends on where they are in life and their relationship. Most want a nice penis because they require a level of being "filled up" and just a tad bit of pain, nothing excruciating though. She just wants to know that you fit well and can get her attention not only sexually, but also mentally. Black women do not like selfish men.

If you're selfish, you'll get one chance, maybe two, and after that, you won't stand a chance ever again. Most of them are loyal. They just require that Black men be loyal, too. The ones that have experienced white or Latino men, or a woman at some point in their lives, become addicted to oral sex and to the way the last person explored their body, so being well endowed doesn't always do it for her. They need and expect their man to be well groomed, confident about his business, honest, and able to communicate. What really turns Black women on is her man's ability to get her to listen to him, handle his friends, family, and co-workers. In addition to that, she enjoys when her man puts her first and can manage many things at once. Black women that have a man like this, will not cheat and will do more for him than anyone ever has. She's ready to give her entire being to him, but may have reservations until he passes all of the tests. You will be tested. Black women suffer from not being celebrated, expecting to always be strong, racism, and others' fear and insecurities. They love hard, too. Most can't wait to be a "Ride or Die chick." They are built for it. Most, if not all of the Black women that I encountered, suffered from a lack of romance. It's a pity I was one-dimensional. She wants to be put first, over your friends, family, but more importantly, she does not want to have to compete with your mother and sister! Take note of that. If you can't handle your mother and sister, you'll lose your woman every time. When Black women orgasm, you have to be extra strong and hold on. Getting them to that point, they become very serving, friendly, and loving afterwards. Make sure to hold them and don't just rush to get off of her. In that moment, be quiet and do what she says, please!

Overall, my knowledge of women varied, and it started at an early age for me. In their early ages, women aren't really into mental stimulation. They're more inquisitive, impressionable, very emotional, and easily led astray. Some, however, look for monogamy but become heartbroken early on. They then develop trust issues and lose trust in men in their twenties, and it lingers on for years. In the latter years for women, when they reach their prime, most settle for sex partners and become comfortable with being alone. They get comfortable with a sexual fix every now and then. By the time they do settle down, they've become quite hardened with no serious expectations from a man.

For the young ladies, being heartbroken is a crucial time for them and some delve into romance with other women. They begin to desire another woman's touch or teachings for many reasons. They want and need answers about their sexuality, looks, body, and sexual confidence. Some feel unattractive when they are actually very attractive, but it's not been told to them or shown by young men that just rush to get into their panties. This stems from younger men ignoring them and their needs or having a mother that despises them. This can really do damage to a young woman's psyche.

If a young lady loses her father early on, due to jail, death, or the streets, she might emulate his ways, unknowingly, and this would create a problem with her mother, especially if her mother had issues with her father. It will create tension between the two of them and her man. Without some form of intervention or therapy, they tend to lose confidence or develop low self-esteem. This will be another turning point in her life, leading to thoughts of polygamy, porn, or prostitution.

You act just like yo damn daddy or his momma! Their mothers might say to them constantly.

When you discard your kids like this, they feel like they're being thrown away, pushed to the side, and abandoned. They will use your words against you as an excuse to become rebellious and look for others that love them, those who act like they love them or treat them better. Be careful with your words. Even though the attention or fake love they'll receive from others isn't genuine, it's just enough. Some women that I dated informed me of this. I knew then that she was missing her dad and had a strained relationship with her mother. She told me that her mother would frown and stare right through her and say, "You look like, walk like, and talk like yo damn daddy!" I know how this feels for young ladies. I was honestly missing my mother in that moment.

My father was a really good man, too. This can happen to women later on in life as well. Some young ladies and women learn from other women what it feels like to be touched and kissed properly. At this stage most mothers take over and try to give their daughter strict and specific guidance about being with another woman. That's if she knows, of course. Mothers don't know in some cases. It does work; however, if the father isn't around, the young lady will tend to look for a father figure in her next man. She'll also begin to lose herself in her needs and have a gaping void in her life that exists to be filled by a man. They become very easy to control at this point, by both men and women. It becomes a hard connection and attraction to break away from when they do find someone to make them feel special, even if it is for just a few minutes, which can also turn into a relationship. Soul ties can begin in this stage. Her sexual needs are deeply rooted and intense. Even though a woman may not become gay, she'll definitely look for the gay woman when her man either isn't there enough, doesn't know her body, leaves, or leaves her hanging sexually, over and over again.

For the man, don't ever be afraid to let a gay woman teach you, mainly how to be soft and gentle, all over a woman's body. I talk about this later in the book, when I met Joanne, the masculine barber.

Things to Consider and Know about Women

Most races of women share these same sentiments:

- Sensual massages
- The missionary position along with kissing brings about intense eye contact and a better connection of the entire body, feeling on the skin, and overall closeness.
- Dressing up and role play, which allows fantasies to be fulfilled.
- Light choking from the doggy-style position.
- Extended foreplay. Start well before the bedroom.
- Porn WITH a storyline.
- Spooning with or without sex.

- Sex games with great wine or good-quality liquor.
- Swings, ramp pillows, massage tables.
- Spontaneous sex, and sex in front of the mirror.
- Dirty talk while having sex.
- Watching her pleasure herself.
- Kissing her while she pleasures herself, without touching her, and touching and rubbing her body while she pleasures herself.

Some may say that this is basic, but it's not. Some women have never experienced this and for those that have, it's been quite a long time.

Young ladies that experience porn early on never forget the images and how it made them feel. Like myself, this can be a life-long desire and need. Their sex drive is more intense than a man's sex drive and lasts a lot longer. They'll delve into making porn for money, satisfaction, and attention. These days, women are more open to performing in porn and this has become highly regarded, respected, admired, and esteemed over their more respectful traits and skill sets, unfortunately.

> *Ninety percent of child molesters are people the victim knows or trusts. Not everyone deserves to be around your kids, family included.*
> – *Child welfare.gov*

Pay attention and don't ever think for one moment that your kids are safe. My parents thought I was when I wasn't. What children see, hear, learn, feel, and experience in their childhood ultimately determines who they become once they grow older. The remnants, residual effects, as well as second- third- and fourth-order effects that are not identified early on can damage kids for life. The only difference between a child and an adult is height, weight, and age, unless they encounter a life-altering event that takes place, sooner or later in life, and if they get help for it. I never got help until I was forty-seven years old, so I remained that dysfunctional child for a long time. At times, when women called me a little boy, they were right. It was all mental, and so I could not connect. Physically, I was trained by family demons and those that never received help either. It was a clear and sad case of early intergenerational transmission of family violence.

I was five when I was first molested and started wetting the bed, seven when I first started watching porn and started to masturbate, and eight when I lost my virginity.

The Virtuous Woman

According to my dictionary, "virtuous" means trustworthy or encouraging. The word describes someone who works diligently, is strong, brave, resourceful, well prepared, generous, wise, and thinks well of others. A virtuous woman is one you would say the following to:

> *Teach me how to love you, because I want to know how!*
> *I'm very interested in your Love Languages!*

For me, I'm fine with being your student. Just be careful with me as I am fragile right now. However, I know you are my rib, a shield to protect my vital organs. You are my prayer warrior to protect me from the demons that I do not see.

Yes, my mother was a bartender. She multi-tasked; dealt with drunken, boisterous men and women; as well as loud music, flirtatious and disrespectful men, and jealous women. She was a manager and a leader. My mother was my first and only Den Mother of my Cub Scout pack/troop 336. She gave me my first job, and she took me to the dentist, football and baseball practice. My mother enrolled me in swimming. From that point on, I've never been afraid to be led by a woman, but she had to be like my mom. Only a few came very close. Women care for us always, from the beginning of our personalities to when our brain supposedly stops developing, at the ripe age of twenty-five; women teach beyond that. As I look back, from kindergarten to when I joined the Navy, there were more women in charge and responsible for my growth and development. Yes, there were and there always will be the men in my life who deserve and will always get my respect and credit for being pivotal in my growth and development; however, I have to admit, there were more women than men.

From kindergarten to the fourth grade, they were all women. In junior high there were two women for the most important classes, English and Mathematics, and in high school, my teachers for English, Health Science, Mathematics, Social Studies, and Biology were all women. That makes eleven in total. There were seven men who taught me subjects like auto-mechanics, art, woodshop, gym, and swimming. My sixth-grade teacher, Mr. Burroughs, taught me everything. I remember him saying to me one time, "Mr. Walker, Mr. Walker, come here young man!"

Whenever he called me up to his desk, for whatever reason he called me, I was terrified, but I responded to "young man" and it felt good. I was only ten years old. Words and certain people are very important to kids. Some are everlasting.

I learned how to swim in elementary school, and though I never used a woodshop after graduation, gym came naturally to me, and mechanics did help a little. All the lessons were extremely invaluable, but the classes that helped me pass the military entrance exam, which changed my life, were Mathematics and English. I was taught lessons that have been and will continue to be useful to me in life. I will always have to speak good English, read and understand paragraphs, and know numbers and formulas. Wood and mechanics are a life skill that I will always be grateful for; even though I kind of forgot about them later in life, they are still very useful today.

Numbers relate to:

- Credit scores
- APRs
- Time, in relation to maturity and patience
- Time, in relation to rest
- Numbers for measuring anything

- Reading comprehension for understanding contracts, blue-prints, a resume, applications, labels, medicine

The Virtuous Woman, a teacher of sorts, has always had me covered!

CHAPTER TEN

The Development of
My Narcissistic Personality

From the ages of five to twelve, when I was abused, I slowly became a loner, having evil thoughts and low self-esteem. I was angry, lost, and embarrassed. They kept touching me and I kept drifting further and further away from life. Where was God? I consistently found myself asking. I blocked those events out for so long, I indirectly taught myself how to separate myself from reality and what I created in my own mind, to be "make believe." Later in life, a psychologist told me;

"Leon, your "make-believe" was built for your own protection and to not allow yourself to go crazy."

"Yes, ma'am, I understand that. But in doing so, I felt numb, like I didn't care anymore."

"Well, you were neglected and abused."

When my therapist told me that, it hurt to hear it. I didn't want that put over my parents.

"My parents were great people, they wouldn't do that to me.'

"I'm not speaking of your parents, but others that did mean things to you."

"Okay, okay. It always felt like I was just here, floating endlessly, like I was conscious of what was going on around me, and at the same time, I wasn't. When I was in the seventh grade, this one girl called me 'dense.' At first, I didn't know what that meant, so I looked it up.

Finding out what it meant really hurt my feelings. That's when I really felt like I was crazy. It was like everyone knew that I was slow, or dense, and were secretly laughing behind my back at this fact, like everyone was in on the joke except me."

"You cared, they didn't. You shouldn't listen to the bad things people say about you."

"Okay, ma'am. I understand. I was just trying to survive."

In my memoir, *Broken*, published in April 2018, I speak of three incidents that had a profound effect on me, an impact that will remain with me until the day I die. I'm kind of glad that those incidents remain with me. Sometimes, you have to visit your past to live life in the present and future, to its fullest.

I take full responsibility for my actions. But I had to process and understand the bad people that started me off on the wrong foot.

Just to let you know, before I knew how to take responsibility, the stress and depression started from my childhood, so it took me years to understand it all. What I began to do later in life was to make every woman I encountered in my life, like my cousins and babysitters, pay for what was done to me. Whenever I remembered the male that touched my testicles and penis, I felt so angry, I wanted to murder him. Funny part was I had the gun to do so. The person that showed me porn corrupted my young mind.

At-risk kids are the way they are because of at-risk adults.

In *Broken*, I speak about a time when my mother shot at my father six times while she was bartending. She didn't kill him, but she tried.

You look like, walk like, and talk like yo damn daddy!

Would a woman try to kill me one day? After all, I was just like my "damn daddy." That gun my mother used on my father remained in her drawer and I knew exactly where it was. It was in a powder-blue box, lying on a thick sheet of cotton.

The shells were lined up next to the gun. The bullets were short and thick, with a copper tip.

I walked into my mother's bedroom and as I pulled the drawer open, I took the gun from the box, then slid the barrel into my mouth. It was cold and had a nasty taste. Then I heard that voice again...

Mr. Walker, come here young man!

I couldn't do it. I didn't want to let Mr. Burroughs down.

Young man, young man...

I wanted to be a man so badly. Sexually, I felt I was more than ready. Mentally, I was far from that being my reality. I was so weak, the lures of suicide felt so relieving.

I was too young to have a double-mind, but voices always followed me.

Mumble, mumble, mumble...the voices carried on, injecting fears and insecurities into my mind.

"I'm tired of this. I pee in the bed, I suck my thumb, my teeth stick out, and my parents are getting divorced. I have cavities and my teeth are turning green." I wasn't washing up regularly then, either. Just another sign of neglect and depression.

I FELT NOTHING—I HAD MY OWN NOVOCAINE!

Our neighbor, Mrs. Shell, was tough. She had five sons and they were all very talented, intelligent, strong, and lots of fun to be around. We feared and respected her. Mrs. Shell looked out for us on Alder Avenue. She'd drink that ice-cold pop and read her newspaper on the front porch. Me and Mike Tucker would watch her from his porch, turn that bottle up, and after six to seven deep gulps, it would be finished.

Mike Tucker was a silly little boy then, and he's even funnier now. Laughter has always helped me.

"Dub, you hear how she sucked that Vernors down?"

"Hell, yea—haaaaaaaa!"

I had lots of respect for her.

As I walked into our bathroom, I slowly opened the window, then bent down and took my laces out of my small, blue and white

Pro-Keds. This was months after I tried to burn the house down, twice. I pulled my shoes off and tied my shoe-strings together, then peeped out the window. It was only about twenty feet down, but far enough to snap my neck if I fell.

"GULP, GULP, GULP—FINISHED!"

I couldn't help but laugh. Mike wasn't with me, but the laughter took my mind off of suicide.

Words, certain people, and for me, certain sounds are very important to kids. Some are everlasting. I get my laughter from my dad, and I thank God for my laughter. When I see Mike Tucker back home in Cleveland, all he says is, "GULP, GULP, GULP, VERNORS" and the laughter starts all over, not the thoughts of suicide.

REFLEXIVELY

It seemed like my motor skills were off, my cognitive awareness was kind of loopy. Here one day, and gone the next. At this point, I developed an intense hate for bullies, child molesters, and rapists. Hurt and damaged people know and operate in their loveless trait(s) long before their actual emotional language(s), depending on their situation, dysfunction, and pain, or whichever emotion comes first. They are always guarded. The emotions they carry are normally fear, anger, resentment, and then they exercise their ability to protect their hearts, at all costs, leaving others in their wake lost and confused.

I mastered this through my ability to "make believe," convincing myself that it was fine to mistreat women, act like it didn't happen, and then simply just walk away. In winning or losing during a marriage or relationship, narcissistic trait carriers take on and experience many mind shifts. All mind shifts must be in their favor. Narcissistic people take flight, remain and cheat, never give up or give in to anyone, or they settle for those that are less than they are, in order to feel superior and possibly die with a broken heart filled with discontent. They will act unbothered when they actually are bothered, unsettled, and feeling uneasy.

As I said, it is a form of either protection or vengeance. We feel the burning loveless traits in our core, before acting or reacting. This gives us motivation to remain above you and it starts with what we hear or feel in our heart. We then process it in our dark mind for an attack, or an exit plan. For me, I harbored what my female cousins, my babysitter, and male family members—all of whom were six to seven years older than I was—did to me. Coupled with that, there was my addiction to porn that catapulted my innocent mind to see women as just sex objects, or toys to be played with, and nothing more. A woman's heart and emotions didn't matter to me, it only mattered when I was in control of their hurt and how much pain I was able to inflict. Revenge was deeply rooted in my childhood; no one was safe.

Narcissistic traits will cause people to ignore the genuine languages given to us by God. Our ability to ignore is due to many things, such as greed and lust, and through this, we render ourselves incapable of loving, caring, forgiving, or being honest. We block it out and develop an innate ability to separate ourselves from reality. We believe what we think; our minds are immersed in lies. This allows us to continue to see you as the aggressor or perpetrator and ourselves as the victim. All along we know that God is forgiving, but we're just not ready to be good and forgive people; our souls resonate with the devil and his ill intent; we seek to injure and damage. For me, that was my comfort zone, extending my hurt onto other women, hoping to see them fall, falter, fall deeply in love with me, and for me to leave them always wondering and despondent. All this was to cause them to create doubt about themselves in their hearts. For me, repenting was being used as a way to reprieve, which was not done the correct way. I failed at it for years. But due to my shadow traits, I used repenting as an excuse to be excused and go right back to doing what I was doing. It never worked because I didn't do it right. I knew that I needed help, but I truly didn't want help. My sick mind attracted other sick minds and that felt good to me.

CHAPTER ELEVEN

How Leon Processed a Woman's Hurt

In my aunt's bedroom, he grabbed my mother by her throat with his left hand, drew his right hand back, and then "BOOM" with all of his might, he punched my mother square in the mouth.

In my first memoir, *Broken: Survival Instincts of a Child*, I talk about the time when my mother was punched in the mouth and had her front teeth knocked out. I was right there with her. Picking your mother's broken teeth up off of the floor and seeing her mouth gushing with blood is a scene that no one should ever see; it's one thing no man should ever do. It will have an everlasting and devastating effect on your child. I should have started seeing a psychiatrist back then, but I didn't. My psychiatrist sessions wouldn't happen for many years to come. One thing was for sure: at that moment, I learned to never physically hurt a woman. Emotional hurt was a different matter for me. I'll explain that later too. The sound of the punch my mother endured has remained with me for my entire life. It was like hearing a baseball bat cracking a baseball.

I wish that I had also learned that hurting a woman's feelings and breaking their heart was wrong and just as painful, if not more painful, than doing it physically. Instead, the vision of my mother covering her mouth with a towel while we were on the bus that night, leaving my aunt's party, is what stuck with me as far as hurting a woman was concerned. In that moment, I was only able to process my mother's physical damage and not the emotional one. My mother became the toughest woman in my mind.

When people read this story in *Broken,* many of them had questions about the whereabouts of my dad that night. He was there and I clearly remember he and my mom arguing in the kitchen before the punch was thrown. Moments later, my mom stood face to face with my uncle. What my parents argued about, I never knew. I didn't develop a means of protecting a woman because I never knew what my dad did to my uncle after he punched my mother. I wasn't shown how to step up and be the man. Was it okay to hit women? This question lingered in my mind for many years.

I replayed the conversation my aunt had with my uncle that night in my head. "Greg, why did you punch Sylvia like that?" I heard my aunt ask him.

"She threw that damn television into my face, shit!"

As I stood between my mother and my uncle in the bedroom, the red light was dim. It was fairly dark, but I could clearly see both of them. I then saw my mother pick up a nineteen-inch television and throw it right into my uncle's face. Blood gushed from his eye and nose. He was cut wide open.

My mother's life was changed forever that night.

Back in the kitchen, my aunt continued her questions as she was behind my uncle while he bent over, and when he lifted his head up, we both saw his injuries. No one knew why it happened, and in 2022, we still don't know. My uncle and mom are both deceased now.

My aunt took care of my mother. For a brief moment, she was conflicted too. "Here, Sylvia, take this towel."

I saw my mother reach out, grab the towel, and cover her face. I held her hand, trembling and hoping that there were no more punches thrown. As I looked up at my mother, I could see the blood fill the white towel as we walked down the stairs and out of my aunt's house to catch the bus home that night.

In that moment, I distinctly remember creating in my mind a way to not allow a woman to get punched in my presence ever again, or to ever hit women.

Seeing the tragic event play out, along with all the gore and sorrow that engulfed my little ten-year-old mind and body, I knew for sure that hitting women was a cowardly act.

It's not okay to ever hit a woman, ever. I started to become a protector at that moment. Violence terrified me as a kid, but I had to learn some kind of self-defense, which came in the form of karate and boxing. It was hard for me to harm people, but after practicing those routines, it started to feel good to punch boys my age, and then men, as I got older. I felt a sense of confidence, my self-esteem grew, but harming others still didn't sit well with me. It was a struggle indeed, yet the better I became at boxing, the more I wanted to extend hurt to people because I still felt an urge to protect my mother, even if the situation had nothing to do with what had happened that night. My mind was set.

What was also odd is that my mother never let out a peep, not even a little squeak. She didn't even cry, at least not in front of me. She just walked away after she got up off of the floor. I understood then that women can endure unbearable pain and their strength is unmatched. That wasn't a good example for me, though, as far as identifying a woman's strength was concerned, but it was all I had to go on at the time. Mom never flipped out, though. From that point forward, she indirectly taught me how to remain calm, and this continued to be good advice through all circumstances I faced in life and in the Navy. It later worked against me and my mom because even though I became a carrier of deep pain, I became a good manager of it as well. I initially cried when I saw my mother's mouth but when I noticed that there were no tears in her eyes , I stopped crying. This hurt me later in life also, because I didn't learn how to process crying or show my emotions in front of anyone, namely women. I had become a heartless and emotionless person on many occasions.

During her crack-smoking years, she was still just as strong and resilient as she was that fateful night at my aunt's house. My mother started smoking crack around 1985. She was stubborn, strong, beautiful, and dead set on what she wanted and what she was going to do. The only reason she stopped smoking crack is because she got sick. My sister took care of my mother that period and later had to put her in a nursing home, and then hospice. I remember the phone call I received from my sister in 2011.

"Mommy is in the hospital. She's sick."

"What happened to her?"

My whole naval career, I don't remember my mom ever getting sick. At this time, I had been in the Navy for twenty-eight years.

"The drugs, Doubleo. She just wouldn't stop getting high."

A drug dealer dropped my mom off at the hospital when she got sick. He was her crack dealer. When my mom got sick, I was in the Great Lakes as a Command Master Chief for Naval Station, Great Lakes. I was proud of every command that I was in charge of, but because of my mother's addiction, she never got to see how successful I was in leading men and women just like she had. Her crack binge lasted for twenty-seven years. Indirectly and naturally, I took on my mother's strength in discarding, silent treatment, gas-lighting, and other negative traits, along with the strong traits she gave me. I know exactly where those narcissistic traits came from. The traits empowered me to keep doing what I wanted with women, in relationships, as I continued to drink my troubles away and get promoted. The drinking part was inherited from my dad. And like my mother, I too had become very stubborn. I missed my mother and her nurturing ways a great deal. I lost a lot during my mother's sickness, mainly how to tap into my feminine side to really figure out what women wanted, needed, and desired outside of sex. Emotional pain suited me better; it was like I didn't think that emotional pain mattered. What did I do to my sister? Why was she so tough, too?

Maybe if I saw my mother cry, wince in pain, beg, plead, or anything else to show her emotional side, I would have been able to process my ability to care for or come to the rescue of a crying woman as a child. Instead, I saw my mother get up, cover her mouth, and take us home that night. Women don't hurt inside, they don't cry, nor are they weak; this is what I settled on. This was my takeaway. My acts of being physical and yearning to fight, or punch, were still geared towards boys and young men, until my sister would anger or provoke me. I noticed that I was slowly becoming a bully, and the first person that I bullied was my sister. It was hard to hit my sister, but after a few times of doing so, sadly, it became fun to me. That was very wrong. I never hit her in the face, but I would hit her back, arms, legs, and pop her upside her head often. It was a sibling thing but it was still physical abuse. This lesson and the bullying of my sister started to leave me around age fourteen, and I'm glad that it did. What I got from those years of bullying my sister was releasing my anger issues, my need to hit and see people in pain. The experience made my sister very tough, though, as she started punching people, both men and women, with ease. I was responsible for that, and I regretted it. I played a part in my sister's need to mask and suppress emotional pain too.

Later on in life, when I made women cry, it was easy to just sit there and watch them cry. Physical pain overrode mental pain, anguish, and mental abuse in my mind. I developed a very uneasy feeling of being defeated by my sister during these times. Sometimes she would punch me and get away with it. That defeat hurt like hell. I can't ever lose to a girl or woman, in anything, especially relationships, or so I thought. Also, I despised bullies, but I ended up becoming one.

My mother passed away in 2012, and her mouth was never fixed!

"Why are you crying, I didn't even punch you!"

CHAPTER TWELVE

Looking for Our Mothers
in the Women We Date

Mothers forgive, heal, pray, and let you back in. That's what they do.

When I mess up, I expect you to heal, pray, forgive, and let me back in, but deep down, I'm asking you to not let me back in. The thing is I'm afraid to leave and see you with someone else. I am a repeat offender. My mother kept me around, so I expect you to do the same. After all, you're a woman, just like my mommy. The umbilical cord was my connection to my mother, but since I am shallow, your connection to me is through your vagina and bonding over trauma. We both know this so well so I can't be wrong.

Sometimes, you must be careful when a man wants a woman like his mother. He might have become used to his behavior being excused. Mothers can and do many things for us as they raise their sons and make adjustments. They are typically:

- Overprotective.
- Overbearing.
- Nurturing.
- Very strict with their guidance.
- Too involved and doting.
- Insightful.
- Fearful.

- Confident because you are there.
- Counselors.
- Very intuitive as far as the woman we pick.
- Teachers about menstrual cycles and menopause. We want to feel like we know you and can relate to one another just like mother and son. It's very comforting and helps us relax and become more open, but more importantly, it's a lifelong, valuable means of understanding our better half!

The Negatives of Wanting a Woman Like Our Mother

Some men are very close to their mothers and some are not. With this type of situation, a young man will follow in his father's footsteps, just like I did until I studied my mom later in her final days. I was both close and at times, really far away, from my mother, but overall she instilled in me very valuable lessons.

The Ghetto and Young-Thinking and Performing Mom

Emotional and spiritual needs are not important to this mom. If a young man has a great relationship with his mom and the mom still seems to have an immature mindset, he'll be attracted to and seek women who have that same type of mindset but will not give her what he gives his mom. Characteristics of those types of moms:

- Materialistic.
- Mouthy.
- Committed to taking their son's side regardless.
- Expect her grown son to still pay her pills.
- Expect to come first.
- She will not relent and continue to make decisions in her son's life.
- Will have a strained relationship with every girlfriend her son has.
- She will text often and call, even while her son is on a date.

- She will always want to be involved in every decision her son makes.

Men that seek these types of women, take care of the woman so that he can feel and remain superior. They know that they will never be superior to their moms and are fine with that because their woman has to be and act subservient. This is the mom that continues to reel her son in but doesn't expect his woman to reel him in. She's teaching him to not be submissive, but only to her, and the only time the mother will do anything with or for his woman is if he tells or asks her to, and even then, it'll be with reservation or with some type of slight.

They both submit to each other, but not to women outside of their mother and son relationship! The woman will always feel and be treated like she's beneath him. Some mothers directly and indirectly teach their sons this. The girlfriend can sometimes sense this and is fine with coming second to the mother, as this dynamic would have been established when they met. She gets what she wants and will not challenge him. It becomes a fair exchange for a woman that feels like a man is supposed to take care of her and put her on a pedestal because her material needs are being met and her emotional and spiritual voids don't matter. Those voids come second and third, just like his mother.

My Doting Mother

GYPSY

My mother never, ever left me. From having her DNA to finally understanding her life of pain, loss, and agony, she was taken away from me and in some instances, forced to live the life that she never imagined, but had to do so. Therapy was by far the greatest thing that ever happened to my mind, mental health, and reconnecting with my mother!

– Leon R. Walker, Jr.

Mommy, why did you change your name?

Because I can, it's my name, Doubleo. I don't care what people say about me, and you shouldn't either.

My mother's name was Sylvia. She changed it to Gypsy when I was about eleven. I would later find out that she didn't like her name, *Sylvia*, mainly because her mother named her and my father always yelled, *"Sylvia"* and that was a reminder. My dad made fun of her new name and so did my friends. I was embarrassed but like my mom, I started to not care what other people said.

"So, I couldn't care less, girl!"

My mother renamed herself. Was this a grandiose mindset, avoidance issues, or both, that I would also later develop? Yes!

As a child, our family hardly ever sat down to eat together, nor did we pray before we ate. I do not remember ever doing that. Later in life, I was the same way with my own family. In addition to that, saying prayer before I ate while eating with a girlfriend or her family, I wanted to always avoid prayer before we ate. It just felt irritating to have to wait to eat. They did pray, but while doing so, I can distinctly remember zoning off. Just thinking about anything except for God.

Although my grandmother attended church often, and carried her Bible with her, my mom didn't. She did mention God often, though. My grandmother did have a mean streak in her—mostly towards the women in the family. Even her son's girlfriends. My mom doting on me was a double-edged sword. I always felt that if my mother could leave me, then any woman would. I was eleven years old when I first encountered and welcomed this into my mind, but she never left me. I would never let the negative thoughts go, either. Having those thoughts made me want women and not want them. It was a full-time mindset for me! I went into every relationship already halfway out! My mother was a permanent fixture in my life, even after her two abandonments (losing our house and her drug addiction). I am very thankful that I went through therapy for as long as I did, because in doing so, my therapist helped me realize that losing our house and my mother's drug addiction wasn't all her fault. I was an angry kid that blamed my mother and so, I became an angry man that blamed everything on the women that I dated. I should have stayed in therapy in my twenties, and gone to therapy as a kid. Had I done so, I would have understood more why I feared or experienced:

- Abandonment.
- An inability to care.

- Commitment.
- Loss.
- Heartbreak.
- Avoidance.
- My inability to make a decision based on my gut feeling.
- Being a flight risk.
- A lack of spiritual connection.

The resonation of the above characteristics that I experienced, became my excuse to hold onto them and not the women I dated. I exercised those in every relationship and they had become a means of protecting my heart, but in doing so—I had become heartless! It was obviously counterproductive, but as my personality had a firm grasp on them, I felt like I was right in doing what I was doing. That's how I saw things. It was truly unfair to not warn these women, but how could I, if I was also greedy and very lustful? I wanted them just enough for them to want me, but not so much as to make them want to stay; most did, though!

Over the years, I had developed a very bad habit of blaming every woman that I dated, for everything. Nothing was my fault, not even cheating, but it was all my fault. For years, practically all of my thirty-two year naval career, I held resentment, fear of loss, and an inability to "hang in there," speaking from a relationship perspective. Although my mother left me, she knew that I would always come back, in some kind of way—and I did, but it was sporadic, or more like—she would come back! This became my expectation throughout life and I had done it without reservation, or without putting any thought into it. I couldn't care less. I can do no wrong, I am always right, and if I do, do wrong, you'll take some of the blame, just so that I don't feel bad, or you might even take all of the blame. I can't and won't process being wrong. Even if I am wrong, it's your fault! You're supposed to dote on me. You didn't do your part, so any of my wrong-doings are your fault. I am not wrong then, right?

Personality disorder

When, not if, I hurt you, blame the other me, not the current me. That's what I'm going to do, so, if you want to understand me, pick one or the other to blame, the good guy will be back shortly and you'll accept me because you see what's inside, but I don't want to!

– Leon R. Walker, Jr.

Walking back into your life, you must accept me, because I didn't leave you, other circumstances caused that. Maybe it was drugs, my past, my childhood—that's everything else, not me. I didn't walk away, circumstances took me away, just like those circumstances took my mother away. You want to see me do better, be better, act better, treat the kids better, but more than anything, you don't want anyone else to have me since you've spent years investing in me. It's just a matter of time before I turn that corner, as a better man, and when I do, you would die inside if you see another woman with me, after all of the work you've put in. The doting wife or girlfriend you are! Be careful with that, even with your son!

I always thought this way about the women that I dated and married. I never gave it a second thought, and it happened every time, except for my marriage. Walking away was easy for me but I had to initiate it. I knew that if the women would walk away from me first, I would be devastated, and that the same routine would transition in my mind (my mother leaving me and then summoning me back). If that happened, the other woman would then have the power to lure me back, just like my mother. I was okay with my mother having that power, but not another woman, no way. She didn't deserve to have that power over me, but my mother did. Women will allow this to happen for years. I know this because my mother did it for years. I expected it without any reservation. My sister always told me that I got away with anything, and I did. I could barely remember my mother spanking me—my dad sure did, but my mother, not so much. I had a hard time forgiving her, but my love for her and my desire to always respect my mother, now that ran deep. While in therapy, many things came out about my relationship with my mother but mainly, how I related to her, her actions, mindset, thought processes, emotions, feelings or a lack of all. I distinctly remember my mother ignoring things, walking away from things, as if it didn't happen or that it didn't bother her, or mattered. I could separate myself from anything or reality and believe it was what I wanted it to be. You wouldn't or couldn't understand how I could do this, but it wasn't for you to understand, just deal with it and keep me alive!

My dad was doted on, too. Family members would always tell me about him and his mom, how close they were. In my first book, *Broken: Survival Instincts of a Child*, I remember trying to burn the house down. This occurred during the years prior to my parents' divorce. I was in the kitchen and my mother was on the phone but I wanted a sandwich. After numerous attempts to get her attention, I felt like she was ignoring me, so I started a fire in the trash, in the kitchen.

The small fire reached the telephone cord, melted it, and ended her call, but it got out of control and started rising up the kitchen wall. We put the fire out, and when my dad came home from work, she told my dad. I was a kid, but even as a kid, I understood our close relationship, until she told my dad. Imagine that, a young kid having the audacity to get upset when his mom tells his dad on him. My dad spanked me pretty good that day and I never forgot that. Yes, it was painful, but I could feel my anger from the betrayal of my mother build up inside me. Not long after that, I tried to burn the house down again. I wasn't hungry, nor did I want a sandwich, I was sending a message to my mother. I was spanked again, but this time, it felt good to try and burn the house down, so there wasn't much pain while I was being spanked.

How soon can a child develop the ability to be vindictive or to want revenge, and at what cost? For me, hurting my entire family (burning the house down) never crossed my mind, I wanted what I wanted, and that was my mother's attention and to be vindictive; both were required! I didn't even think about the second- and third-order of effects. It was all about me, but I didn't realize it, although I knew that I wanted that effect. My parents, after a while, seemed to be just existing. I saw that.

As a kid, those thoughts are pretty extreme. As an adult, I had the same mindset. It wasn't to burn any house down, but it was to burn my relationships down. I wanted to send a message to her, and there was no pain involved either, at least not from me. I wanted revenge, to be vindictive, and constant attention—it was all about me. Losing her never crossed my mind. I wanted what I wanted—attention! Don't betray me! I became addicted to my mother's attention, and her doting. Being able to get away with anything, and then being allowed to come back like nothing ever happened, even if I was burning the house down. The house is repairable, and so is the relationship that I had broken down to just—existing with one another. I am comfortable with that living condition.

Now that I am older, who's going to spank me, hold me accountable? If you dote on your son, you must dote on me—it's what I know and believe in, nothing else. I know all about it. Is the damage irreversible, is it always a good thing to dote on your son? Yes, I am old enough to know better (this chapter represents Leon between the ages of 20 and 45), to make good decisions, to not act like a little boy, but I want what I want, and it will always be that way until I get therapy. Until then, I need you to dote on me!

"If you act a tad bit like my mother, I'll enjoy that, but don't go overboard or I'll become offended, angry, and upset. Give me what I need, just like my mother, but you can't be her, okay?"

I do miss the doted-on little boy, but that's not your sole purpose or job. If you overcompensate, I'll go into little boy mode, I'll shut down, leave, shun you, become disrespectful, lie, and act disobedient. Can we talk about it, please? Just be careful as my feelings and emotions are by far the only thing fragile about me, besides my ego! I won't tell you this about me, but if you find out, again, please be careful with me!

Believing that my mom was the sole reason for our family breaking up, and giving my dad all of the credit for keeping us alive and taken care of, I would despise all women because I felt like they had the same agenda, sooner or later. I was wrong. Some women are pushed to survival. Mentally abusing them will do that. I was guilty of that, too.

If I don't go to or get therapy, and you remain with me,
I am truly who you want, so don't expect anything else!

CHAPTER THIRTEEN

Caught Between Two Women

I have a story for you...

I was taught, directly and indirectly, how "not" to care.

Over the years of studying my parents and grandparents, I learned so much. Mainly physical violence and verbal abuse. My uncle verbally abused my grandmother, my grandfather verbally abused my grandmother, and my grandmother verbally and physically abused my mother.

Cleveland, Ohio in the 1970s...In my book, *Broken*, I explain why I hated Christmas. On this day, Christmas, all I wanted was some collard greens. My grandmother was a great cook, and during this time the house was filled with adults, kids, food, liquor, weed, and cigarettes. Everyone smoked, drank, or did both while the simmering smell of collard greens, ham hocks, macaroni and cheese, and dressing floated around the living room. As I sat there on the small, cotton, leopard-colored couch, gazing at the well-developed women, my stomach began to growl. My grandfather was often mean, but really sweet to the ladies who were my mother's friends; not so much to me and my sister. He was a provider and always kept nice, clean Cadillacs! I was afraid of him, and he really didn't smile that often at me. He and my uncle (my mother's brother) were the bullies of the family. They were treated like kings, and I wanted that so badly, but during those times, it never came. Because of granddad, I sat on that couch frozen stiff, but found a way to get my mother's attention.

I watched my mother entertain the crowd and when she was free, I caught her attention. Through my very young eyes, I sat there with my legs crammed together, and my hands smashed between my thighs. I raised my eyebrows, swiftly, two or three times, and sharply cut and gestured my eyes towards the kitchen. My mouth was sealed tight, with a smile that stretched across my face. My stomach grumbled.

My mother slowly walked towards me. She was always beautiful and smiling. "Boy, what are you over here thinking about...lil sneaky self?"

I whisper in her ear as she bends down to me.

"Ma, can we at least taste the greens, I'm starving"

"Okay, come on."

We dodge the grown people standing around chatting, and then walk into the kitchen and I can see the smoke billowing from the heavy pot, the bubbles popping as the greens come to a nice boil. My mother uncovered the greens and the steam rushed towards the ceiling.

"Wow, these smell really good, ma!"

"They sure do. Back up, let me get a spoon."

My mother opens the kitchen drawer and pulls out a large, wooden spoon. She stirs the greens and dips the wooden spoon deep into the pot. She removes the spoon, with a heaping serving of collard greens and bits of smoked turkey necks, then slurps the collard green juice and takes a small bite of the greens, and turns towards me.

"Here you go, lil boy!" She smiles and she steadily and gently brings the spoon towards my mouth. I tilt my head back, open my mouth, and enjoy the savory, delicious greens as they ease down my throat.

"Be careful, they're hot, Doubleo!"

"CRACK!"

I gulped the greens and the juice burned my throat. My mother dropped the spoon and I quickly grabbed her hand.

"CRACK!"

"Sylvia, don't you ever do shit in my kitchen, you hear me!"

"Momma, why did you slap me?"

I quickly grab my mother's hand and tears stream down my face—I'm silent.

I began to wet my pants while holding my mother's hand. I felt the power of my grandmother's hand-slap across my mother's face, ease down into my hand, as if she slapped me. I look up, my mother's jaw begins to turn red and puff up a little. My mother became quiet, as she always did when she was slapped or punched.

"You okay, Mommy?"

"Mhmm."

My mother gently rubbed her face and took me back to sit on the couch. My pants were soaked!

The party continued like nothing ever happened.

Intergenerational Transmission of Family Violence

For years, my mother internalized her pain—and so would I.

CHAPTER FOURTEEN

The Cold Stare

Cleveland, Ohio, in the 1970s. Christmas the following year...

My mother cooked the same food as always, just like my grandmother. Greens were a must. We're enjoying family time, the music is blaring, and the food is on the stove and in the oven. My grandmother heads to the kitchen and opens the pot of greens, takes a gulp, and begins to choke.

"UGH, UGHHH, UMPH–UMPH." My grandmother grunts, and grunts, and grunts.

My mom and I run to the kitchen, and then follow my grandmother up the stairs as she's struggling to breath. Within seconds, my grandmother is heaving over the toilet trying to clear her throat. She's struggling! Her hands grip both sides of the toilet, her knees scrape the floor, and her head is hanging inside the toilet. My mom stands there holding my hand, and as I try to bend down to help my grandmother, my mother holds me back.

"NO!"

I could see my grandmother shake and suffer as she tried to clear her throat. My mother does nothing but stand there and look down at grandma. She's silent! Tears stream down my face and I watch my grandmother struggle to stay alive. She finally cleared her throat, but we did nothing but watch her suffer. My grandmother gets up, looks at us, and walks back downstairs like nothing ever happened. I felt like grandma blamed me, too. It seemed like I was always there when tragedy reared its ugly head!

To this day, I don't understand that exchange of unpleasantries, but I felt like it was very vindictive. I do know one thing for sure: Later in life, I could easily become extremely cold, calculating, and vindictive so that I felt absolutely nothing when it occurred, just like my mother and grandmother. When I was "Caught Between Two Women," or even more, my ability to care about their feelings was non-existent. All they got from me was "The Cold Stare!"

The Topic of Spirituality

Certain women and moms of this mindset attend church for status and possibly titles. They go for the attention, to gossip and stare at the pastor, and let people know they're part of the high society in church. They go to make people think they know the Bible, or to show off their new outfit, expensive purse, shoes, and jewelry.

Bitter—Lonely—and Divorced Mom

This kind of mother has the following characteristics. I caused these traits in many women, so her traits were my fault.

- Always negative
- Absent in the grandchildren's life
- Everyone is guilty until proven innocent
- Grumpy
- Unreliable
- Becomes a recluse
- Holds grudges
- Argumentative

Please, I'd love to be very clear on this.

Mothers that continue to harbor hate and discontent, do so because of a lack of therapy, being done wrong, abused, forgotten about, mistreated, disrespected, abandoned, hurt, and cheated on.

They probably didn't have a relationship with their own mother or father, and have been misunderstood for a good part of their lives. There was a time where these types of moms were good, or even great people but took a path, or were put on a path of destruction to themselves and others.

Mom Accepting the Girlfriend

Some women will do anything to be accepted. If mom feels the slightest bit of competition, she'll take note and you'll feel it because she'll keep you distant.

Being put in the "Distant Zone," you'll experience:

- Shallow conversations
- The cutting of eyes
- Being left out of plans and conversations
- A clear lack of reciprocity by the mother
- No response to text messages
- Receiving cheap gifts or none at all.

The only time the mother will like the girlfriend is when the girlfriend comes second to her, doesn't speak up for herself, and doesn't challenge her in any way. In living like this, you'll find yourself being who he wants you to be and not who you want to be. The years of unhappiness, being unfulfilled, always coming second, and even being disrespected, will more than likely never end and there's a great chance that he'll never marry you. These types of moms have run their own husband off and will run the girlfriend off too, eventually.

You have no authority in such an arrangement, so expect to function more like the little sister. Mom will be a part of his decision-making when he selects the woman for the two of them. You will never have, receive, or experience grace.

A woman who spends months or years in a relationship, always coming second to the mother, will one day explode as a result of all the disrespect that she's been receiving. Once she does this, she begins to look after her interests alone, and it's almost guaranteed that you'll lose her forever, first mentally and then emotionally. She'll go so far and deep into herself, and you'll feel ignored, disrespected, and worthless. After months or sometimes years, it will become obvious how much of her life she has lost. She'll see everything she does as fair and will be honest about her revenge. At this point, she'll have become extremely bitter and resentful. Please bear in mind that not all mothers are like what I discussed earlier. The ones that are most likely didn't have a great relationship with their parents or guardians. It's also most likely true that no one ever challenged them in those formative years; they probably have tons of childhood trauma they're completely oblivious to. They're not only obsessed with exercising control over their children, but they also feel really good about it, too.

I was attracted to older women at an early age, especially those that had endured many ups and downs in life. Even though I was very close to my mother, emotionally and spiritually, indirectly and directly these women taught me how to receive a woman on her level and not from a masculine mindset through a lens of obsession and pure lust.

While a strong woman brought out the best in me, an afraid and abused woman allowed me to bring out the best in her. I was only on my bad behavior whenever I got horny, and this made me a predator. One thing that I mastered was the "art of listening," and that was my most disgusting trait when used maliciously. When I was genuine, I listened to learn, to teach, and to just enjoy good conversation. At this point, I was at my spiritual best. It felt really good to communicate when sex wasn't on my mind.

The Positives of Wanting a Woman Like Our Mother

It is also very healthy and helpful to have a great relationship with your mother. There are many traits that we derive from this. For instance, a man that has great conversations with his mother, will expect the same from his partner. If he sees that his mom and dad doesn't talk much, he'll desire deep and consistent conversations more, as he will surely experience the lack of communication between his parents and also how his mom reacts to it. In addition to the man desiring communication, he'll also desire his woman to serve him his meals, if his mom does so. If his mother doesn't do this, for whatever reason, he will not think that it's the role of the woman. I didn't see my mom serve my dad that often, from kindergarten to sixth grade, but I'm sure she did, as I was a child and didn't relate to anything in their marriage except for bills being paid, school clothes, food, and trips. However, after my parents' divorce, I never saw that again. As a child, when I did see it with my grandparents, my grandfather would do it in a demanding way. I learned verbal abuse far too early. Women down South, for the most part, are raised like this, and so are Latino women.

Psychological Manipulation through Reciprocity

Whenever I listened, I immediately began to look for how to attack a woman's mental and emotional side, to create an imbalance of power in the relationship. In order to do this, I had to read, be conversant with many topics, and come off as intelligent to her so I could control the art of psychological reciprocity. My answer had to be just what she wanted to hear.

Note: I had little respect for any woman in that position, even though possessing and deliberately using this trait made me have no respect for myself. Women don't want to be in charge. They prefer to be pampered by a man who really understands them and is in tune with their needs and desires. It's a pity I didn't see things that way back then. Since I was using the information she had given me against her, I was afraid she was going to do the same to me. She had every right to do so. I just didn't want to be like my sister the first time I hit her: defeated. I was emotionally stunted.

Emotionally Stunted People

These are some of the characteristics of emotionally stunted people.

- They get angry over the littlest things.
- They are extremely self-centered.
- Everything revolves around them.

- They get upset when things don't go their way.
- They consider other people beneath them and treat them likewise.

You might find it interesting to note that even during all the times of manipulation, God had me. The women who my manipulation did not work on were truly connected to God. All I was doing was shamelessly exposing myself.

CHAPTER FIFTEEN

Trigger Alert

I could choose when and where to express this toxic trait. I could turn it on and off like a switch depending on her conversation, eye contact, body language, and upbringing. In *Loveship*, I talk about how important it is to get to know someone's past; however, you have to realize that you should exercise extreme caution when you expound on your past. It could work against you, especially if you're involved with a toxic person. Some of the ways that it could work against you are:

If I know you're missing your dad, I'll be your daddy.

If you were raped or molested, I know you'll be guarded and afraid to open up sexually, but I'll be patient because I know you'll eventually have sex with me. If you were touched by a woman, I now know that you want, for the most part, slow and soft sex. At that point, I also know that I need to perform oral sex on you, like a woman would.

I would do everything you wished your previous lover did, but didn't for whatever reason.

If you are overconfident, I'll work on breaking you down just to show you that you are not confident, only delusional. Doing this will make you second guess yourself, and every time you second guess yourself, I'll blurt out some version of "I told you so." You'll begin to believe in me, more and more. This is where you begin to lose yourself, lose your ability to challenge me, and lose sight of your good qualities. And you'll remain my girlfriend because I'll never marry you.

If you have an issue with your mother, I'll suspect that it's because she's jealous of you.

I'll be nurturing like a mother. I'll talk to you about womanly things, a feat most men will not even attempt. I'll talk to you about men among other topics, such as the one thing that you wanted the most from your mom but never received.

Also, you should know that if I do marry you, the side piece(s) will all know, approve, and stick around. The truth is you all are the same; the only reason you made it to wife status is due to some extra qualities such as the following:

- Being low-maintenance.
- Having a good credit score.
- Being dependable.
- Being docile.
- Your entire existence must revolve around me.
- I am your everything, your master, your leader, but not your family.

Back then, women with low self-esteem made me feel important and on top of the world. I was in charge of two rotten, weak, and delirious people at that time. I told all of the women that were like me about all others that were just like them. Most of the time, being brutally honest is for the benefit of the narcissists.

Remember this statement I made earlier?

"Please don't like me, I am no good!"

This is clearly a red flag of emotional abuse. If you ever hear this from a man or woman, be advised that they will emotionally abuse you, be it directly or indirectly, soon. It's a subtle waring.

Our greed is skin-deep and sky-high. It's only skin deep because it's a sin and God doesn't allow the sin to run to deep into the temple that he has created for us.

I knew about women that had acquired the same street-lifestyle as my mother and would therefore understand my lifestyle. For those that were deep thinkers, like my mom, they challenged me, kept my attention, and drew me closer to them. I remained worldly and articulate around them long enough to keep them interested in me. When I eventually started to become attracted to them, I would exercise my emotional detachment to deflect any serious advances or possible future commitments.

I'm telling you all this to let you understand that I had "mommy issues" and was always looking for a woman to fill that void without hurting me. I would quickly get on the mother's good side. Mothers deeply appealed to me, and when I saw a mother and daughter being very close, there was a good chance that I could have that motherly bond with my woman. I knew that what I was about to do to her daughter would be devastating, but when the mother takes your side, that's about seventy percent of the battle. I struggled with missing my mother, loving their mother, and then hurting the daughter. It was a real mess.

A Lack of Personal Boundaries

"Leon, sometimes with you—I feel like I'm going crazy or losing my damn mind."

I actually enjoyed hearing these words, because it gave me a sense of control. I would never respond when I heard them say this, but I could feel my devilish thoughts growing into doing more things that would keep them aloof.

I lost my mother three times in my life. The first time came when we lost our house. Losing our home was extremely hurtful. I go into that later on in the book. I was sent to live with my mother's friend, Irene, for a year or so. I felt neglected. Abandoned was the right word. You know how it goes, during the divorce proceedings the father is told to leave the home and the mother gets custody of the children. The second time I lost my mom—and this was the most damaging instance for me—was when she started getting high; the third time was when she passed away. I try to keep her close, though. Losing touch with her during her trials and before her death, I also lost a very important lesson in understanding women. The women that I dated could only help me so much. Their cries to me were all about telling me what I wasn't doing right as far as maintaining a healthy relationship was concerned. Honestly, at that point I wasn't interested in having or being in a long-term relationship, much less a marriage, even though I found myself in three long-term relationships anyway. I remained in the relationship because I was scared of the women leaving me. I was a "thirty-percenter." I didn't have the willpower to just walk away even though I had a lot of experience doing that. I was extremely jealous of seeing her with someone else, so I knew exactly what to do to keep them around and interested in me, enough for them to not allow anyone else to have me. I was a thirty-percenter for many years; I gave great sex, cleaned up the house, and contributed financially. The main things I lacked were being romantic, communicating better, being a good listener, and being faithful. However, if their mother liked me, I was definitely in.

I would find myself loving, listening to, and supporting the mothers of women that I dated. I was a totally different person around their mothers, not because I was fake but because I still felt the need to be nurtured by a mother. I was always on my best behavior in their company and always gave them the utmost respect.

As I became a recruiter in Cleveland, I fell in love with the mothers of women I dated. It was easy for me to be honest to moms when they asked me questions. My answers were painful but at times, funny and honest.

"So, Leon, what church do you go to?"

"Well, Mrs. Johnson, honestly I don't currently belong to any church. I did go as a kid though."

"Okay, okay, that's good. What did you learn, Leon?"

At this point, for some reason I usually found it hard to pause and think about what I wanted to say. The answers came right out.

"I didn't pay attention. I went for the milk, cookies, and the little girls, Mrs. Johnson."

I stared in silence, waiting to be chastised, just like a little boy but her mom never became angry nor did she judge me. My mom was the same way. I missed that so much.

"I get it, Leon. Heck, her brothers never went and when they did, they probably did the same thing."

Whew, I thought to myself while I was biting down on my teeth and my toes were popping in my shoes.

"You and Sheila come in here and eat."

Sheila had a great mom but her dad was a player. They had been married for over twenty-five years and had a large family with siblings spread across Cleveland. We dated for about six months and I watched her mother closely every day. Sheila suffered from some type of personality disorder, and she clearly wasn't like her mother. I met Sheila a year after my heartbreak in San Diego, so I had a lot to do with her disorders. I wasn't ready for a relationship, but had she been like her mother, I might have married her. I had more respect for her mom than I did for her. The major reason I didn't respect her was the fact that she had let me turn her into a psycho. She had character and integrity until she met me. She'd been a pure and clean young lady but soon after I met her, she was smoking weed, drinking, and fighting like a thug. Girls that go to Catholic schools are, for the most part, good girls until they meet a menace. And she met me, the biggest menace of all.

Such girls have been sheltered and immersed in the Bible their entire lives. They are wonderful souls. Be careful if you ever meet one. Endeavor to do the right thing. I didn't do the right thing. My goal was to bring out her inner freak. That was wrong, but I did it anyway. I brought out a little fiery demon that I wasn't ready for.

Remember when I asked, "Will a woman try to kill me one day?" I was just like "my damn daddy." My mom was right.

I am driving my Ford Probe, 1992 through downtown Cleveland, on my way to have dinner with another young lady. Suddenly, a car gets close to me and slightly bumps my car. I pull over in front of my old high school, Shaw High, close to the gas station. An argument ensues and the police pull up. They tell Sheila to leave and then tell me to go in the opposite direction. I waited too long to call my dad; I knew Sheila was headed to my dad's house.

"Dad, if Sheila comes over, please don't let her in."

"Too late, man, she just left, and she did damage to your room and clothes. When she came into the house, she spoke, gave me a hug, seemed happy, so I didn't think anything was wrong. Then she went upstairs to your room."

"Okay, I'll be there shortly."

"I told you to treat that girl right, man."

"Yea, I know, my bad..."

Moments later my car phone rings.

"Leon, this is Mrs. Johnson. What did you do to Sheila? Where are you?"

"She caught me with another woman, while I was driving down Euclid, Mrs. Johnson, I'm sorry! I'm headed to my dad's house!"

I let down quite a few mothers and I hated that feeling, I really did.

"Don't apologize to me, you know I trusted you with my daughter. Her sister is here crying, and she's mad at you too. You need to head to the hospital, Leon."

That night, Sheila tried to commit suicide.

For some reason, I was addicted to women with drama—drama that I caused. It actually felt good to know that she was crazy about me. I would later kick it with Sheila again. It didn't go so well. I honestly wasn't trying to console her, it was more of trying to feed my addictions to the drama. The victim will chase you all day, neglecting friends, family, and even their kids. The perpetrator will see it as a serious thrill; I know I did.

Note: Having or making someone crazy about you, gives the aggressor more freedom and latitude in the relationship. It's very dangerous, misleading, and harmful.

Impressing a mother just enough for her to see me as better than her daughter's last boyfriend was enough for me to be in. I then acted like I wasn't promiscuous, and they rolled with that. I would learn later that even though I loved the mothers of women I dated, I made myself believe that I wasn't lying to them by treating their daughter better than any other man they had dated, even though I was cheating. That wasn't love for a mother at all. I was still missing true and authentic love.

Proselytism

I didn't even know how to love God!

My parents never forced church on us, so Christian women would always have a hard time with me. Once they spoke about the Bible, I would either shut down or walk away. This hurt me when it came to knowing the Bible, but my mother made sure I believed in God. It felt good and natural to have it that way. There were times that I lost my way with God, though. I liked that church and religion wasn't forced on me. I only had one relationship where it was kind of forced on me, but that didn't last long. I was rebellious as hell back in 1992. My girlfriend eased me into it and I appreciated that; it was a good feeling. I still lost my way with God again. I believe that her way of teaching me the Bible, or trying to, was the best course of action for myself and any man.

Note: Please let your man's passion for God come naturally.

Please keep that in mind. As a kid and even as an adult, if forced to go to church, I would sit there and think about women and what I wanted to do to and with them. Leave me at home on a Sunday to watch ESPN and football all day. I wasn't so naughty and was more loving when you came home from church. Keep that in mind, too. I know it sounds disrespectful, but it's not meant that way. Men just enjoy their alone time, even if we do miss church. Even if you're the type of person that goes to church frequently, has a relationship with God, and has knowledge about the word, refrain from imposing that on him.

Ask yourself, is he living by those scriptures that you know so well? That's surely something you need to keep an eye out for. If so, that's his natural course and he'll slowly make himself better with his relationship with God.

Note: You should never use your pastor as a measuring stick for your husband. If he wants to do that himself, please allow him. Let it be his decision and not yours. I may not be able to quote a single scripture in the Bible, but if I can live by that scripture, or many scriptures, this should suffice for our matrimony.

The problem that women will have with this is that when we marry you, we're supposed to follow certain rules, regulations, and guidelines, according to our wedding vows. Well, who made these rules and guidelines? The state, the government, church, the pastor, or God? If God made these rules, and they were made back in olden times, how many times have they been changed, and by whom? There's a huge disparity when it comes to this. The disparities consist of different churches, pastors, versions of the Bible, one's beliefs, upbringing, and so on. I had a hard time believing in certain people who regularly read the Bible and preached the word, and then lived a separate life right after church was over. It's important that you do not force your beliefs on your man, regardless of what you were taught. Most mothers will not do this; they allow their sons to make their own adjustments, and live their lives based on what they believe. Most women want their man to live how her father wants her and her family to live. This will be a major problem with your man. It was with me.

Women have asked me if I was saved, and then they would say, "Well if you're not, then I can't date you." Some of them were lusting after the person on the pulpit, even if he was married. To me, they weren't saved either. That was my way of being evil and informing them of what I saw and knew, just because they wouldn't date me. I was very vindictive.

Please bear in mind, I'm speaking to you in character. A character which was dysfunctional, molested, touched and suffering from many addictions. Your current man may have experienced this, too. We are timid at times, fractured, worried, fragile, unsteady. Just hold on, hold on to us. The reason we date or marry a woman like our mother is because we're looking for unconditional love. And also, we need a woman that's easy to talk to. Some other reasons are:

Men want a woman to listen, care, understand, and not judge us, especially if we are in our most vulnerable stages. We need to hear that it's going to be fine, whatever it is, with solid and concrete backup and support. This is what our mothers say to us.

We do not want to be controlled, managed, or pushed around. Mothers are welcoming, approachable, endearing, and teachers, and we want that in a partner. We do enjoy being taught, but not at the expense of a woman holding it against us that we don't know something. Mothers don't often tell their friends that their sons don't know or can't do something.

Mothers don't gossip about their sons to other women. They may scold us, but it's forgotten and forgiven. If they gossip to other women about their son, it's usually a grandma, auntie, or some trusted confidant, and they receive proper feedback, too. Men enjoy their finances. Do not try to take control of what he has or what he makes. Believe me when I tell you, if you act like and treat him like it's his money, you'll get more that way. However, once you become intricately involved with his spending habits, he'll lie to your face. I did this, without remorse. The argument here is that women will resort to their dad, the church, your past, and whatever your mom recommends, in that situation. It's still his hard-earned money, and if you don't know how to treat him with his money, you'll inject the thoughts and recommendations of outside people and you'll lose him.

- His friends are his friends. Please don't judge him but be aware of who they are. Some are real, and some are fake.
- Keep him informed and allow him to make his decisions.
- Don't manage his time.
- Stay out of his phone.
- Ask him for his input.
- Don't tell him what to do.

CHAPTER SIXTEEN

Comfort-Covering Safety and EMIQ of a Mother

It's important that you know about your man's mother. It'll be the principal trait in his knowledge of how he treats you and your mother. It is also important that you pay attention to this. If his mother was there and nurtured him as a child, he would have her qualities, regardless of how manly he is. This means that he'll understand your thoughts, mindset, vision, and more importantly, how to relate to your traits. If mom was absent, he would be inept in his understanding of you and your relationship with your mother, and all mentioned above. There's a good chance that he will harbor and hold on to some regrets and deep hurts, and would possibly be experiencing emotional detachment as well as Repressive Masculine Norm.

Masculine Norms

- Heterosexual presentation
- Risk-taking
- Emotional restraint
- Power over women
- Dominance over his territory
- Self-reliance
- A winning attitude

Masculine Norms will make a woman feel worthless. In this situation, a man takes on a dominant role, while she becomes docile and totally submissive, sometimes against her will. These must be clearly identified in the dating stages if she expects to not have issues later on, unless this is her natural role, as taught to her by her mother, in which case all is fine and dandy.

Repressive masculine norms will cause women to want to act in a masculine manner. She'll fight this as long as she can but once she has decided to take over, respect will be lost in the relationship. Everyone would suffer in the household, and oddly as it may seem, the son would see a role that he doesn't want to emulate and the daughter would see a role that she wants to emulate. Or the opposite can occur as well.

Now, I came into all of my relationships a broken man. What I depict above is not to be excused, but I needed help. I should not have been dating while I was in such a mental state. I clearly had issues and should have been in therapy, many years ago. Regardless of what a man wants or desires, he has to earn it and not be an exception at any time in his life. When we earn your trust, it's easy to then date without reservation and a guarded heart. I was not ever to be trusted.

Fighting His Safe Haven, and Hers Too

When a woman truly loves a man, she'll cover him, but if a man isn't familiar with her covering, he'll focus more on the passive neglect from his past. If you don't know anything about his past, you'll feel like everything wrong in the relationship is your fault.

When passive neglect occurs, it can come from an aunt, sister, babysitter, grandmother, or teacher. It's not always from the mother. My neglect started with my two female cousins, like I mentioned earlier. For women, it could be an uncle, dad, male cousin, or an ex.

We take a woman's covering and love for granted. I know I did. I became comfortable and because of this, her needs became secondary. When a man has been starved or neglected as a child, he will not realize the woman's covering, care, or support; instead, he'll fight it.

He'll become extremely independent and, in this case, he'll lose all his morals. His independence causes a lack of remorse as well. He feels that if he can survive and doesn't need many people, then you should be the same way, too. As a result of this, he will feel like he doesn't need you. Some men are kicked out of the nest far too soon. As a result of this survival trait, which they develop early, a woman starts to feel like she doesn't have an active role in the relationship or can't add any value.

Passive Neglect Triggers That Prevent Covering
This goes for both, male and female.

- Yelling and screaming
- Being domineering
- Not trusting them
- Not forgiving them
- Apologizing then repeating the same behavior
- Controlling the kids and excluding them
- Not preparing meals on purpose
- A lack of compliments
- Refusal to extend reassuring confidence
- Constant reminders of their mistakes

Comfort Zone

- Make sure that she knows that she matters!
- Stay on your "happy toes" and not just on your toes.

When you become comfortable, you get complacent and civilized. Her forward motion and thinking begins to slow down. This is when we begin to push a woman away. Comfort resonates with a man's soul; it's like being in a warm, safe, and secure nest, like a fetus in the womb. But in his comfort, he must continue to respect her in his belief and actions by reciprocating. Any man can say what he wants to about this ideology, but there's no greater fear for a man than to lose his woman to a man that just simply gets her, a man that understands and appreciates her, and refuses to become comfortable. A man that doesn't mind residing in her soul, spirit, and the mental security of her womb while being covered, nurtured, and protected. A man who is on his job, secure and aware.

When women leave, it happens mentally first, and then once her mind is gone, her body becomes cold. You are no longer welcome in her warmth or womb and your touch will not matter regardless of your sexual prowess. Her vagina has shut down.

The Woman's EMIQ

Empathy: "I understand that baby, how can we fix it?"

Compassion: "I want this relationship to work, I'll give it my all."

Passion: "I love you with my entire being, honey."

Courage: "Let's work it out, we can get past this, baby!"

My relationship EMIQ was extremely low.

Leon's EMIQ

Empathy: "I understand how you feel, but oh well."

Compassion: "I'm sorry, but look what you made me do."

Passion: "I'll make it up to you. I have a nice weekend planned, you down?"

Courage: "I cheated, I don't really like her though, I feel you more."

CHAPTER SEVENTEEN

Dance for the Vagina

I was really crying out for help, but the crowd of women only clapped for me, flirted, or offered me more work. I wish they had asked me why I was stripping. Then I would have probably been more articulate. I just wanted answers from a woman about my breakup in 1991, but I clearly went about it the wrong way.

Bond Court Hotel, Cleveland, 1994.

I was pimping myself out, on the side! In the daytime, I was extremely professional—at night, I turned into this wicked monster. People admire military members, but in all honestly, we join for most reasons aside from being patriotic. Seeking attention, trying to prove something to ourselves and others, the exotic women, an abundance of sex with exotic women, and many other reasons. Military men and women can join and hide or suppress who they really are or once were, and most people will never know, except those that really know you. I was a Navy recruiter back then, with four percent body fat and a head full of wavy hair. I weighed 185 pounds and was as cocky, conceited, and as lost as they come. I was searching for my own identity, still heartbroken from my last relationship. I was always the one walking away, but when it happened to me, I wasn't ready. I was dead set on getting revenge, but sadly, it was at the detriment of my own health, self-medication, and mental cutting.

Narcissists can't handle "escapism"—she got away without me getting my much-needed trophy!

My drinking was at an all-time high as well, but I didn't care, not one bit. I drank excessively for two years; most of the time when I was behind the wheel, I was blind drunk. None of the police officers that pulled me over ever arrested me or gave me a ticket. Cleveland loves professional athletes and the military. It was as if I could do no wrong. Wearing my Navy uniform proved my allegiance to America and also showed that I was patriotic. Serving my country was cool to black people back then, but white people have always loved it. It was a badge of honor and respect.

The people in the bar at the hotel, buying me drinks and on some occasions, food, had no clue that I was there to perform as a male stripper.

Before attending any job as a male stripper, I would wear my uniform into the bar, or wherever the event was being held. This was my safe haven, because I knew that there was no trouble getting into these places. My change of clothes was in the trunk. I wasn't even doing the stripping for money, honestly. I did it to expose myself to women and invite them to do whatever they wanted to me. I wanted the word to get back to my ex, that I had let other women see me half-naked, and had even allowed them to touch me all over. The news traveling to her never happened. I had hoped it did!

I had a death wish. I wanted to go out by any means necessary, be it a violent car crash or being killed or injured by crazy women who'd been driven over the edge; I just didn't care. I wanted to tease them with my body, lead them on, and then have sex with them and leave them, breaking their heart. When women are hurt from an emotional standpoint, nothing or no one can stop them from getting revenge. I became addicted to hitting their "crazy spot." Never do that to a woman, it's not right and you will pay for it.

Recruiting Office, 1993

LQ, from Detroit, taught me a valuable lesson. She was twenty-two years old, five feet nine inches tall, and very good looking but also very crazy. She weighed 135 pounds and had short hair and large breasts. I met her at a local bar in Cleveland and invited her to one of my stripper events. She attended, and then we went on a few dates. This was when I started playing games with her. Later that year after being caught with other women, lying, and ghosting—she had had enough. I'm sitting at my desk making phone calls and setting up appointments, school visits, and talking to the other recruiters.

"Yo, Walker, O'l girl wanna holler at you outside."

"Who?"

"I'on know, the one you been kicking it wit, she's outside."

LQ burst through the office door.

"Uhh, muthafucka, we need to talk—*bitch!*"

I sat in my chair, stunned and freaked out, and then stood up.

"Girl, why you tripping?"

"Come outside, Leon—now!"

LQ had done time in the juvenile system and she could fight. She came to my job with a butcher knife in hand, in front of my co-workers. She didn't care who was around; she didn't mind where we were, either. LQ didn't cut me open, but I surely paid her to leave me alone, and it was worth it. She claimed to be pregnant but I think she just needed money for rent, food, and weed. I didn't care what her reasons were at that moment, though. I was so terrified of her that I began to quickly peel off my twenties and fifties. Six-hundred dollars worth.

Let's talk about what happened at Bond Court Hotel some more. When I arrived, I sat at the bar for about an hour. I usually did this before any stripping event. Looking dashing in my uniform, I drank three straight shots of gin; all of the drinks were on the house. I went to the bathroom to change and came back to my seat at the bar. The bartender, a white guy, started talking to me.

"So, are you here for the party, man?"

I had on a green suit, no shirt, and a green bowtie.

"Yea, how do you know?"

"By the way you're dressed, I suppose. You're the stripper, aren't you?"

I laughed, a loud embarrassing guffaw before proceeding to take my next shot of gin. The alcohol made me wince. I eventually swallowed, and responded.

"Ahhh, yea, the group of women upstairs booked me for an hour."

"Ahh, I see. Hey, see those two ladies at the end of the bar? They're looking for a boy toy."

I slowly cut my eyes towards the end of the bar, and two middle-aged white women stared back at me. We nod, hold our drinks up, and take sips together from a distance. They wink.

"Are you interested in being a gigolo?" the bartender asked. "Man, I'm telling you, there's plenty of money in this type of work. The women that come here are deprived and depraved but they're also filthy rich."

My mind quickly went back to the encounter with LQ. When white women are hurt or misled, their revenge is different. For the most part, they might not wield a weapon, but they will come to your place of work. They would also speak to the people at the top: police, lawyers, psychiatrists, you name it. They work their way from the top down. I didn't want that. Although it was very tempting at the time, I had to decline.

I did meet women that gave me free massages and made me clothes though.

I blamed my job for making me into a monster, but it wasn't true. As a narcissist who avoided all forms of responsibility, I had an excuse for everything wrong with me; it was always other people's fault, never mine. I had used that same excuse all my life to continue being a menace to women. Like I said, everything that happened to me was always everyone else's fault. The truth is that people affect our lives in numerous ways; however, once I knew who I was and why I was doing those things, I had a choice to become a better person. But I chose to immerse myself in my job, craft, and work ethic; nothing else mattered. People are forgiving. America itself is forgiving, but not me. I wasn't even forgiving to myself. I became Recruiter of the Year that year, thanks to all my hard work. And the harder I worked, two things happened. I partied harder and my job let me get away with anything. Stripping for women made me some good money, but I was still unhappy and felt really empty inside.

CHAPTER EIGHTEEN

Feminine Energy

I was so afraid of getting hurt that I gave no one a chance to get close to me. I would much rather do harm to myself, by being immature, lonely, embarrassed, or anything else deemed unhealthy, just to keep people at a distance. It was easy for me to deflect hurt that way, when it came from a woman. I didn't dance to attract women. I did it to see who was into me, to help me. I battled all of my different personalities all my life. Although I was never diagnosed as having more than one personality, I just knew, somehow. People expose themselves to a large audience for many reasons, be it money, lust, fake love, or help, and I needed help badly. I was killing Leon and trying to keep him alive all at the same time, relationship-wise. I was only able to process the needs of a woman from one side of my brain, the left side. This, for me, and probably many men, consists of things that are action-oriented or have to do with problem-solving. I failed at both miserably because my anger issues clouded my judgment and any hopes of her getting through to me with logic went out the window. As a child, like I mentioned earlier, anything connected to love terrified me. Women are receivers and men are releasers, but not one woman received anything from me worth holding on to. I just wanted to Enter without a Course.

Intercourse with a woman is one thing: it's about physicality. Lust. Love-making, on the other hand, is when she lets herself go, when she becomes completely vulnerable in the company of a man that she trusts and has chemistry with. For many years, I thought that I was in her good graces because she had intercourse with me. I was so wrong. When a man releases his lustful energy into a woman, it's different from what she releases, and if there isn't any chemistry, she will not release on a wholesome and loving level. She knows when she's not giving herself to you, but the man doesn't, especially if he's entering without something I like to call "a course of action."

I think a woman's vagina is the last thing she thinks of as far as purity and virginity are concerned. She wants first, closure for her mental well-being after a break-up or divorce, followed by other things like peace of mind, clarity, time to mourn her loss, as well as answers to why her marriage or relationship failed. Most women ask themselves, "What could I have done more or better?"

Good Girl Gone Bad

Most men fear these types of women. However, just like broken and untrustworthy men, she deserves a chance, too. Good guys attract broken women who are looking for help while they're unconsciously searching for a man that has no street credibility. He's an easy target for them and they know he can't really handle them. This type of woman wants to have her cake and eat it too. She's more masculine than feminine; she either loves her father, misses him, or never knew who he was; however, she realizes she's just like him. The streets are a lure for her, everything from strip-clubs to exquisite bars. Even though she may have made mistakes, lived as a wildflower, struggled with addictions, and so on, once she's on her path to recovery, growth, and forgiveness, believe her. Make sure you take your time with this, especially if she was the masculine, domineering one. Her transition can be scary at first when her partner is the caring, loving, and nurturing one, but take note and pay attention. There's a chance that she's done with the streets. She's definitely confident and has the work ethic. The streets have done that much to her.

Mourn to Recovery

After a breakup, her vagina is connected to her refusal to participate in fornication. Her happiness and intuition, which stem from desiring to be treated with respect, becomes her goal. Being motivated by her man is one thing, but being inspired, highly regarded, rehabilitated, transcended, and exclusive is the ultimate.

When she's happy and trusts you, her desire to be showered with love makes her creative juices flow. Her "girl" pulsates and gets wet at this; that's why women give their vagina a name, because it sometimes has a mind of its own. When she's sad, hurt, or has the intuition of your cheating ways, it dries up and goes home. However, on the flip-side, during this period, women mourn their losses, losses of children, and definitely the loss of a man she tried to build a future and family with. They take their time before jumping in bed with someone else. These are women, after all, not little girls. In an effort to satisfy themselves and avoid becoming promiscuous, their mind will draw from a past partner, a good guy who things didn't work out with for whatever reason, and who they still respect and hold in high regard. With this memory in mind, they begin to pleasure themselves. They do not need penile penetration for pleasure. The next guy, even though he may not be as endowed as you are, will be in tune with her emotions, feelings, mindset, plans, goals, and more importantly, he'll know her Emotional Languages; she'll make sure of this. Don't get too comfortable, though. Knowing the Emotional Languages leads me to talk about my next topic.

Developing Balance for Positivity

I never took the time to get to know women on any level. Men want the relationship to be easy and also fear that women change after marriage. Some women still reserve the thoughts of their mother and father being successfully married for forty to fifty years and the roles of both of them from back then. They expect that the both of you will have the same dynamic, but you must consider that things have changed now. You must recognize your ways, traditions, tutelage, and his too. How was he raised, and does it match how you were raised?

Forget the fact that you may have heard that he's a momma's boy; listen to his mother. In some cases, listen to his sister, too. An aunt can be helpful, a neighbor, and close friends. You may think that this approach is too intense, but it's not. If you are into this man, and feel a good connection, then you need to do your homework and do your due diligence. He should do the same about you as well. He may one day be the father of your kids, and both good and bad genetics are passed down. Never settle. Endeavor to remain intuitive, fair, and honest. Never sneak around looking for your answers about your man. Don't let insecurity creep in. In this matter, trust is crucial. If he's real about the future he plans to build with you, then it's a good idea to talk to any available person. Pay close attention to his father and his father's ways. Most men take on their father's habits, especially if they're toxic. We forget that since we get half our genes from our mother, we don't have to be carbon copies of our fathers, especially as far as toxic traits are concerned. Taking on your father's problematic ways, solely, makes you lose sight of who your woman really is, what she brings to the table, her capabilities, drive, and effort, and her ability to make you better. Knowing my mother's ways taught me a lot about women. There was no way that I would listen to a woman intently, nor submit, until later in life when I read what submitting was all about.

CHAPTER NINETEEN

Submitting Is an Art

When done and understood properly and without reservation, submitting is a holy act. The church, made up of both men and women, collectively submits to God. We all freely and happily talk about the art of war, the art of kissing, and many more arts, but no one wants to discuss the art of submitting.

In an effort to make yourself ready and willing to submit, you must understand first of all that you are not surrendering. Neither are you giving up power, being a coward, or losing any ground in the relationship. You are not being fearful either. People know how to submit to God, but when it comes to their partner, it becomes hard. When submitting to God we ask, "What am I here for?" Have you asked your partner that? Back then, I had never thrown that question to any woman I dated. For years, I lived a counterfeit life.

Submitting Your Soul

This involves sacrificing your Ungodly desires of:

- Shame
- Pain
- Loyalties
- Self-vows

Now, to make it easier and clearer for men and women like myself, especially those that either do not go to church for whatever reason, or are not that well versed in the Bible, here it is in layman's terms.

In a healthy relationship, both man and woman are not forced into submission. Submission is an act that is expressed mutually and voluntarily, out of love. Being submissive helps us to be less self-centered and allows us to consider the other person's desires.

For many years, both men and women have misinterpreted the Bible's version of submitting. Some have used the passage to justify controlling, dysfunctional, and abusive behavior. In my fifty-seven years of existence, I have only sat and listened to the preacher speak a total of two times. Once was at my uncle's funeral. I didn't understand what the minister was saying that day, but I saw all of the people he spoke about as clear as day, in color! It terrified me. The other time, a friend of mine was speaking here in Illinois, and this time, I saw what he was saying, in black and white. Both times, I felt detached from the experience; they felt like movies in my head.

How Women Fail at Being Submissive

A. By not letting a man be a man. You've heard the saying, boys will be boys. Well, men will be men as well.

B. By becoming afraid of being vulnerable, especially if she's with a man that has cheated before. In that situation, she'll feel that he will never be the man she wants him to be. Once he cheats, his word no longer means anything to her. She'll even become more guarded about their children. Cheating reduces trust, drastically. I get that. I lived that life once upon a time.

C. By holding him hostage.

D. By building strong, permanent walls. This prevents both men and women from loving in freedom.

E. By being taught by her mother who is or has been bitter towards men.

How Men Fail at Being Submissive

A. By listening to men that have misinterpreted the word "submitting."

B. By thinking that women are inferior and less than us. If she cheats, the man will feel insecure, inadequate, and extremely fearful. He'll become more domineering within the home as far as finances are concerned. He'll be less loving or domineering in bed. The vision of another man will always stick with him. His first thought will be of his penis being smaller than the man she cheated on him with, or his inability to satisfy her orally like the man or woman she cheated on him with.

C. By being narcissistic or having some of the traits.

D. Living by ancient traditions.

E. By not trusting his partner.

F. Listening to other broken men and their toxic advice.

G. Failing to open up.

H. Always talking about likes, dislikes, etc., to his benefit.

I. Not sharing goals, fantasies, as well as what's on her mind.

As a Command Master Chief in the Navy, around my twenty-fifth year, I witnessed another senior Sailor totally submit to another man. This bothered me. It bothered me because he was a minister in a well-known church, preaching the word every Sunday, speaking about how women are supposed to submit, and not totally the man, and yet he did the opposite when he came to work.

I was always unequally yoked. I was absent from God and pitched my tent with the devil. Once I knew that the devil could not affect the woman that I knew was for me, I understood that he didn't have power over me.

This was when my transition started. I had to be fine with God being the husband of all women. If I wanted a wholesome woman, I had to know, accept, and believe that I would always come second.

CHAPTER TWENTY

Seeing My Dad Cry,
I Knew It Was Okay to Cry

Shut up, boy! Quit crying!
But it hurts!

I was eight years old and my uncle had damaged me for a long time by then. The vision of my strong dad helped me, though. Uncle Greg bullied me and told me not to cry. He stood there in front of me as I stood against the tree at my grandmother's house as he threw prickly plants into my face. From that point forward, it took years for me to cry again. I lost trust for men at an early age because of that incident.

Abusers first abuse, and then the abused also abuse. Hurt people hurt people. I'm sure you're familiar with the saying, "When I would make women cry, I didn't feel a thing." My uncle taught me that. I was eleven years old and we were in the living room in our house on Alder Avenue. My dad was drinking a beer.

"Sylvia, I have something to tell you."

"What is it, Leon?"

"I have a son in Alabama."

I stopped in my tracks and looked at my mother.

"Well, he can't come here."

Instantly, my dad started to cry. My dad was my hero and when I saw him cry, it opened up wells of emotion in me that had been shut tightly for years. I walked upstairs and cried for him. It felt so good to release those tears. I thought to myself, if this tall, strong man can cry, then maybe it's not such a bad thing to cry. Before that, aside from being bullied, I was told repeatedly that only girls cried.

Seeing my parents argue about a brother I had never seen was hurtful. I suppose my mom considered my dad a cheater. I never found out when my dad had a relationship with another woman, or if he cheated, but my mom didn't want to accept my brother and I heard her utter those words to my dad. I too would later cheat on my wife and also have a child outside of my engagement and marriage, some thirty-one years after my parents divorced. I cried when I found out that I had gotten another woman pregnant. Before my other uncle died, my brother and I would go see him. He was extremely sick and would always cry too. Maybe this crying thing was from my grandfather? I only saw men on my father's side cry, not the ones on my mother's side. I remember that well.

CHAPTER TWENTY-ONE

Emulating My Dad's Dating Pattern

For the young men that did not have their dad around growing up, please do not discard him now that you're older. Whatever his reason was for not being there—be it death, jail, or even if it was just an irresponsible absence—remember, you still have his DNA. Listen to what people say about him, good and bad; learn about your mom, his mom, and other family members. Do your own research. If you can, find him, reach out to him. As it stands right now, you are more than likely to emulate his ways, both positive and negative, so make sure you pay attention to that and adjust accordingly. My dad was always there for me.

Regardless of what people will tell you, remember that he had his reasons for doing what he did. We all get a fair chance at life, but some of us don't get help when we are derailed. Black men especially are not known to embrace therapy as an effective way to solve mental issues. This makes us suppress our feelings a lot. When we do this, it becomes very damaging to the family structure and future relationships. We will then begin to blame others for our actions, inabilities, inactions, and unresolved issues, even though we're much better than who we currently present. I was guilty of this for years.

The routine post-divorce can be very heartbreaking: move out of the house, make room for another man to be around your kids, get the kids every other weekend, every other holiday; deal with the pain of having to drop them off at a certain time, rotating birthdays. It can take a toll on your mental health. My kids were never kept from me, though, and I appreciate my ex-wife for that.

Try not to repeat those actions. I did the same thing when I got divorced thirty-one years after my parents did.

Most, if not all men want to be just like their dads, and rightfully so. I mean, I sure did. In doing so, sometimes, we lose sight of our mom's ways. We have a tendency to lose focus of what women need, how to treat them, but more importantly, how women think. Or we think it's too feminine to study and get to know women on a deeper level; we're only interested in them sexually. Men need to realize and be comfortable with accepting our mother's DNA side as well. Once we're comfortable with that, and really understand it, it'll be almost impossible for any other man to make you think differently or adopt his ways and beliefs. However, when we favor women in certain areas of relationships, because of their intuition, foresight, and hindsight, we're categorized and called many names:

- Weak
- Simp
- Henpecked
- Captain Saver
- Wimp
- Soft
- Imbecile
- Wuss
- Sorry excuse for a man
- Pencil neck

When favoring and respecting women due to certain qualities they possess, you become enlightened, and those that categorize you as any of the above will be very stereotypical and critical of you even though they do not have the power to uplift you. There are more men in the world that feel the opposite of what I am saying; they feel if you want to become popular, all you have to do is put a woman down.

Listen to this: Building them up might be unpopular, but it's definitely the right thing to do.

Part of being confident is being sure of who you are and being fine with others not understanding you. Knowing women requires thinking in a different way, adjusting your mindset. You'll need to appreciate her worth, ask for her input, and not view the relationship from a masculine perspective alone.

I wouldn't make sense if I was speaking and teaching as if I was a virgin or someone that hasn't dated women, but I am far from that, and the years spent in and out of relationships gives me an abundance of experience and exposure.

Men that put their woman first, exercise chivalry, and show respect for their better half, live better and healthier lives. However, taking the path of least resistance— a path that allows you to seek only women that need and depend on you— won't keep you safe. It's only a shorter road to death. Some women add life to you, and some take it away. Men can be like this, too. Don't make your companion's decision based on your needs, greed, or lust, which are mortal sins. You must understand that when a woman is really there for you, it is something to be happy about, something to be reciprocated. You must repent of any of your previous sins and start afresh with her. Treat her like a queen.

Some men will argue this point forever and will take the side of those who think less of women. I have thought less of women before, but I don't do that anymore and I am not afraid to speak on why I no longer think less of women. Naturally, when men are hurt, put in jail, need answers, and so on, the first person they call out for is their mother. When there are issues with their girlfriend, they call "mama," not "daddy," yet they listen to and follow male chauvinists when they feel less than a woman or are involved with one who is too strong for them. The "theorists" that are turning men against women or those that have a misogynistic mindset straight out of the 1930s, will also die alone. They will never settle down, will keep multiple sex partners, and will always share a woman with other men; the women would be aware of this but he won't. We need women in our lives and society at large for many reasons. I am a practitioner and have always either wanted a woman or needed one in my life. I am proud to say that and not fearful of what other men think. Some men are afraid to admit how much they love their woman, and some will even put their friends before their woman, by getting embarrassed or afraid to tell them they can't or don't want to hang out because they want to spend time with their woman. But we expect women to do that for us.

The same men that give others a problem about spending time with their woman are the same ones that will try to have sex with that man's woman, or wish that he had her. The ones that are against marriage are the ones that are usually caught cheating, just like me, so I know where they are coming from; however, it's wrong to teach other men that.

We immerse ourselves so deep into being like our dads alone that we fall prey to hypermasculinity and chauvinism. In today's society, we men suffer from a lack of mentors. Look at all of the professional athletes that get into trouble. I'm not saying it's all their fault, we know that's not true, but we need to have more discipline among us males. I had mentors during my time in the Navy, but I didn't take heed to the mature men. I feel horrible for irresponsibly spreading my seed all over the world; it's disgusting. That wasn't my dad's way.

Let me carry on talking about my dating pattern...

Sheila was a beautiful woman, at five feet six inches and 150 pounds. She had long, flowing, brown hair, and college degrees, which only made hotter somehow. Ertha was a homebody, short and thick, loved Winston cigarettes and liked having my dad around. She made sure he was well-fed, too. Pearl was a super crack-head, smoked Newports, had patchy hair, and was missing a couple teeth. She wasn't this way when my dad met her. My dad was six feet two inches and stood at about 220 pounds when he was healthy. He had dark skin, a full beard, a head of thick hair, and a mouthful of strong teeth.

When my dad would disappear during the day, while we lived on Hough Avenue, my sister and I knew exactly where to find him. Pearl, a serious crack-head, literally brought my dad down, which ultimately led to his death. He stayed with her the longest. I believe it was about sixteen years.

"Hey man, if Sheila comes by, tell her I'm not here, okay?"

My dad always avoided Sheila and I never knew why but I did have an idea.

Men emulate their dad on many levels. I never thought that I would pick up the same dating traits as my dad. I knew that I was a generous person like him, enjoyed the company of people, worked hard, and was extremely outgoing, just like him, but I didn't figure out that we would be attracted to the same type of women. I suppose if we weren't living in the ghetto, my attraction would have been different. Sometimes I wonder about that. I know one thing for sure: I appreciated the women on Hough because they were pretty simple and it resonated with my personality. Not saying that women else-where weren't simple, but living in the ghetto, people are much more grateful for what they have or don't have, and most of us didn't have much. The women on Hough were tough and a lot of them didn't have much time for love. They hardly ever challenged you, too. Unless you were caught cheating, and even then, they would take you back, with a fight, literally. I truly believe that cheating as a kid without any serious consequences followed me for the rest of my life.

Not being challenged in a relationship and just having to take a slap or two when I got caught cheating made me comfortable. Women don't slap hard. It was not a repercussion I was scared of, by any means. I was clueless about what women wanted. I had already developed a mindset to walk away from women without thinking twice, but sometimes I stayed because we were both addicted to the drama. We saw the adults do the same thing: smoke, drink, fight, and argue. The fighting couples became very popular on Hough. I was twelve years old when this mindset was formed in me. Back then, having sex at that age was common. If you were still a virgin, the kids in the neighborhood made fun of you.

I saw grown men and women dating on Hough and I saw the men being violent towards the women. Pimps were as constant as sunrise and sunset, and prostitutes were a dime a dozen. I saw women completely differently once we lost our house in East Cleveland.

The women on Hough Avenue and the surrounding areas were mouthy, and could fight just as well as the men. Very few were lady-like, the environment didn't allow that, but after dating a few, I would come to find out that they were very beautiful, strong, and classy women. Women from the hood have a totally different mindset. Most men can't handle them because of their strength and how they were raised. They love hard because they've had to deal with the loss of their parents, as well as other things like losing their virginity at an early age, living in a place with a high crime rate, and having to grow up fast. Lots of them became babysitters very young. Some went astray, but most were committed and down for their man. The women who lived in the suburbs were automatically scared of them.

The first thing to come out of their mouth whenever they were confronted was, "Bitch, what—dis ain't whatchuwant!"

And then they'd remove their earrings, shoes, and tighten up their ponytail. They'd be talking the whole time too, swinging their arms and biting their bottom lip. Apart from systemic racism, and segregation, substances such as alcohol, cigarettes, heroin, and cocaine dealt a deadly blow to black families in the country; it made them start to fall apart. Every day, during my encounters with girls in East Cleveland and on Hough, I had to switch up my approach—the way I spoke, and what we talked about. The two places were two totally different worlds.

At the time, East Cleveland was a thriving suburb and the young ladies were very classy. On Hough, they had class from time to time, but most times they were always ready to get down and dirty, ready to fight, smoke, drink, and have sex. East Cleveland girls required some dating before sex. Not on Hough, though; sex was instant there. Cheap! This was my struggle.

My dad was a monogamist. I didn't learn how to cheat from him, and from the time of my parents' divorce in 1976, I had only seen my dad with those three women I mentioned earlier while I saw my mom with only one man. The homebody and the crack-head suited my dad well. This lesson taught me to like women for who they were. I did notice that being monogamous was a trait that I inherited; however, I discovered that trait too late in life. Finding that trait early on would have drastically reduced the number of dating and sex partners I had.

I'm not saying that I settled, or a man or woman should settle, but women settled with me and my ways, so it was fair, I suppose, to be forgiving and understanding on many levels towards them. I never saw my parents really date people after their divorce. It seemed like they were just in a situation. This is where I became very comfortable with just existing with a woman without all the additional stress and implications of marriage. I'd never thought of it too much, even in my childhood.

Seeing my parents give up on marriage sealed the deal for me; there was no turning back even if I did try later on.

In their situation, they stayed at home, drank liquor, smoked weed, ate good food, laughed, and sat on the front porch watching the numerous street fights as well as the crack-heads and beggars walking by. From that experience, I wanted to do more with women. At this point, I felt myself becoming a serial dater. My grandfather, from what I was told, was a provider. My dad and his siblings had cars, a house, and enough food on the table. My dad treated us the same. In my era, lavish gifts, eventful dates, movies, plays, great restaurants, and buying nice jewelry were what men did. I was all about that. All of the women that I had, all received the same thing. I just rewound my game plan.

This trait did not diminish my dad's role as a father or as a man. That was a valuable lesson for me, too.

From watching my dad date, I noticed a few things in the women he chose. Two of them were needy and looked to him for support and to be up under him all the time. Sheila would wear London Fog trenchcoats, high heels, and nice perfume. Her hair was always neat and beautiful. The other women didn't come close to matching Sheila, but those are the ones my dad chose. I didn't understand why he liked cigarette-smokers, but later I found that it was more of a stress reliever and conversation thing. I would later not mind a woman that smoked; it showed that she was being herself really. These days, women smoke cigars as a social and conversation piece as well. Most men actually enjoy it. My dad didn't mind shy, loud, patchy-haired, or wig-wearing women either. I also didn't mind the wigs, as long as they were taken care of, but not the patchy hair, or the ones that were loud. That's where we were different. Eartha was neat and even though she dressed nicely, she always stayed in her apartment waiting on my dad. We saw very little of her. Pearl had patchy hair, missing teeth, and smoked crack all day. She took my dad's money for years. I don't remember her ever working for a long period of time. What I do remember is her not working for many years. My dad wasn't the same after he had his first stroke in the 1990s. He didn't have a woman to take care of him back then; all he had were his children. Sheila and Ertha were long gone. They would have been the best choice to nurse my dad back to good health, but over the years he had gotten worse. Think about your woman you have now; if she's loyal and has taken your disrespect over the years, she might not want to take the responsibility of nursing you back to health one day if you fall sick. She will do it, though, if she's virtuous. The other ones that just want you for sex, money, or status will not be there when you desperately need them as you age and battle different ailments.

Later, when I studied my dad, I realized that the trait of providing, being relied upon, and being fine with a situation, was something admirable in a man, and so I became that same man. When I got married in 1995, I wasn't ready for marriage, I was merely fine with it. During my dating years, I had six years with Terry, and another six with Tara, and I didn't marry either of them. I know my parents and back then, their situations after their divorce had a lot to do with that. Terry and Tara both mentioned marriage to me over the years, but they let me get away with just being a provider. I relied on them, too. I did them wrong and I know they deserved better. Both of them are married now. When I did get married, it was because she held me accountable and it wasn't about a situation. The two ladies that I didn't marry, I was more in control of and much more comfortable around.

Sheila was one that held my dad accountable. Not that he couldn't do well with her, but the path of least resistance kept him comfortable. Ertha and Pearl in no way challenged my dad. They loved him for who he was, for his physical qualities; he was tall, dark, had a full beard, a head full of hair, was in good shape, had a wide, healthy smile and laugh, and was fun, fun-loving, and outgoing. Sheila was looking for a husband, while Ertha and Pearl merely wanted a nice-looking daddy to take care of them. I saw that my dad was very confident when he was providing and not being told what to do. Submitting wasn't on his agenda, and I saw that, too. I also became very confident when I was providing and not being challenged or told what to do. This pushed me further and further away from thinking that we had to be married. In my mind, my woman was set and well taken care of. During this period, I also liked the fact that I was still available to other women because we weren't married. Being married didn't mean I wasn't available. Sadly, that was the mindset I had.

"Don't force me to marry you or I'll remain single but double-minded in my mind."

When women look at you as a father figure, they are more obedient and easy to control. They will not talk back but will instead love you unconditionally. This wasn't good for me, as I felt extremely powerful, unstoppable, and did what I wanted to do. Even when their mothers knew I was a provider, they were told to just go along with what I said. Performing in this manner was very disrespectful and I almost destroyed those women. There were many times where I was financially and emotionally absent just like their own fathers had been. I found myself a lot happier in those relationships, though.

It wasn't that I deprived her, it was merely a control thing. I'm sure other men filled in. How could I get mad? I'd been a side-piece a few times too.

I avoided well-kept women. I looked for those that didn't have a father figure in their lives and thus felt that they needed me for everything. I was comfortable playing the role of daddy. Sheila surely didn't need my dad, and he avoided her. I was the same way for many years.

Black males are being incarcerated and killed at an alarming rate. The ones that are not in a gang are considered soft, by both young men and women. Weed smoking is at an all-time high; same goes for the playing of video games. Parents are friends to their kids and not parents. Young males disrespecting their mothers is common. The young black ladies are being forgotten, reduced to an afterthought, and just used for sex. The role of a mother is too tasking; mothers are expected to be and do more, and since the ratio of men to women is so low, men can walk in and out of stepfamilies without a bother. Young white males are emulating black males more and more, and so are the young white females. The "N" word is being used by everyone, Latinos, Puerto Ricans, Asians, and even whites! Kids can yell at adults, but adults can't yell at kids. The government controls the kids and not the parents. We are all very soft and afraid. Kids overseas are more grateful and tough. I wasn't a good role model or example for young men and women back then, as far as relationships were concerned.

Our Left Rib

She comes from our side, not our back.

When we come together, we're in our original state. Becoming more than we can ever be on our own. I never engaged with a woman on a spiritual level, and this is why all of my relationships failed. Whenever a man or woman defers too much, the one that defers has their life take on the rules of their partner. This brings about resentment, detachment, loneliness, and discontent.

The Thoroughbred in Horsepower

It was men who built the infrastructure of this world, but we can't work with a healthy mindset without a stable home or woman. Men have power, but with an added thoroughbred, we have horsepower. Women, for the most part, add the base, groundwork, support, footing, the root, and the underpinning. This must be understood by all men. If all these things are not there, then it's just a house, not a home.

Both are needed regardless of what society teaches or forecasts. In fact, I get my leadership abilities from my mother; I know this for sure. Yes, I am strong, confident, supportive, and handy because of my dad, but without the ability to envision, have direction, foresight, and the sense to infuse those qualities as a leader, I am just a pillar with no one to lead, guide, and direct. Without those things, I'll just stand alone, strong with no influence.

Motherhood has changed drastically over the years, such as how women are now expected to be masculine, step into roles normally reserved for men, and sometimes take on both parenting roles. This can stem from how divorces are processed through the court system. The perceptions of women being barefoot, pregnant, and in the kitchen are long gone. This has brought about hyper femininity, a condition where some women rely solely on their sexuality or capacity for romance. Some of them have replaced men with toys and their imagination, causing them to think that they do not need a man. Men have become secondary. It's getting worse because some men do not like when a woman is independent. I don't have a problem with this at all. Independent women still have wants, desires, and needs. Those who are not independent only have needs.

I believe the gap is widening between men and women, especially in the black community. We do not get therapy as often as necessary, and instead of working things out, or even divorcing amicably, we look to harm one another during the process. Black male lawyers are not recommended to black women by other black women because they have an assumed bias. For this reason, most black women hire a white lawyer instead of a fellow woman, bitter and scorned. She tells her lawyer to run the father of her children into the ground financially. "Let's get him for everything he's got," she might say. This mindset has taken hold for many years and it still persists today.

I deserved everything I got, all the repercussions for my indiscretions. At first, it was a hard pill to swallow, but I couldn't be bitter because it was my fault. Therefore, after many years of replaying my divorce in my mind, I decided that it was fair that my ex-wife decided to keep a white man or a bitter woman on retainer. I was the one responsible for their assembly. If you look at it from the perspective of a cheating man, the impending gathering was set in motion by my infidelity.

I had a black female lawyer; she was extremely fair, though.

I caused all of my breakups and I paid dearly for every one of them. We have been taught to believe and fear many things. The fear causes the divorce rate to rise as fatherless homes become more common and a lack of discipline exists in the household. Men get destroyed in court over child support and alimony. For whatever reason, the relationship or marriage didn't work. There are children at stake. Women get destroyed in court, too. The ones who have good jobs and have a solid life and future but chose a man who promised heaven and earth and failed to deliver. These are reasons why men are afraid to marry, and some women have given up hope about healthy relationships and marriage. Women now know that some men decide to marry later on in life to have a woman take care of them and live her life for him. Women outlive men by at least five years. The life expectancy for men is 76.1 years, and for women it's 81.1. It's expected to increase too as time goes on. This is why most women decide to remain single, staying happy and healthy for the rest of their days. This was something only men did for many years. We divorce and move right along and the woman mourns for years. Not anymore. It's not that they have become masculine, no, but they have decided to not wallow in their misery and instead enjoy all the goodness that life has to offer.

A woman's happiness resides in the care of her children, as well as things like her finances being taken care of, a nice home to live in, constant peace of mind, close friends, and making sure the kids see their grandparents. Sex is prominent but much lower on her list at this stage. Women can go right to sleep after masturbating and be totally fine. They use their vivid imagination, which is so efficient and clear that it almost seems real to them. This is why when they masturbate, they rub themselves all over; they even kiss their own breasts. Men don't like to masturbate, rub ourselves, or kiss our own chest. We need to be inside of a woman for satisfaction, we need to experience that release. Releasing does many things for a man, and this is why women that love their man, will receive him regardless of whether she wants to or not, just to satisfy him. We are not in-tune with our minds and bodies like women are; our mindset is one of sexual greed, releasing, and self-satisfaction. A man will feel incomplete without a woman's touch. Women love a man's touch but can adjust if they don't get it. As men, we are self-serving with respect to cars, money, big houses, clothes, jewelry, and this is where we begin to lose touch with a woman and her needs. During mating season in the jungle and even in the ocean, the male species have to show their dominance to be selected. This ends in death for some animals. In our world, and for materialistic women, titles, status, and material things are what grab a woman's attention. A man that wields power does this, too. The men that are considered broke or the ones that do not possess power or material things, are left out. Those types of men are looked over and are most of the time the ones with much more substance, honesty, respect, and longevity.

I lost my girl to an ugly dude, but that guy knew all about touch, holding hands, cuddling, and hugging. He was just better than I was. Women want security first. They can see the beauty in a man outside of looks. When a divorce happens and the mother gets custody of the children, they begin to lose touch with their father and get subconsciously angry at their mother because of it.

Women are being forced into masculine roles more than ever before because of a perceived shortage of men, among other reasons. And since women are leaving their feminine roles behind now, men are also forced to see life from a woman's perspective, if they are willing to be fair about it. We still fight this notion, though, because we have been taught and groomed differently. I don't believe that the role reversal and women stepping up in jobs normally reserved for men is caused solely due to a shortage of men, but now, women are beginning to desire equality and have proven to the world time and again that they can work and lead like men can. The man who has a problem with this will be uncomfortable and agitated all the time.

Women are leading in the military, on various huge platforms, playing sports that were reserved for men, becoming CEOs, being selected into Special Warfare programs, getting into boxing, the UFC, and many more things. Women lose respect for men when they find out that they can do what we do, and the fact that men don't give them credit for it is salt on an open wound. As men and women, we must consider changing our worldview. We've become so accustomed to women being masculine that it's become toxic for everyone.

They say we're hunters, right? People fight that notion knowing at the end of the day, we're texting, emailing, calling, and waiting on a woman.

CHAPTER TWENTY-TWO

Double Mind

I must go into character again. This is my memory and there are prior addictions that I still have to manage. It gets easier and easier the more I talk about it, and I genuinely want to see people heal. I don't ever want to lose my gift of confident transparency. The damage I did to myself isn't permanent, and I want to make sure it isn't for the women that I damaged.

Being double minded is very bad for your health. You will be uninhibited, and this is very risky. I was sixteen when I first contracted gonorrhea. She was fifteen and acted just like me. I never knew that I had a high tolerance for pain, as the dripping and burning really didn't scare me that much. My other mind took over so that I could hurry up and have sex again. Two shots in my butt cheeks and ten pills later, I was back at it. I suppressed my pain not because it hurt but because I wanted to go against the doctor's orders.

"Leon, no sex for ten days, and make sure you take all of your medicine!"

"Okay, Doc, I got you."

Mumble, mumble, mumble.

A double-minded person will always be in a hurry to get back to their evildoing. Their flesh craves it. They are heartless and reckless. A double-mind will allow you to write off your heinous acts as being "not that bad." It doesn't just occur, we make it happen, so as to process things easier in our favor. Back then, I could detach myself from reality and believe that people believed in what I said and how I acted. I got this from my mother. Everyone around you, a double-minded person, will get hurt and you won't even care. You will apologize but will not change your behavior.

I was undecided, vacillating, and unstable in all of my ways. I never took relationships seriously. I wasn't relating at all. I wasn't a believer, so I was always separated from my body. Faithless, always changing my thoughts and ways, constantly changing what I said and did. A sickness of the heart and the inner man.

They say that this cannot be corrected by medicine, and I believe that. I am a practitioner, so I knew that I could change my double-mind. I did this by implementing certain practices. First, I started by asking for people to pray for me, implementing different ways and thoughts, apologizing, admitting when I did not know something, keeping my word, listening more, being humble, talking to God, being honest with myself, practicing patience, having positive thoughts, looking at things from a woman's perspective, and becoming better at not getting upset. During my career in the Navy, I had to speak with three psychiatrists, one psychotherapist, and one psychologist, none of whom knew about my double-mind. I never brought it up, because I knew that what I had to say would hurt and make me cry. I was already crying sitting on the office couch and that was hard enough even though it felt good to release all the built-up emotions. The therapists that I sat with actually hit on a lot of things relating to my double-mind but they didn't know the full story. Or maybe they did. Our discussions were not spiritual and her job didn't permit her to go there. That's how my mind operated; it's how I was wired for my entire life. I'm sure the pain and anger associated with my PTSD had a lot to do with it.

Who was the master of my two minds, me or my demons? Most of the time it was my demons. Leon was different, period. I allowed them to enter my mind based on what I wanted or needed, or when I was upset. No one else or nothing else was responsible. Feeling sorry for myself was my way of building up a fragile ego. I needed my ego stroked; it was like a drug and I was addicted. It wasn't even about material wealth; I never had that to begin with. As a kid we were taught to be humble and grateful for what we had. I found it boring but I kept that mindset my entire life. I wish that I was grateful to have just one woman, but again, I soon became bored of that, too.

Being complimented all my life made me feel like I wasn't meant for just one woman. I needed to lose myself to find myself, yet I was afraid to let go of Doubleo.

"Doubleo, what's up for the weekend, dog?"

I loved my nickname but hated how I would transition from Leon to Doubleo whenever my boys called me.

"Shiiiit, you know how we do, girls, girls, girls, hit me up, cuz!"

Doubleo was a nickname that my mom gave me. I resonated more with him than I did with Leon. Leon was the professional guy who came out when necessary. As a kid, I was never diagnosed with any type of personality disorder—it was sure to come, though, but I could switch my mind up with ease. My mother gave me that name because I was fat when I was a baby. I had two chins. It's a cool name and I have never met anyone with it. I made him into a character, even though he wasn't supposed to be. I could act like I was loving, caring, passionate, compassionate, courageous, sympathy, you name it. Doubleo was my name, but my mind was infiltrated by people with soul-ties and sex demons. I was too young to know or understand this, but they weren't. Striving for singleness of mind meant that I had to be good and do right; having one mind gave me no other choice to live in purity; I couldn't because I didn't want to. My worldliness wasn't to have knowledge of people and culture, but to become an international lover. I had the most beautiful and spiritual chance to do so when I went to Israel, but when I met two women that smoked weed and drank alcohol, the day after we left the *Wailing Wall*, I blew that chance. Even in the Holy Land, I turned away from being holy. I wanted to hurry up and just go to heaven already, but I knew it didn't work like that; I had to cleanse my soul and spirit first, and then rid my heart of all discontent. I played with God, because when I saw him, I knew that he knew that the people I had met along my life's journey were responsible for making me into the little devil I had become; I hadn't just chosen Satan's path.

I took a lot of pictures in Israel. I rode camels, visited the Sea of Galilee, the banks of the Jordan River; I even saw where Jesus was anointed. As we walked around and toured the Holy Land, I took pictures of almost everything I saw. One man warned me not to do that. He was short, dark in complexion, and with smooth but heavily wrinkled skin and a long black beard with splotches of gray. The only skin that was showing through his Kandora was his face and long, skinny, veiny arms. He wore a very colorful turban. As I raised my camera up to my face, one eye open, the lens pressed firmly against my other eye, I saw the man waving a finger at me. I felt like he was looking through my soul. Seconds later, a short Jewish lady ran up to me and gently grabbed my camera and lowered it.

"Sir, no, no, you can't take pictures of the men and women here, they feel like the camera takes their soul."

"Oh, wow. Sorry, I didn't know that."

The tour took us to where Jesus was anointed, and I began to snap pictures of that, too. The Jewish lady appeared again, and again, lowering my camera every time.

"Sir, sir, no, no, that's sacred. You can't take pictures of that."

I did it anyway and she just looked at me and walked away. I studied the tomb, walked around it, took three, maybe four close-up pictures, and left quickly.

We were on deployment that year. It was 1996. Our ship headed back to Norfolk, Virginia where I would get my pictures developed. I couldn't wait. All pictures came out fine except those pictures of the place Jesus was anointed. They came out as three black photos with nothing on them. No glare, nothing, just blank, black pictures.

All my life, I've always received signs. I wasn't a good listener, which is crucial in communication.

Doubleo kept me evil, lustful, and without fear. Transitioning to him was easy and fun. I did it without reservation. Lots of times he came out depending on who I was with. It was easier for me to relate to other double-minded people than with those that were single-minded and single-hearted. Those people were good for me, but too mature and boring. I didn't mind risking any woman that I was with when I was Doubleo; he was the one that got two women pregnant at the same time, not Leon. It's not easy to speak about this other person as if he wasn't a part of my psyche. Back then it was easy to do and even to talk about, but not anymore. I feel horrible for leading such a disrespectful lifestyle. I let many people down, and was the infamous destroyer of all women. I want you to know that when a person is living this lifestyle, take note of their actions and place yourself at a safe distance or you will suffer; many people who failed to do this are suffering the consequences. The mindset of separation is pure evil. Whenever I pulled myself back from the edge and out of the toxic mindset of Doubleo, I would feel the guilt of everything I had done in that state. As I went back to being Leon, the weight of these occurrences came rushing at me like a flood; however, the lures of evil were stronger, (and somehow weaker at the same time).

Doubleo was the predator of vulnerable women. He lied, deceived, misled, and even slept with friends of other girls he met, sometimes the very next hour. Leon was lonely and trying to be a better person while Doubleo was on the prowl. I hated that character, despised everything about him, but he controlled me. Doubleo always had a body odor from the excessive sex partners, was prone to frequent headaches, drank often, drove under the influence, disappeared for long periods of time, and continued to watch porn when he was engaged and even after getting married. You can only live this way for so long, but God, for some reason, kept me alive while I was at the apex of my sickness.

A person's heart can only take so much, and I had always felt some big repercussion was waiting for me, as a result of my lifestyle. It finally came in 2013 when I had a heart attack and spent five months in rehab. I was taking nine pills per day. Embarrassed and ashamed, Doubleo had to face Leon. It was time to rest. I spent one week in the hospital where I received a stent and became a heart patient for the rest of my life. I had broken women's hearts in the past and now mine was broken for real. Leon had suffered greatly because of Doubleo. I was forty-eight years old at the time.

They say a serial killer is one that kills three or more people. I was no different. I never murdered any women in cold blood, but I killed the hopes, dreams, and spirits of many women.

CHAPTER TWENTY-THREE

Loveless Trait #2: Broken Communication

"Be quiet, Doubleo. If you say anything, no more quarters or candy!"

It was always about me. Women felt like they were growing when we talked, but not connecting. So, what happened was, we were taking turns talking but I still had to dominate the conversation. My talks were just for a one-night stand. I acted like I cared, but I didn't. The gift of gab is only a gift if you don't use it maliciously, but if you use it to do harm or for your own pleasure, it becomes the *Curse of Gabble.*

I liked doing it to women but hated when it was done to me. When I met a woman that liked to talk a lot, I couldn't stand it. As I became older, I had to realize that she might have been silenced as a child, left out or abandoned. I started letting them talk while I listened intently. Women love a man that likes to listen. Put yourself in her shoes, in your mind's eye, look back at yourself, your facial expressions, eye contact, and see yourself gazing into her eyes and you'll see and understand how she feels when you do this. Ladies, it's all about your delivery when you want to teach us something.

Whenever I had an orgasm, I would shut down. I never let out any emotions.

Be quiet, Doubleo. If you say anything, no more quarters or candy.

While I was being molested, my cousins, babysitter, and uncle all told me, *shhh...be quiet,* and I realized later in life that they were responsible for my being quiet while having sex as an adult.

About ninety-nine percent of women like to talk, express themselves, look for validation, agreement, gain confidence, and feel included. In order to be able to manipulate their mind, to remain in control at all times, I studied two things, psychological reciprocity and emotionally disturbing.

Psychological Reciprocity

From deep and intense listening, I was able to develop my own answers, which was nothing more than making them her answers coupled with my compliment and infusing just a tad bit of something she either forgot or didn't know about. It then became my answer alone that carried a sense of being desired, being listened to, and feeling important, which is what she was really looking for. On subsequent occasions, I knew that she was not only listening to me but playing with herself. This is a form of mental stimulation.

Women feel enriched when they experience mental stimulation and the environment just adds to it. The ambience is the cherry on top. I knew to cover both her internal feelings and her external visual attraction.

Emotionally Disturbing

Narcissistic people are able to do this based on being great listeners. Be cautious and extremely careful in what you tell me. Your deep thoughts and conversations shall always be considered sensitive and time-sensitive. There's a time and place as to when and what you tell me. This includes *any* and *everything.* Please be careful!

What I am about to describe to you is pure evil and not recommended to do, to anyone! By being attentive and focusing on what she didn't like about herself, like how she wanted to improve her looks or lose weight, I became well versed in those things. Her priority wasn't mine, but in order to keep her drawn in, I had to make it seem that way.

My words were sharp and piercing but harmless. I was teaching, but more importantly to me, I was noticing things she could improve on. In delivering my comments, recommendations, or pieces of advice, I had to be blunt but respectful and offer a solid solution to whatever she was suffering from. Most times, women are confused about their partners. If I could be strategic in my thoughts, it made her feel good, comfortable, and eventually, she opened herself up to me. My delivery had to be attractive to her. When saying things without any hint of spite or bitterness, women tend to listen and engage more and not be afraid or skeptical. When you build a woman up and she begins to believe in you, give you her all and totally submit, she thinks that you now have a union, that you're now together—all sorts of things of that nature. If you don't truly care about her, it would be easy for you to leave but hard for her to let go. You'd have damn near planted yourself in her DNA by this point. Her life would now revolve around you.

Please take note that I do not recommend mastering either psychological reciprocity or emotional disturbance for malicious purposes. Soon, I'll tell you a short story to explain why you shouldn't do that. I used it in a malicious way and I didn't like it. It doesn't matter if you are demonic or claim that you are godly (which is a lie when operating in this manner), you will be punished dearly and possibly give your life for it. I enrolled into a class for this back in 1992; it was called "persuasive selling." After many years, the corporation that I was a part of deemed it an unprofessional term, and removed it from the curriculum. I supported that decision as it was very dangerous for me and the people I came in contact with.

Also, when used properly and with good intent, psychological reciprocity together with emotional disturbance becomes a gift that can take you and your partner to unprecedented levels of love, intimacy, as well as growth and development for one another. Study it together and please use it wisely. Emotionally disturbing people has to be done cautiously and without malicious intent. This garners precise and understanding communication without any kind of disturbance, and the emotion is felt in a caring manner.

Pushing Her to Her Limits

The place was Cleveland, Ohio, in 1993.

Leon, do you have a minute?

Lisa came to see me at work; she had an eerie look in her eyes. The night before, I had slept with another woman, and I sensed her arrival before Lisa walked into the building even though I hadn't seen her yet. Lisa was four-feet-eleven inches tall, and weighed slightly over a hundred pounds; she had long black hair, full lips, pretty eyes, and a dark, smooth body. She was naturally built. Extremely smart, Lisa graduated from one of the top Catholic schools in Cleveland. Once I found that out, I deduced many other things. She was sheltered and clearly not street smart. I took advantage of that.

"Yo, what's up, Lisa?"

"Don't 'yo' me, Leon, where were you last night?"

"Lisa, don't start tripping. Let's go outside and have a chat in your car."

She agreed, surprisingly.

"Lisa, I can remember that you like to talk, so as soon as you pissed me off, I became silent for days and then weeks. But as soon as I wanted you and your body, I became nice, I touched you in your favorite places, I gave you compliments, and watched you watch me take over your emotions. I was heartbroken and very vindictive. I'm sorry."

"You dirty mothafu..."

"Watch your mouth, Lisa!"

And with that, she took off, speeding down Euclid Avenue, running all the red lights, and heading straight into Lake Erie. I fought and fought to hit the brakes and grab the steering wheel as we tussled. She had a strength that I could not handle, but by the grace of God, we stopped the car at the big boulders right at the water's edge.

"I should kill the both of us, asshole!"

Lisa was many things—smart, beautiful, strong (as I found out that day), wicked, and hurt. But overall and above everything else, she was emotionally disturbed because of me.

For years, I was on a mission, on a path of destruction and I didn't care. I maneuvered through life with reckless abandon.

Bad Communication

If a woman that likes to talk, gets married to a man who doesn't, it's either there'd be no communication in the home or the both of them would keep sending and interpreting mixed signals. If you and your partner are not compatible, it reflects in so many ways such as lacking the ability to relate, not understanding each other's love language, and so on. This can lead to crucial mistakes being made, fatal assumptions and whatnot. Bad communication is a "Loveless Trait."

The Silent Treatment

This is used as a weapon to make you bend, give up, give in, or totally submit under certain conditions.

I'll talk if it makes me feel good or if things are going my way!

I enjoyed it when you were quiet. My evil playground was able to build and build and build.

I already have you and I am not going to marry you; being boyfriend and girlfriend is good enough.

I know you'll continue to ask me the same question. "Leon, what are we doing here? I don't plan on staying like this, okay?"

"Huh, what do you mean?"

"You know what I mean."

"I don't, and that's why I asked. Now you think I'm stupid, just like my last girlfriend. I don't need this shit, for real, I'm out!"

This was my way of *avoiding* any and all questions. Once you get tired of me walking away, leaving the house for hours, you'll stop asking me about it. When I eventually come back home, I'd always bring you something to eat but I still didn't answer your question and I wasn't going to. You didn't want me to leave, again, because I sure would.

Sadly, I could do the "silent treatment'" for long periods of time, not even caring about the damage that I was causing.

Broken Home

A broken home, or breaking a home, didn't mean anything to me. That became my comfort zone. I was very strong in being alone, simply repeating my childhood tragedy.

I was conditioned to just get up and walk away. I blamed my childhood on everything, just to keep you listening to me about my problems, and putting yours on the back-burner. Dysfunction was a function of mine. Your family was good, mine wasn't, so you wanted me to experience that, by any means necessary, even if you just sat back and took what I did. Feel sorry for me if you want to, I know you will, and every time you do, I'll get worse to make you stronger for helping me, but weaker for keeping me around.

I really spoke of my past so that you would spend more time giving me more of you, than I would of giving you me. You will excuse all of my indiscretions, too.

You'll suggest help, therapy, and even counseling, and this is where I begin to get angry and blame YOU as to why I'm silent.

Our sex was good. We had vehicles and a nice apartment and I knew where to take you, bought you nice things, perfume, jewelry, shoes, and even took you to the best restaurants. Your friends and family liked me because they didn't know that I was abusive, both verbally and silently. The pros outweighed the cons, so our communication being off, was a settlement.

"I don't need no damn counseling, girl."

"Leon, yes you do."

"I said...no I don't." Pause. "Now I'm pissed."

"Okay, okay, I'm sorry."

This is where you slowly give me what I want, *silence,* until I'm ready to talk. I wasn't violent, but I had become verbally abusive. I would say things that I didn't even mean just to cut you down and make you cry. I did this so that when you tried to get me to talk again, I would remind you.

"Now, you know I'm going to say something hurtful, why are you making me do this?"

Although as odd as it may sound, it was a little hard for me to say bad things, but at times, most times, it felt good. When the feelings of feeling bad came up, I could easily suppress them. I had to keep the upper hand. You couldn't know that I felt bad about what I just said. No way!

I know women like to talk, listen, and rehabilitate, especially if there's time invested. Losing my family at age eleven, and just taking my parents' divorce as if it were mine in a way, affected my family morals and marriage. With that, my ability to not care about closeness, unity, being as one, commitment, and proper communication left, too. I didn't want to talk about my own embarrassment as it was too hard, so I learned how to hide and suppress it. Had I talked about it, someone might have made fun of me. I remember when my parents got divorced and one time when we didn't have any utilities, kids laughed at me. I remember those days and times. From that, I became a grateful man, grateful for the small things I did have, but when I lost or failed at something, or didn't have certain things that I should have, or know something I should know, I had to hide it. The mental torture was too intense to share. I held so much in I didn't have to. I learned about loss very early on, but didn't process the fact that I could regain things, or that it would be okay.

"Leon, it'll be okay, it will, I got your back."

I never believed that.

"You're not my family yet, so how do I know?"

No one told me we would lose our house, no one told me that my parents were getting divorced, either. Don't play with me!"

I will not open up to you because of these things. You will open up and expect me to, but I just can't and wouldn't. I acted like things with me were solid when they weren't. I had to lie, ignore you, or walk away. Ignoring you felt better to me, because it was a form of punishment. You couldn't make me talk. I also became really good at walking away, leaving for hours, and talking to other women to make myself feel better, even though you had asked me simple questions. Your questions were triggers, triggers because we never discussed my past in the beginning of our relationship. I wasn't fine when you met me, and I knew that it would come out later on. My smile and social personality hid it all.

Talking against my will felt like I was being weak and defeated. I didn't tell you this, so you kept trying to get me to talk, and as you did, I thought of other ways to punish you. All I had to do was open up, but that feeling of feeling vulnerable or you possibly laughing at my pain, was terrifying and infuriating to me.

Now that that's established, you'll try and try again, and the more you try to make me open up, the angrier I become. This is where I took it a step further to gain control of you wanting to talk.

Raise the Intensity

At first, while sitting down, I would argue with you a little, but my anger was so intense after feeling like I was losing the argument that I would have violent thoughts and begin to bang on furniture. You were winning but didn't know it. You knew of my violent thoughts because this was the only time I would get up and look into your eyes as I walked up to you. I did that on purpose. I wanted you to see and feel a totally different side of me, up close and personal.

Cursing

Cursing comes from a weak mind—a mind that doesn't have a better choice of words. This is caused by two things: poor behavior control and anger issues.

I would curse at you, extremely loudly. Cursing and being loud was my way of scaring you and making you feel intimidated, coupled with walking up to you while accepting defeat. It was like a curse word every step towards you. The quieter you become as I walked up to you, the louder and more powerful I felt. It had to be total chaos. Once I saw the fear in your eyes, we both knew you had just lost, because you either backed up or got quiet. I wasn't going to hit you, but you didn't know that. These were my insecurities coming out.

I felt better when I saw her tears.

Physical Violence

I controlled this because I frequently remembered my mother getting beat up, and seeing my grandmother slap my mother. I remembered my mother's face, her look, the blood, embarrassment, you name it, and I didn't want to do that to a woman.

Domestic violence meant jail time, but not adultery or cheating on a girlfriend. As sick as it sounds, this is how I processed it.

Nasty Words

Even though I didn't mean these words, and could not handle them if they were spoken to me, I said them anyway. It was my way of sealing the deal and making her think that I didn't care about her. I did try. I was just afraid to give my heart away.

"Leave, I don't care, bye."

"No one's going to want you, anyway."

"You ain't shit and you'll never be shit."

"That's why I'll never marry you."

"I can help you leave right now."

"Go ahead, run back to your family. You'll be back. Watch."

I had a verbal abuse trait in me, deeply. Every time I uttered those words, they came back to haunt me. I remember when my dad yelled in the house, I peed my pants, stood still, and just got quiet.

I never forgot those times. Later in life, I started using it against my girlfriends.

Walking Out

The next thing that made me feel good was storming off. Believe me, the separation from someone that's either a narcissist or is challenging him or her, is like getting out of jail after months, or years, even if we only walk away for a couple hours. We don't just walk away, we leave to go smoke, drink, flirt, or cheat. It's very satisfying and sick at the same time. But we still blame you, so that we don't feel bad.

You made me do this to you, again, damn, girl!

My level of revenge depended on how mad I had gotten.

The time away becomes longer and longer, depending on how long it takes me to control your mouth. I'll be gone for a very disrespectful amount of time, knowing that you were going to

be pissed when I got home, and you really did nothing wrong. As soon as I come back, and you start again, I'll walk out again at the slightest provocation.

When we dated, I talked a lot and it was very draining for me. You didn't know this, though. I made myself worldly, so as to seem intelligent and attractive to you. I really was worldly, but that came naturally because of my time in the military.

Bottom line is this: I didn't want you to know that I either wasn't ready for marriage, didn't want to get married, didn't think we needed to get married, was very immature, and was only a physical type of guy. I wanted a woman to always be around me, as it made me feel good. But again, due to my mom leaving me and my cousins and babysitter molesting me, I still had fears of what women were capable of, even if I had been good to them. My childhood pain had me thinking of suicide and I didn't want to think or know where my mind would go when heartbreak happened as an adult. The closest I got to my mind slipping away was being a stalker. Her silent treatment drove me to that place again. That was my karma.

A woman's silent treatment towards a man is much worse than a man's towards a woman! As men, we're silent because of anger—a woman becomes silent when she's planning her exit strategy. We don't pay attention and that's why it's so shocking when she leaves. That's when were vulnerable!

Domineering Through Insecurities

For men and women, if you scream at your partner often or are always pushing them around with negative words, you'll be in great danger of losing them. Some people intimidate people when their flaws or weaknesses have been exposed with no hope of recovery. Overt narcissists exploit and expose as a means of controlling your sharing of their wrongdoings. Treating people in this manner will make them fall into the arms of people who will just listen to their opinions without berating or demeaning them. They will open up and talk more, too.

Bossy

Bossy people build fear in others, establish unhealthy boundaries, and make people walk on eggshells around them. People will not only find it hard to like you, they will also never love you. You will create a lot of bad blood and negative energy if you keep treating people this way. And at the end of the day, you will wind up lonely. If you always show up with your status, titles, and sex drive, then that's how you will always be seen. I've dated plenty of women like this, and all I had to do was stroke their ego, listen to how great they were at work, and then give them some wine. They are the easiest to abuse, in a passive way. If your bossy ways no longer bother a person, be careful—it's probably because your mouth and words irritate them but someone else's body makes them feel good!

Compartmentalizing

This is when a hurt person or someone that doesn't trust you anymore, compartmentalizes their relationship with you, pushing you away.

Once their mind shuts off, their body will surely follow. A mental disconnect is by far the worst way for a relationship to go. You've probably seen such a situation before, where people remain together for years even though they have lost sight of one another. This is a death sentence for some. There is no longer trust, compliance, or respect. The spark, the vibe, is dead and gone.

Men that cheat will no longer have a voice in the relationship.

Compartmentalizers keep you right in the part of their mind that takes their loving ways away. This is usually due to something you've done to harm or hurt them. Your chemistry will be destroyed, as well as your communication, touch, as well as the joy derived from spending quality time together. Almost all of the love languages will vanish, sometimes forever. Once this happens, you'll develop Loveless Traits towards one another. The kids will also be affected. These are relationships that either end up in divorce or where people stay together for the sake of time invested, kids, or finances. It goes without saying that both people will be miserable in this arrangement.

I dated a woman that I felt I liked because I told myself that over and over. The truth was I secretly loathed her. We never talked, and when we did, it was about other people. I felt so detached from her, from her mind and spirit. It was a waste of time. Yes, she was beautiful, but after dating her for a few years, I started to enjoy other women with beautiful personalities and wasn't moved by looks any longer.

I used the silent treatment as a weapon, and it worked well until she used it against me.

Listen to Gain

Women that have deeply rooted fears don't talk too much. I studied them closely, and once I realized that they didn't open up fast, I already knew they were scared and maybe even scorned. This made me gentler with them as they clearly needed care, time, and passion. After that, it was only a matter of time before they gave in. This was about the only time where I was patient, if I really liked her.

The ones that did talk, fell into a trap of telling me, indirectly, about their deprivation, what they yearned for, and what they were missing. All they were doing was inviting me into their body without outrightly saying so.

Learning how people receive you is also a key component in communication. One of the first traits and signs of broken communication, or the inability to converse, is talking over each other. Both of you are trying to get your points across and it quickly turns into a competition where you are trying to "one up" each other. When people listen intently, it means any of these four things:

1. *They really like you.*
2. *They want to know more about you.*
3. *They miss talking and having good conversations.*
4. *They want to learn your weakness or what you deeply desire, to be able to manipulate you or to be able to grow.*

Broken people aren't ready to grow, though. Upon meeting someone, observe the way they communicate, what they say, things they repeat, how emotional they get when speaking, and so on. All of these are indicators of where they are in life, what they want, what they haven't been receiving, and any unresolved trauma in their past. This creates a large number of triggers. To resolve this, both parties in the relationship must be reminded about their deficiencies, but from a place of concern. It is easier to resolve when you all care about one another.

The Interrupter

When a person consistently interrupts or cuts you off, it's because they haven't been listened to by their family or their other partners. Be patient with them. It's not that they are angry or lacking the ability to listen, it's just that they have a low trust factor, based on what people have said and done to them. These people want to be heard, healed, understood, and are on the lookout for someone that can mentally stimulate them. It's probably been years since they've had this kind of connection. A lot of them are hurting in some way, have been used, abused, or forgotten about. The best course of action is to just listen to them. They have a lot of people relying on them at work or at home and do not have an outlet to unwind, except through their bleeding heart, mind, and mouth. They mean well, they are just that way due to being surrounded by energy vampires and fake people.

They've been doubted by their peers, disrespected and cast off.

When a person lives with, dates, or marries someone that doesn't talk or doesn't know how to communicate, the person seeking conversation will yearn for it. In their yearning stages, when you meet someone like this, you must be careful, as they will use you to fill a void and eventually explode on their partner using your actions as an excuse. Be careful giving advice, too; it's easy for them to believe in you, especially if they haven't heard your counsel before. Hearing positive thoughts and great ideas sounds beautiful to them; it resonates deep in their soul. This could be as a result of many things:

> *The way your voice sounds.*
> *How thoughtful you are, and how what you say makes sense.*
> *They can also make themselves believe that you have some*
> *level of care for them. They crave knowledge and love to*
> *be appreciated.*

Good and great conversations can lead to healthy relationships and trustworthy partners. This might not happen on the first few dates or times that you see this person, but if you both decide to stick together, this is where it starts. Only be consistent. When we are attracted to people, we tend to say anything to get them to like us more. We act a certain way around them, and use big words in our conversation. However, you should not feel the need to use big words to impress anyone. Keep it simple. Talk about what you know. Never volunteer your experiences unless it is asked for or it can add value to the conversation.

The Too-Talkative Braggart

These are people trying to prove a point. Their intelligence precedes them, and they want you to know it. It's a turn-off. Most are living in the past. Some are materialistic, and talk about their clothes, jewelry, cars, and house. Let them talk and they will always tell on themselves! These types are serious time-wasters and "hope" you believe everything they say. Men can be easily tricked by women like this, and good natured, wholesome women will give men like this chance after chance, only to be let-down in the end.

Communication is beautiful when souls come together. Talk to her, nice and slow, while kissing her from ear to ear.

The Make-Up Artists

Making up stories just to be accepted is the quickest way to be disregarded, left alone, or ignored.

"You caught me in a lie, and I lied about the lie you said I lied about!" Communication is a crucial aspect of a relationship. It will either take you off your crutches, or make you become a crutch.

Uninterested in The Word

God has always communicated with me, but for years, I never listened!

One day in church, in Cleveland, I got a small tap on my shoulder. A man leaned in, close to my ear. His breath was stinky and hot, and smelled like an old attic.

"Young man, please pay attention to the minister, have some respect."

I never disrespected my elders outright, but I suppose I did that day because I just stared at him as he walked away. He wasn't going to let me off the hook.

One group of people I'm put off by are those who stay in church scanning to see who's not paying attention. I was always called out for that.

The man came back.

"Did you hear me, son? Please follow along."

I couldn't wait until service ended so me and a few others could huddle up and talk about the "pay attention" monster. That was wrong, but I was so angry with Mr. Attic Breath.

As I sat there with my eyes roaming and scanning the room, I started thinking about the women dressed up, the sweet smell of perfume lingering around them as their ruby-red lipstick flashed in my face. I stared intently at the lead choir singer. She had a wide mouth, pretty teeth, and golden-brown hair. As she turned around to face the choir, I watched her thick buttocks sway from side to side. Her golden-brown hair color caught my eye during the church services as it was the same color as my babysitter's hair. When the pastor spoke, everyone picked up the Bible that was sitting next to them, except me. As he spoke, my mind continued to wander off, trying my darndest to flirt. No one was available. I don't remember what chapter he was reading, but as he spoke, a jolt of electricity went through my entire body. This was the best feeling that I had ever felt in my life. I could feel myself getting warm, excited, and nervous. I stopped gazing, sat up, focused, and became afraid, so I walked out of church in the middle of the service. The feeling was so intense, I thought someone had heard it shoot through my body.

That was another sign for me. I wanted to pay attention so that I would learn, understand, and be able to communicate about the Word, but I failed miserably. I could not speak about the Bible because I had a forked tongue.

I wasn't into the service of God, but the service of myself, even in his house. And what's more, he knew it.

I never thanked God for the women in my life, and I should have, because all of them kept me safe, even the ones from Satan. They were my mirror of karma.

CHAPTER TWENTY-FOUR

Loveless Trait #3:
Untouched and Not Kissed

My third cousin was a full-size, built, young lady but she had soft lips. She was about five years older than I was and weighed about 190 pounds. Big for her size. As sick as this sounds, she always kissed me in my mouth!

At five years old, in the first grade, I was guilty of incest.

Since we played "spin the bottle" as kids, I was already well versed in kissing. My cousins had taught me how to kiss. That morning, I lost a tooth. I tasted my own blood as the pressure of their mouths covered mine. They didn't know my tooth had come out before I went into their room, and I didn't tell them.

The damage would last for many years. I received answers about this while in therapy, too.

"Is it still good to you?"

Some women can't answer that question. A lot of them haven't been kissed in years, be it a nice peck or a deep, sensual kiss while holding her face gently or the back of her head.

Ways to Kiss Her

- Slowly.
- Prepare your lips, do not kiss her with crusty lips.

- Make sure your lips are on hers and not under her nose and by her chin.
- Keep your teeth away, no clashing of teeth.
- Always have fresh breath.
- Gently, gently, bite her lips.
- Do not shove your tongue down her throat.
- The tongue must be soft and gentle, too.
- Kiss her while breathing slowly without using your tongue.
- Hold her face softly when you kiss her.
- Tell her nice things while you kiss her.
- Don't kiss fast.
- If you are on top of her, move your body weight so she's not suffocating and is able to enjoy the kiss.

Upon getting my physical for retirement in 2015 and speaking to my psychiatrist during the first six months of that year, I would attend every session with a straw, toothpick, or something in my mouth. I never knew why until my last therapy session.

"Mr. Walker, can I ask you a question?"

"Yes, Ma'am—go ahead."

"As a man of your military stature, you do know that it's quite unprofessional to come into my office chewing on something. Can we discuss that?"

At first I became offended. Then I dropped my head. I had finally come to terms with the reason I was in her office.

"Yes, you're right, it's wrong to do that and, ma'am, I always bring that to my Sailors attention whenever they're chewing gum or have something hanging from their mouth while they're in uniform, but no one ever told me about what I was doing wrong."

"Okay, let's start there today."

"Okay, I agree because I want to fix this issue too."

"How old were you when something oral happened, Mr. Walker—because it's a fixation issue!"

"Well, the first time was in the first grade. I was five. And then another cousin did it when I was about seven or eight. She would always hug me tight, and then kiss me on the forehead; it progressed from there. They were all much older than I was. Then they started putting their tongues in my mouth."

"Well, you'll have to forgive them, in order to move on."

"How do I do that, they're both dead now?"

"Just do it, pray and ask for forgiveness?"

"I don't pray, for some reason, Doc—I hate doing it."

Amongst the other discussions that were to come, we also talked about the straws, toothpicks, and Starbucks stopper hanging from my lips. After talking to her, I found out that because I was molested, I had an oral fixation addiction from my childhood. I even chewed my shirt collars as a kid and was made fun of. I eventually begin to be open to prayer. I remember my aunt praying before we ate during Thanksgiving—it really irritated me. I had lots to work on.

I don't think any adult should kiss children on the mouth, it's not necessary. Fathers kissing their daughters or mothers kissing their sons is wrong. From the age of five until I was about eight or nine, it was something I did a lot. I developed that addiction early on.

Cousins aren't expected to do that, either. I never told anyone about those incidents. The truth is most kids don't. They hold it in for fear of retaliation, being disowned, or that their family will not believe them. As a result of having this mindset, the atrocities went on for years, and it soon started to feel natural to me. This became an outlet for me, while my parents fought and argued, just like the porn. I thought that I had major addictions. I mean, I did, but it was only because I was looking for comfort, something or someone to make me happy and pacify my urges. Sadly, I found it in my female cousins. It was such a severe, oral addiction, I never thought about mononucleosis even when we were deployed overseas. I was an international kissing bandit!

There were different sizes and types of lips, and sometimes they were very misleading to me because I wanted and liked full, thick lips, just like my cousins'. For women that didn't have full or thick lips, my mind would automatically wander off to other parts of their body, but most times that wouldn't help; I was mentally stuck on lip size and shape. Some women are the same way with a man's penis size. If the man they first encountered sexually, regardless of age, was well endowed, they'll have the propensity to look for or even crave size and not passion. Years after high school, I would finally start to think differently about lip size and shape.

I know that this also had a lot to do with my race and what I always saw, for the most part. I learned that it wasn't always about the size or shape of her lips, but how she used them, that was very important for me. Some women have full, thick lips but haven't been complimented on them enough or kissed passionately enough that they no longer feel like their lips are an attraction. They just need the right person to pay attention to them.

Because of my one full-sized cousin, I started to like women her size, but they had to have full lips just like her. I didn't care what my friends thought of me and that full-sized woman, either.

It's still hard to admit what they taught me, but I forgave them. Both of them are deceased now; one was killed by her boyfriend and the other died from alcohol poisoning.

Her Neck

"Choke me papi!"

I first heard of choking women during sex when my ship was on deployment. A white guy mentioned it to me and I thought he was weird and crazy. Later in the deployment, he would become violent with women and had gotten in trouble for it.

Some women climax or squirt from this alone.

The only physical pain that I was able to inflict on a woman was deeply rooted in sexual exploitation, in the form of choking. I was afraid to do it though, as I didn't see any form of intimacy in it. I would put my hands on her neck slowly, and then take them off. The vision of my uncle choking me as he put his hands in my pants just would not go away.

The white guys in the Navy were cool, fun, and wicked. Jake was the porn king on the ship.

"Hey, Walker, have you ever choked a hooker?"

"Huh? Man are you crazy, nooooo!"

He began to explain. "See, either two to three things happen. She'll take your hand and put it around her throat, she'll tell ya to do it, or hell...since we're payin' em, you just do it yourself. Either way, you'll learn something and both of *ya* will be satisfied. Trust me, I know."

I just stood there getting dressed to go on liberty.

In 1984, we visited Panama, and choking was what the women in the brothels liked, aside from our Navy paychecks. They were rather small women, so my hands fit around their necks easily. I initially struggled with this form of aggressive sex, but somehow found a way to blame the Latinas for teaching me. It wasn't my fault when my hands were around her neck, I told myself. There I was blaming others for my actions again.

At age eighteen, I felt a deep urge of control and dominance consuming my entire soul. My mind would always go back to the times in my childhood when I was in the company of a woman, my cousins, or my babysitter.

I wonder if they felt like this when they controlled me? I'll never be molested ever again.

And remembering the woman I was with, I thought, it can't be painful if she gets off.

I looked into her eyes. This was a very dangerous time for me. Anger, ecstasy, together with my desire for an orgasm and memories of my hurtful past, all flashed in my mind. She can take it and not even cry, I thought. This became a huge turn-on for me. However, there were times when I would choke her to tears, and at that moment I would begin to feel extremely closer to her. I was aware that women cried a lot but if it wasn't during sex, it didn't matter to me. I choked her and she grabbed me tight but I could not handle that, it was just too much for me.

I still had serious reservations about harming women. Choking just seemed so brutal to me. Jake was accused of raping a woman and was sentenced to jail time by the local government. He also had to deal with additional punishment from the Navy. On that ship, there were about 280 men, and we all had an addiction to porn. One officer had his own program called FFF—Friday Fu&* Flicks. Most of us would watch porn all day and night, work, eat chow, then porn and when we pulled into port, we would emulate what we watched. Overseas, that was easy to do.

Touch: Her Skin Is Hungry

Affection deprivation. Our skin is our largest organ. When a woman isn't touched often, in some way, regardless of where—her body begins to ache and crave touch! Touch-deprived women will get it one way or another, either by rubbing up against you on purpose—where you apologize, or maybe even allow you to tap her on her back, shoulder, or a gentle handshake. They get off on it at that moment, but will never say anything.

My touch was so off, and I know women could tell that I was losing interest or had just touched another woman. I wasn't passionate at all, only when I wanted things for myself. I knew she couldn't feel any kind of warmth or compassion from me, none at all. I was so disconnected!

"Leon, you haven't touched me in a long time, what's wrong?"

"Huh?" I was frozen and my eyes were wide open. I was clueless of what a woman desired. My non-sexual contact was off!

When I was cheating and touching another woman, and then came home, my "touch energy" was off. That was the first dead giveaway and indication that I was physically removed from her at the moment.

God always protected women from me. I was always exposed by my inability to give proper attention when she needed it but she didn't know. My hands and body should not have been shared like that. I thought it was because I was tired from being with another woman, but no, God spared her from my evildoings, just moments, hours, or days earlier. I had to be rejected like Cain, I suppose. Or was it that I was just with Satan's wife?

I first learned how to give massages when I was eighteen, in the Philippines. Those little women would walk all over me, literally. I not only enjoyed their massages, but also paid attention to how they did it. It wasn't always about a "happy ending." I knew one day that I would be there for a woman when she was sore, tired from work, or just wanted to connect in a non-sexual way.

Women who only get massages because they're sore miss out on the beauty and pleasure of sensual human touch. Some haven't even been rubbed on by a man in years.

Ways to Massage Her

Get a potpourri jar or anything you can add heat to, and fill it with coconut oil. Make the bed or massage table comfortable. Satin or silk sheets, or 300-count cotton type.

Soft towels are also nice to have if you have a massage table, for the head and face area. Cheap towels are a bit rough; the more expensive ones are thicker and softer. Have a music playlist. Calming music is the best for this. Rain, blowing winds, thunderstorms, sea waves, or her favorite singer.

Headphones that cover the ears are really good, as it prevents outside noise so she can go deeper into her relaxation.

Dim red lights, and make sure the room is dark.

Ask if she likes deep rubdowns or if she wants it soft and gentle. This is very important.

Hot towels for her feet, wrap the towels around her feet, one at a time and massage while the towel is on her foot. Squeeze the feet and apply pressure, through the towels. The heels of her feet need a deep massage.

Start with massaging her scalp and work your way down, slowly to her shoulders, neck, arms, back, and entire spine. Concentrate on those areas for a while before moving to the legs. Massage her hands and wrists, too. Fingers are done individually. Apply the oil while it's nice and warm. Do not squirt it or drip it on her. Lather your hands and apply it with minimum pressure, or to her desire.

Massage using the palms of your hands, elbows (gently), forearms, fingers, and the sides of your hands. Massage each toe individually as well. Massage her entire ear, forehead, and eyebrows.

Women that are starving for touch are very vulnerable and guarded. If they are single, the physical touch starvation period makes them afraid to be touched for fear of falling for a man or woman too quickly. Sometimes you can brush up on a woman by mistake and her nipples will immediately get hard; this means she is going through a touch-starvation period. She really can't control her nipples popping out. In some cases, it's a dead giveaway.

Touching can and will transmit a sense of being cared for. When a woman experiences great and soothing touch, it brings about lower levels of the stress hormone, cortisol, and she gets more relaxed. This comes more often from hugging or holding hands. This is something I failed at for years. Touching also stimulates the production of oxytocin and improves interpersonal communication. It shows a form of attraction and security for the woman. It creates a bond.

Being Sleepy around Your Partner

If you are happy and relaxed with them, it brings about a few things.

When you're comfortable, the brain switches to sleep mode. Serotonin and dopamine are being released when you sleep together. I truly believe that women with insomnia can be cured if they sleep next to someone that they really like or love.

Ways to Improve Your Touch with a Touchless Man

- Touch him first.
- Put your breast on him.
- While in bed, lay your leg across his.
- Grab his hand and put it on your private area.
- Do not touch his private parts, until you have him in the mood. Some men are more confident when they're erect or getting there.
- Walk around with a thong on, or some sexy panties/lingerie.
- Wear his favorite perfume to bed.
- Do your hair before getting in bed. Wear it in a style that he likes, something that doesn't take much time. Men enjoy sexy ponytails.
- Do not ever wear a bonnet to bed, or a scarf tied in the front.

Mouth Passion

Kissing isn't just for the lips and it does count as a form of touch.

Speaking of cunnilingus, it's imperative that you know or ask her how she likes it. Some women want or need constant pressure on their clitoris and vulva area; while some want you to take care of it like another woman would, soft and gentle. People don't kiss passionately anymore, and I understand why. Women are very careful with whom they kiss. Even when they do, it's only a peck. They feel that kissing too early is too passionate and personal. They like getting to know the man first. Kissing is not usually intimate in the first few encounters. If a man can't kiss on the first day or any time after that, or if it happens that soon, there's a good chance she's already uninterested. There's a serious disconnect at that point and lack of chemistry, which leads to women feeling like there isn't any compatibility. It's not a sexual thing. I mean eventually, yes, it is; however, in the beginning, women want to know about your passion and intimacy. They don't feel as though a grown man has to be taught these interactions; they wonder why he does not know how to perform in this manner. The lack of touch is on a whole different level, and people feel the same way about this.

When we do not start the act of touching and kissing in the beginning, it causes a relationship to falter and remain off-kilter. We now lack many things conducive to sexual health and companionship. If there are connection issues, women will begin to think and feel like a man doesn't want to touch them, doesn't want to see them naked, or that there isn't a complete and total attraction. This happens when women settle and don't speak up instead of taking a temporary role in leadership. What also transpires during this time of getting to know each other is that the man may refuse to open up and listen to her cries.

Learn how to massage each other. Massaging is one of the most intense and pleasurable connections a couple can have as far as touch is concerned. Get back to being attracted to each other. What you did months or even years ago, to draw that person in, should still be a part of your routine. People submit at work and then come home to raise hell; they are afraid to submit at home, and this takes the relationship compass and puts it in a spin, creating a vertigo-like feeling. We both need to play a submissive role. It's not about "bowing down" but more about bowing in. Preparing for bed doesn't always have to be about making sure you are ready for work the next day, it must also be about making sure that you are ready to keep your partner turned on and interested. Some of us give more to our jobs than we do to our relationships, and this is how we lose our spouse.

It all depends on whether or not you reinstate touching in your relationship. If you do, things will get better, if you don't, this is the beginning of the end.

Note that just because you're well-endowed doesn't always mean she's happy. Also, just because you use your mouth well, that doesn't mean it is always what he needs.

Even though I screwed up all of my relationships, acting like I didn't care was one thing that kept me safe. That didn't last, though. I was a jealous man because of the way I was treating women. Jealous because that was my given shadow trait, and I had no control over it. I began to gain strength over my loveless traits when I identified them and accepted who I really was. I was faking it, so I was attracted to fake. Just like real recognizes real, we forget that fake also recognizes fake. My mistreatment wasn't a physical way of mistreating her, but I was guilty of destroying her temple, only touching what I liked and not what she needed touched. I was a "leaver," leaving her unwanted, untouched, and unhappy. By leaving a real woman, due to being unprepared, you're preparing yourself for a "leaver" as well.

"Girl, I don't need you, you know how many women I can get?"

This was my favorite line, and after spewing those evil words, I had the audacity to sit there and watch her cry. That was my security: "Me first, *you never*, and you'll never see me cry." But the fact is, I was drowning on the inside holding my feelings and tears in.

One thing that got me on track was seeing my ex-girlfriend with another man. I couldn't stand the sight of that.

My touch was always partial and cold because I was halfway in. I had "leaving power," which wasn't power in any way.

Regaining Touch

The forehead kiss: a form of admiration!

How Women Can Regain the Touch

- Stop wearing a rag to bed. If you do, make it pretty and sexy.
- Rollers are a turn-off, too.
- Before you scrub your face at night and look like someone else, get him turned on and locked onto a visual. Before you

take off your make-up mask, make sure he's nice and horny before retreating to the bathroom, and try not to take too long.

- Wear some nice lingerie or easy-access pajamas.
- Keep your hair sexy and smelling good, healthy.
- If you wear a rag to bed, tie it in the back. We want a little bit of thug, not Aunt Jemima.
- Don't become crabby in the bed.
- Don't try too hard to make him cuddle. Simply back your butt up against him and put his hand on your breast. He'll cuddle fast as hell then. I wasn't a "cuddler," but backing it up against my lower area caused me to become excited fast. Men enjoy non-verbal contact, especially the ones that aren't able to communicate for whatever reason.
- Start the rekindling on the couch or anywhere before you retreat to bed. It makes the transition to bed much easier. At this point, you've already told him subliminally what you want.
- Sleeping naked really helps. Skin-to-skin is extremely hard to resist. A woman is sending signals by doing this. Ignoring her could be devastating.
- Men do not like to be wrong. The same goes for women, but a very intellectual conversation and one where both are in agreement at the end, makes for an intense night in bed. Mental stimulation is also important for women who have a low sex drive. It's important to find out what she likes and is interested in, and then show interest in that. This is her energy zone and a time where she'll feel important and appreciated.
- Stop sleeping with your head propped up and not wanting to be touched. During the day, buy and wear colorful lipstick.
- Wear lip gloss with flavor.
- Allow him to observe Kegel exercises with you.
- In everything you do, be gentle.

How Men Can Regain the Touch

- Shower with nice-smelling soap.
- Shave or be decently groomed before getting in the bed.
- Wear nice-smelling deodorant.
- Dry yourself off, completely.
- Clip your toenails and keep a nice pedicure.
- Ensure that your breath smells nice. Get some orange or any fruit-flavored Listerine tabs.
- Give her nicknames that only you two know. Pet names make women feel special.

The things that I mentioned are all items you can work into your routine. If you just decide that you will not budge on any item, there will not be any improvement on the physical touch aspect and your marriage will continue to suffer. We must learn to make compromises and also improvise. Never be impulsive, as it will feel like you already forgot and then somehow remembered and are trying to make up for last time. It's going to be rushed and without any feeling or emotion. This kills the mood. As we get older, there are some permanent changes that happen in our bodies, but a change in desire, as in a loss of desire, is not permanent. We may lose weight, gain weight, gain wrinkles, and so on, but any change to our outer appearance doesn't have to affect our inner love and respect for our partner. Both men and women are visual creatures. Make no mistake about that. We must pay attention to this fact. On your way to becoming a better couple, here are some things that you must work on and believe in:

Stop being one-sided. You need to create a balance of fairness, harmony, understanding, flexibility, and willingness to compromise in your relationship.

Be clear. In your intentions, acts, and plans. Make sure to follow up and keep your word.

Have no fear. Don't be scared of letting go and receiving your partner regardless of past issues.

Look to discover and explore. We all have new ideas, thoughts, and places in and on our body. Make yourself ready to go there and then have fun.

Be each other's best friend. Treat each other accordingly. Truly enjoy each other's company more than anyone else in your life.

Intensify the love. Make it count, cherish the emotions, and appreciate the flow of intimacy and chemistry. Take it to higher heights of intensity by synchronization. This goes back to exploring and paying close attention to body language.

Walls down. Be open to having a deep understanding of your connection with your partner. Be willing to unfold so they can enter your world of ecstasy.

Stay. Be it after sex or a deep conversation, an exchange of mental stimulation, remain in that vein of care, passion, and caressing. This rekindles everything, connects auras, improves energy, and reignites the connection you have with your partner.

Learn how to cuddle. Women love this. Do it without wanting to have sex. This tells her you respect her body, mind, soul, and spirit, but more importantly, it shows her that you enjoy touching her and she'll feel protected. The man will also learn self-control and understand more about nonverbal communication. It's a win-win.

Stretch Marks

For years, stretch marks turned me off. What got me to like them again was when I met a woman that had them and didn't hide them. Her confidence was a turn-on like I had never experienced.

"Leon, look, I had kids. If my stretch marks are an issue for you, then you can move on. I'm not going to hide them."

Most women are insecure about their stretch marks because they care more about what a man thinks about them as opposed to the beautiful reason she has them. It could be from having a baby, weight loss, or being voluptuous. I had to mature to the level of understanding this before I gave her marks credit or positive attention. I'll make this short and sweet, as stretch marks have been a problem for both men and women. I had to learn that stretch marks are okay, and that they do not play an important role, or at least they shouldn't, in anything as far as physical attraction is concerned. I stopped complaining about them as it doesn't do any good; only bad comes out of complaining. What really made me stop complaining about stretch marks was when I realized and accepted flaws that I had and which women didn't like but accepted as well. Here are a few reasons why we shouldn't complain about stretch marks:

- Some of our testicles are lopsided, and women see them as we age.
- We grow gray hairs on our testicles.
- The sack shrivels up.
- We have stretch marks, too.
- Our chest begins to sag as we get older.
- Fat necks.
- Nappy or tons of hair on our back.
- Cottage-cheese legs.
- Small hands.
- Dirty navels.
- Double chins.
- Dirty necks.

Touch Leadership

Some people are in a marriage but are not really married.

Knowledge and awareness are very important. Someone has to step up and take charge and lead when the communication is broken about likes, dislikes, wants, needs, concerns, and desires. We tend to gain insight and focus about deeper attractions and desired intimacy when we express ourselves clearly. I didn't want to know or do this, but I do now. Conversation about touch was hard for me. I felt like she was essentially telling me, "Leon, you only pay attention to certain body parts. I need more, and I feel vulnerable!"

It hurt to hear that, but she was right. The narcissistic Libra wasn't trying to hear that, and because of who I was back then, all of my relationships suffered. I crave a woman's touch so much now that I wish I had listened. This is why I am writing about these lessons. This was a time for me to work on my communication about my lack of touch for her. She ended up getting it from another man because I was cocky and didn't listen. I acted like I did care, but I didn't. Most times, when I tried to care it was just an act, though. Instead of fixing what I lacked, I took it out on other women by depriving them, too.

Understanding, listening, feedback, and reciprocity in nonverbal communication are significant beyond measure when paying attention to why she needs touch. Sometimes we just take turns talking and in doing so, we'll never get anywhere or get anything done. That can then lead to complaining, leading to anger and short conversations, keeping your partner in need and vulnerable, just like I did.

Make sure you don't become offended when she tells you what she needs as far as touch is concerned. Needs have to be met, or someone is going to cheat or leave. There must be a sense of redirecting, as well as accepting both the redirecting and the exchange in power at that moment when the other partner should be in listening mode. I had a very hard time with this. Just make sure that in your reversal of the leading role, your delivery is handled in a professional and loving manner.

- Make your partner comfortable enough to listen.
- Don't surprise them.
- Always refrain from saying "We need to talk." This puts them in defense mode, and they can become nervous. Instead, say "I miss talking to you, when can we get back to that? I do enjoy talking to you, but really...I get turned on by looking into your eyes!"
- Do it in a comfortable setting.
- Try to wait till when they are in a talkative mood.
- Compliment them first, about other things.
- Ask them how they became good at other things.
- Tell them what you like by doing it to them when you all are talking.

Women are receivers, but men are, too, and if you want your man to listen or respond or to just talk to you, then it's all about how you say what you say, to him, or what you ask of him. This is very important. You have to make sure your man feels like he has some input and is not just in listening mode. When your delivery is off, men go into "little boy" mode; we shut down, tune you out, and do things just to piss you off.

Delivery and Inclusion

Speaking gently is your motherly role, and you must approach him like you would a son that you love and want the most and best for. The worst thing you can do when leading in your relationship as a woman, whether temporary or permanent, is to talk down to or at your partner. The problems and issues occur when people seem desperate, worry about their biological clock, and have just given up on dating and relationships. Your emergency approach will cause your partner to lose interest in listening to you. You will have a tendency to rush your thoughts and expectations, and also impose your will on them. Your expectations may not be our "ready reality." Timing is crucial, and you must prepare him to talk. Just like the man desires that the woman talks to him, you must do this for your man as well; catch him in his energy zone. Grooming must always be a part of any relationship. We all need it, regardless of the desire to put on a front and act "manly."

Men and women abuse the communication skill of proper conveyance when they've been hurt, neglected, not included, or disrespected. During this time of emotional neglect, they'll talk over their partner and not believe anything they have to say. Some would even do it in public, or at family gatherings.

For the man, it is important to know her and what she enjoys. Read books, take advice from monogamous men, and listen to what she tells you. I mention taking advice from a monogamous man and not a promiscuous man like I was, because as a promiscuous man, I didn't care about her wanting or needing a special touch. I was far removed from her sensuality.

When we listen, then perform, a woman takes pride in our ability to match her life, energy, sexual course, and mental connectivity. One thing that helped me with touch, was that I actually studied diagrams, illustrations, and learned how to give massages in an effort to change her negative emotions. I first had to be fine with taking a role in receiving her. It's one thing for a woman to not feel good about her kids, co-workers, and so on. It's a different type of disaster when her partner becomes one of those people that she's at odds with; it affects the entire household, and that's just how it is. It's also our duty to right the wrongs in every aspect, and that's just how it is. As men, we need to be prepared to lead and take initiative in all relationship matters.

For a long time, the masculine man has been put through the wringer by many things in society. Things have sped up: food has changed, communication, transportation, and so on. Everyone is in a hurry. Most people aren't patient anymore, and this takes away from things that are important.

Always be willing to learn about your partner's sensuality.

Benefits of Leading the Touch in a Relationship

You'll learn their erogenous zones.

Non-sexual touch refers to holding another person without being horny; it's controlling your hormones so that you do not rush and become impulsive in that moment. Some women, if not most, enjoy being held closely until she falls asleep. We must respect her comfort zone. It's about how she receives you in times when she needs to be consoled.

- Talking on a deep, sensual level while rubbing her scalp.
- Reconnect after a disagreement.
- Come to bed, don't go to bed.
- Reconnect in other areas of the house, before the bed.
- Make eye contact.
- Give hugs.
- Allow your partner to have and make their own choices.
- Listen before you judge or get upset.
- Do not hold their past against them.
- Get to know them, continue giving them what they like, and don't be manipulative.

Negatives of Not Taking the Lead in Touch

- Lying in bed, facing out from each other
- Flaccid penis
- Dry vagina
- One or both partners will immerse themselves in the kids only, or a pet
- Insecurities
- Lack of intimacy
- Becoming unfamiliar with each other

You must be careful when yearning for touch while struggling with your faith and religion. If you do not cleanse your soul from the other people you've been with, and take care of your physical needs, you will suppress your character, integrity, and morals. You know and want love, but many times, your desire for lust will override that. Once that happens, the nearest person that you've had history with, will suffice, regardless of how toxic that relationship was. This is called "anchoring."

Anchoring is heavy, controlling, and sways you from left to right, leaving you full of confusion. Regardless of how far the anchor chain is let out, you are still linked to that person. Just like a ship at anchor, it swings, and maybe even drags the anchor chain, but it never lets go.

How to Detach

You have to first realize your weakness and then get serious about letting go or moving on. You need to stop being fine with sharing bodily fluids, demons, and soul-ties with strange people and also stop being content as a first, second, or third loser.

A woman has to have personality, class, a decent job, respect for herself, be cool, confident, caring, and fair, too. However, what seals the deal and what will have him coming back, or attracting the right man with morals, is simple: Vagina Discipline.

My friend Chris Burns told me—"Doubleo, you don't want a "cold" woman—you want a "cool woman!" She has to have CPP— Class, Pizazz, and Personality!

CHAPTER TWENTY-FIVE

Loveless Trait #4:
Titles and Status

When I was selected Sailor of the Year, and Recruiter of the Year, I felt untouchable. It became much worse when I was initiated to Chief in the Navy! I wore my khakis and combo cover all day. Putting those anchors on my shirt collar, sealed the deal. I would stare at them, too! My arrogance went even higher when I wore my choker whites and a splash of some nice cologne...I just stood in the open so people could see and smell me!

They have all of their life, education, and corporate "checks in the blocks." Their gains and accomplishments are to make them seem polished. In the Navy, I checked off many things, Sailor of the Year, Recruiter of the Year, and yet my happiness was short-lived, but I acted like I was extremely happy. I was very cocky and arrogant, even when I would get promoted. I was easily influenced by the same type of people. The connection to them wasn't genuine, the connection was from a pretentious feeling or because we all knew that we weren't really real! These people just want to be honored, and popular; they want to be shown love, but won't show love. During their quest for titles and status, they miss out on key components of relationships and are very shallow. They get their energy from dating, leading, supporting like-minded people, or marrying people much less established than themselves. This gives them a sense of security, which is actually false. They need to be able to always look down on you. While dating them, the money is good as well as the sex, but the neglect is high. Sowing is at an all-time low. These types of people are control freaks and will not power up until they want something for themselves. If you decide to stay, you'll be a stay-at-home mom or dad and nothing else. More women fall into this role, and while some are happy, a lot are miserable. You'll become a host for the other neighborhood VIPs, work CEOs, and anyone who shares the same titles and status as your partner. You'll have the desired big house, plenty of cars, access to lots of money; however, after many years, you'll just be like the furniture in the house, maintained, vintage, or at a standstill. After child four or five, you'll notice that you might feel youthful, but won't look like it. Time has passed you by and you've lost your connection with friends and family. You won't find yourself (and I am not recommending this, at all) until either after divorce or you become a widow. As for the man that falls into this category, the stay-at-home dad or one that works and does a lot around the house but feels unimportant, unappreciated, etc., he'll lose confidence, hope, and look for answers constantly. These types of men will also be used, abused, and neglected. He's a good, moral type of guy. I wasn't a good moral type of man. Normally, he'll remain just like the good woman, or just decide to give up on being married. He becomes a "role player" or a prop to keep the outside looking like the marriage or relationship is prospering; it's not. It's more stagnant than anything.

I don't believe that there is ever true love here, for these types of people. She loves comfort, and he loves that she's a robot. The same goes for a woman with titles and social status. In his case, he gets the cars, maybe his own club, and the nanny.

Professional Community Property

Some people search for these types of people, though. The women that are passed around from the NBA, NFL, NHL, to Baseball teams are always available; they are not looking for love. Titlists and status types of men aren't available until they find a woman that's very submissive and docile, a lady who is very traditional and domesticated. Meanwhile, they are not looking for love either. The PCPW (Professional Community Property Woman) will be forced to live the life of a woman from the 1950s; that's if she is ever taken seriously and manages to settle down, of course. Most of the time, neither will happen. Because of her attraction to these men, her run will only last for about five years. She'll circle back but will never be taken seriously. People like that wind up alone. After years of living this way, you'll finally notice that, yes, the bank account is nice, the house has had some additions, you've had every car imaginable, but nothing has been paid into you!

Good and moral men and women die inside; you just haven't been laid to rest yet; you probably already have your own burial plot. It's never too late, though. That's the first mistake you'll make— thinking that your life is over. In many ways, you have been preserved, because for many years you've been taking care of the family, honoring your vows, and not serving only yourself. In doing this, you're covered for sure. There will not be any spiritual regrets!

The Ego

"The sycophants, yes men, and yes women keep us afloat!"

We have a tendency to treat others at work, better than those at home! I have seen numerous athletes and military personnel fall into deep depression after it's all over. Once the career ends in both, and the lights go off, the curtains close, and the fans stop cheering or people stop kissing their butt, it's a very hard pill to swallow. The first person that becomes a part of their wrath due to emptiness, is the spouse, and then the children. They become very insecure, cocky, and arrogant; most do it with nothing, it's all based on a "has been." No more trophies, full paychecks, fans, and admirers. *It's over.* Most try their best to hold onto their past and wind up looking foolish, but deny even that. I think in their mind, they are still who they once were. When the spouse or even prior friends refuse to see them as such, they start to discard them, or even demand divorce. This is who they really were before the promotions or all of the accolades. They were allowed to hide it because people put their status or uniform on a pedestal, and that's what people saw, instead of someone that wasn't grounded! People morph into a false sense of security, based on their status that's given to them because of their athleticism, or evaluations that helped them get promoted. They just might be driven, passionate, or even intelligent, but that's what got them there and not a genuine heart and soul! Those people that groomed them, saw their potential or even a future gain. Groomers are those that will eventually use you as a pawn, minion, or for financial gain, speaking of the potential athlete that looks to make a lot of money. As far as military people that are groomed, the groomer has future plans for you to be their go-fer. This isn't true in all cases; some people are genuinely building a solid team and great friends who will later help with a successful team, or a thriving business.

Note: For those that are wanting, have, or are addicted to the "Titles and Status" types, there will be a few, insanely, and degrading emotions that you will experience:

Sex deprivation: Now that you have the kids, the house, cars, and nice bank account, you'll begin to notice that there hasn't been any kind of love-making for months, or possibly even years. At times, you're expected to just perform oral sex, every now and then, and that's demanded normally when they're on-the-go! Nothing is in it for you, at all. After so many attempts, demands, or performances, you'll lose your desire to do so, and you will not be able to conjure up any motivation to continue. This is more than likely the last phase of sex that starts the sexual decline!

Devaluing: You'll do this on your own, because of the loss of your identity from years past. Your partner may do it as well, but in losing who you were and are, it will be even easier for them to do so, directly or indirectly. Some do it to keep you mentally paralyzed. Your role as mom/dad/husband/wife is what's expected of you, and not much else. I have much respect for homemakers; it's a really tough job, but as the kids move on, so does your youth and life. Once you sign up for the "Titles and Status" types, prepare for years of not feeling loved deeply and genuinely. The love will come from the children, though, and this is why some women, if not most, lay their life on the line for those children and no one else, and in some cases not even for the provider. That person has left you many years ago, in an effort for you to concentrate on the home, how you all are perceived, the appearance, reputation, and them. They can handle themselves, but you—you must handle them and everything else.

Stonewalling: Unknowingly, you will be put into "stonewalling" so that you can and will master your role, a role that will be identified in the beginning. During my military service, I've seen men and women stationed in Great Lakes, as someone that was a great mother, father, husband, wife, or homemaker, who have never even seen the great things that Chicago has to offer, let alone Wisconsin. I had to catch myself when asking my friends if they've visited certain places in Chicago with their family. I got the look, and I knew then to drop the conversation. Stonewalling will make people dive into themselves, gag themselves, lose confidence, and in some cases, start thinking that they're a problem of some sort. You will feel unappreciated, unimportant, and in some cases, unloved or even used.

Some people have been sex deprived, devalued, and stonewalled so much that they may begin to lose their morals, and cheating begins to seem okay with them! They become just as risky as the narcissists!

In some cases where the man or woman seeks those that make less than them, there's usually underlying insecurities. Those types of men and women usually lead their life and conversations with their job, education, fraternity, sorority, nice car, big house, and a business card. People that normally make less than their partner, have a tendency to not speak much, in and around the house. These are "back-seaters" and most have lost their momentum and self-esteem early on in life through abuse and neglect!

CHAPTER TWENTY-SIX

Suppression and Repression

I was closed off like some men, and here's why.

The year was 1987. After the USS Stark incident, I decided to suppress and repress my experiences. I served in the Navy for another twenty-eight years with severe PTSD and I had no clue. I knew something was wrong with me. The nightmares about the USS Stark are still with me. I take sertraline and prazosin to level my head. I'm telling you this story because apart from severe PTSD, I also had the trait of suppression and repression from my parents. The PTSD just made it worse and almost unbearable. Acting like things weren't what they were became my go-to defense mechanism. Lying became easy, deceiving was automatic, and I just didn't care anymore. At times, I found myself bold, impaired, showing a lack of empathy and remorse. I find it disturbing that when we feel these things, we don't allow ourselves to self-diagnose, through awareness, as a means to get ahead of any disorder, saving others in our path. Society thinks that if we're not determined to be sociopaths or psychopaths by a professional, then we're not. I find this to be false, and after reading and doing my research, I discovered I could have some of these traits. I never had abnormal or violent behaviors, but I did envision, or even fantasize about, violence towards people that I didn't like. One person I thought about in this manner was my mother's boyfriend after she and my dad divorced. I felt like he wasn't a good stepdad and didn't care about me or my siblings. I found that very disrespectful. My other traits that I knew were in my head were being:

- Superficially charming
- Egocentric
- Easily bored
- Manipulative
- Shallow in emotional depth
- Lacking in empathy

Please, never be afraid to call yourself out. Once you at least try to self-diagnose, you can start to work on yourself. I don't believe in "self-diagnosing." We don't know enough about anything medically related to our mental issues and the brain, nor are we clinically qualified to do so, but once we become aware and want clarity, along with wanting to do and be better, then that's a start. It doesn't take any type of doctor to tell you about these traits. Tell yourself who you really are, what you're feeling, and plan to work on them to make yourself a better person. Study your family tree, not where they come from or where they were born, but things you may have heard about family members in the past. People always told me that my mom was crazy, she wasn't. I do know that she was never diagnosed with anything; actually, she declined that type of help, which most people do, especially blacks. Stick to it. Inform people that you trust and those that love you, of your own self-diagnosis (what you feel or how you have been thinking), and allow them to hold you accountable, to enroll in treatment and therapy.

As a naval navigator for my first twenty-one years of service, I had to have my act together. I spent fifteen years out on the seas. Half of my naval career was spent on ships, and twelve of these years were spent on the same class of ship, but not the same ship that was bombed in 1987, the USS *Stark*. I had fears residing in my soul during all of my eleven deployments, which were mostly in the Persian Gulf and other hostile territories. I became an actor. I had to. The nightmares persisted and the smell of burning flesh never left me. Burning flesh has a weird but sweet smell and some of our Navy chow had the same smell. I had a very hard time eating chow on many occasions. The story ties into my narcissistic traits because of my ability to act like the bombing never happened, just to make myself comfortable enough to go out to sea and into harm's way year after year. I needed to pretend it was all a bad dream. Because of that mindset and thought process, I was never shocked when I was put in harm's way in relationships. Putting on an act in relationships is what allowed me to protect my heart. Yes, I lost and pushed away plenty of women and screwed up all of my relationships, but I was just being deliberate in keeping myself from hurt and loss. While onboard the USS Stark, the same thing occurred. I began to feel extremely, mentally numb amongst those thirty-seven dead men. I then learned, even more so, how to transfer pain and then transition away from their loss of life, tragedy, fear and tears like it wasn't reality—but it was, just like the ghosting, gas-lighting, the silent treatment, and other traits that also pushed those women away. No one was safe, regardless of how tragic it was.

My mother was a suppressor and repressor. I truly believe that her traits started from childhood, suppression of emotional feelings, but definitely during the years from 1979 to 1982, when her brother was killed, she divorced my father, her father died, and she lost my sister and I. Also losing her relationship with her own mother. Six people lost in three years; how does anyone stand up to that? My mother sure did and indirectly, I did too, in any given situation, be it relationships, or death. I became very nonchalant. Doting transfers a mothers vision and processing of pain also.

The hand that I was dealt never made sense to me. I knew that I was off but I didn't know why. It became clear to me as I got older, that I both feared and loved women, but overall, I wanted to hurt them. I needed to have an understanding of how women were made up and what made them operate in any fashion, before I could make sense of what I was feeling. I could have become a serial killer, gay, a child molester, even a rapist. But I became none of those things. Instead, I grouped all women together and, in my mind, all women were the same, so I took the course of least resistance. I had a voracious appetite but they all received the same menu. Mine was different every time yet I was giving all of them the same treatment, both good and bad, while not wanting to be held accountable. Instead, I wanted to hold them accountable, to blind them, shower them, mislead and misguide them just so that I could remain a *serial cheater!*

CHAPTER TWENTY SEVEN

The Start of It All

An innocent face, showing all thirty-two, as well as a hearty laugh, were just a shield hiding the way that I really felt. In every relationship, I started off as genuine, pleasing, charming, thoughtful, and caring, but my study habits were intense. I studied women more after high school, than I did in all of my schooling years studying any topic. I was destined to turn them out. I studied women in porn, to hurt women outside of porn. In my studying habits and techniques, all I was doing was practicing and acting on her to make sure I had it perfected. But it wasn't for her. This act was for the next two or three women. The current woman entered a test lab, and she had no clue because I knew that I would eventually go back to my old ways of comfort, fear, and ineptitude. I would leave her empty and vulnerable.

They will always go back to the scene of their crime, whether it is in church, the club, gym, you name it. Wherever you are, whatever places you frequent, narcissistic people and those with the trait will show up there. They feel the need to keep tabs on you, looking for your growth but hoping for your decline and testing to see if they still have their hooks in you.

I was my own champion, poised to destroy and keep any part of you as my trophy! There were two trophies. First, your mind, which controls your heart. And then after that, everything falls into place: tears, breathing, and your ability to not think rationally.

Narcissists study you before we walk away, because we will walk away. We become you, we imitate your ways, focus on your needs and your desires. You may desire us, but we desire to be your world. We want to be your core, for you to revolve around us and maximize our intensity within your body composition. Knowing your body composition, we're able to tear you down, and then build you up. It's a form of control over your emotions, physical appearance, confidence and self-esteem, emotional circuitry, and mental make-up.

Narcissistic people will always look back at our victims. We'll call and text, just to make sure we keep you hurting, wondering, crying, and lashing out. Your anger is our addiction; we need that attention. It's a way of feeling attracted and connected to you, knowing you still care deeply about everything that concerns us. This is a massive turn-on.

We thrive on the drama that we create. It's our way of being a manager or supervisor of your every move, reaction, and daily activity. We really enjoy "breaking up to make up." At this point, we pay attention to your deepest needs, knowing full well that you desire to be held, comforted, and touched in a way that frees you from the pain we inflicted on you. You will always want to know that we are okay and still there. This is how we reel you back in and continue to control your mindset and level of comfort. It's connected to loneliness and trauma bonding. We are afraid of being conquered, so we are always on the hunt. We enjoy making you cry, either before, after, or during sex, which is when you are at your most vulnerable.

Sexual and Emotional Bombing Narcissist

After they have shattered your mind, your body will belong to them. They keep looking to shift your emotional paradigm.

"Hey, how are you? How you feelin'?"

You'll hear this a lot during a phone call or in person. Sex usually comes up, too. Once you giggle or partake in the sexual conversation, you're done. Their push for it becomes very powerful, albeit sprinkled with nice words and a fake attempt at uplifting leadership.

When they know that you have been sexually deprived, the goal of the conversation becomes getting you extremely uninhibited and mesmerized. A simple yet emotional drug will be mentioned or recommended, and you'll happily oblige.

This is when you'll hear them say, "I love you!"

They'll hug you then, and their hands will be all over you, like never before. You'll still remember how it felt the following day, but they will make sure they make you think that it was no big deal. You'll be taken aback by what they said, but you make yourself believe it.

"Damn, he loves me?"

Nah, he doesn't. He loves his power over you. It's really that simple.

At this point, the intensity will be so amazing, you'll neglect your faith, morals, integrity, and character just to experience that feeling over and over again, and only with them. Now, it's more about feelings and not so much about emotions.

Their sexual energy is at its apex now, and it's the best sex you've ever had.

But remember, size does not matter. Protect your G-spot!!

Once your fluids are released by the sexual narcissists, this is where the control begins. For some women, their G-spot is their crazy spot, not the clitoris. This is very dangerous.

The control and mind screwing begins when you orgasm, and they don't. This is done on purpose. You are a part of a numbers game here. Sexual Narcissists are only serious when it comes to sex.

We master this to be able to use every part of you. If you are inexperienced, you won't be the same when we're done with you. We can sense your fear. The lonely, the ones that aren't complimented, and the ones that feel undesired, will fall easily into our trap and suffer the most. I know you want to impress me, because you know that I know that you feel sexually unimportant and you're lacking skills in that area. This hurts your pride, but you really want to make me feel better than you do even though you need it more than I do. This way, you'll follow the rules and become extremely obedient. Crying during sex, and seeing the tears flow while you are quiet and when we enter you, takes our narcissistic personality to unprecedented levels. It makes us feel powerful.

If you're happy without us, we're sad, if you're sad without us, we're happy! You will never know, either way.

Narcissists know what your voids are and how to fill them, from the crown of your head to the soles of your feet.

We must know how you are. If you're still trying to heal or move on from a troubling past, and you give in, we'll start all over again. We are serial killers, not as in murderers, but we'll crush your spirit and soul just like the way we've crushed the souls of many others. This is as a result of our winning and rotten spirit. We must always keep a part of you with us for controlling purposes. We will never reconnect, to make things better, only worse. We love trophies!

You must learn how to ignore narcissists and stick to your decision. They can be very persuasive. Regardless of how you feel about us or how addicted to us you are, our doors are always open, but just know that we will hurt you over and over again. To be completely free, you must close your door and move on for good.

I needed the doors to be closed; that's the only way for you to help me help you.

The Narcissist's Playground

There are three rides. There might be more for some, but it's just three for me. The door remains open because I want you to come into my playground.

The Sliding Board: You go up first, alone, after I recommend it and then I coach you. You slide down, surprised and a bit afraid. I come to meet you at the bottom and then we discuss the ride. You informed me that it was a little spooky, being alone. Then I go up with you next time and hold you as we slide down. You feel more comfortable. Now you believe in me more. Your security is rising.

"See, not so bad, right?"

"No, not at all, Leon!"

The Merry-go-Round: Now that you trust me just a little more, and you believe in me, I'll ask you to get on the merry-go-round. As you do this, I spin you around and around, you get dizzy and I spin it faster and faster; you have no control. As you spin around, I walk away to talk to other women, flirt, make plans, and get their numbers. You're still spinning and spinning, holding on, dizzy, but holding on tight. I come back, slow it down, let you gather yourself, and rescue you. You have no clue what I was doing while you were spinning and trusting me, yet you remain confident. I help you get off and we walk over to the seesaw. This is by far the worst ride a narcissist can take you on.

The Seesaw: You get on first, then I get on to balance us out. At first, we're even, looking at each other from either side. You smile and I smile back. Then, I allow you to lower yourself and raise me up. You do so. You smile and enjoy it. While I'm up in the air, you take care of me, raising me slowly and lowering me slowly. We go up and down a few times, still laughing and smiling. Now, it's my time to come down, and you let me down slowly. As I come down and get my "feet on the ground," you are up in the air. Your feet are off the ground, and you're unstable. I swing it slightly to the left, and then to the right, making it shake and tremble. I then instruct you to hold on, grab the handle, lock your legs up under you, and as you do so, I see the fear in your eyes. You want me, you need me, and you can't wait to hold me. I'm your security blanket, but I'll leave you up there dangling. While I was up there, in the air, I was looking for other women, but while you're up there, you're looking down at me. I become your sole focus. All of a sudden, I hop off and as you come crashing down, you roll over, get up, and I am suddenly nowhere to be found. The seesaw is by far the worst ride of them all. It's the end of a buildup, followed by impending doom. No more love or sex bombing, just a total bomb. This is the period when your body starts to ache, and it's not from your period! Even that will be off.

CHAPTER TWENTY-EIGHT

The Narcissistic Traits: Libra in Leon

The best thing you could do was reject me, but please, stay strong and do not let me back in! If you ever leave me, make sure it's when I am down!

I always had a guilty conscience! I thought you were doing what I was doing. My mind would not stop, as long as I was doing wrong!

The Pop-up Narcissists

This person knows you well and thinks that you don't know them. We sit and wait until we think you're weak and vulnerable just enough for us to come back and win. Our capacity for empathy is very low, if at all. I don't just get satisfied seeing your pain, I feel a sense of accomplishment too. I hated myself for being this way, but loved the journey of claiming who I was supposed to be, a demon without grace working with the devil. I know this sounds asinine, but I chose this role and journey as it felt much safer for me, more than genuine love.

For many years, I felt like two, possibly even three people. All of them helped me and all of them hurt me. It was in your best interests to stay away from me, but you couldn't, and I wouldn't let you. You filled me up and I depleted you. You became addicted to me, and I became addicted to hurting you.

My childhood trauma stayed with me for the rest of my life. My two female cousins, uncle, and babysitter really, really messed me up. I didn't suspect at the time, and neither did my family, but I knew that something was off with me mentally. My family eventually found out in 2018 when I wrote my first book, *Broken: Survival Instincts of a Child.*

Every woman I crossed paths with for over forty years was aware, though, because I acted out all the effects of my childhood issues on them and they all paid for it. I was paying for it too.

If you told me that you loved me, that was the worst mistake you could ever make. I was suffering from emotional dysregulation. Monogamy was a game to me; I had never planned to take it seriously. Promiscuity, now that was a different story. From the Asian persuasions to the fiery Latinas, Canadians, Aussies, to Saudis, the Greeks, and to the meek and mild Japanese women. It almost drove me insane because I was chasing a feeling and experience that I'd had since I was molested, both good and bad, to get satisfaction and revenge, oddly. It wasn't even about quality, more like quantity. I gave out lackluster and bad penis, but I didn't care, I was just trying to see if you were willing to give me your most cherished possession. You were only a number.

I had many traits. I was a bit weird, off, and a tad bit crazy, yet I was also loving and unloving. I was forgiving and unforgiving, weak and strong, flawed and imperfect, and also spiritual and demonic. I chose God one day and the devil the next, based on what I was feeling and what I wanted. I learned that God isn't a choice we get to make; he chooses us, but I played with him for years, and yet he never let me go. With the devil, yea, now that was a choice; he never had me, but he used me. I tried to repent and then I didn't try. Living right and doing right was just too boring to me; the wrong path, wrong people, and wrong-doing seemed right for me to pursue. Hell was my comfort.

I held my pain in and took it out on innocent people. I lied with ease, and hurting women didn't bother me. I was conditioned to walk away from relationships and start another one, just as fast. I am an alpha male, with no omega in sight, just adrift, and comfortable with beta females that wouldn't challenge me. I did no wrong in my eyes and had a hard time accepting that I could even be wrong. I was the epitome of flirtatious, sneaky, social, anti-social, unsure, bold, daring, egotistical, self-centered, worldly, aloof, and despondent.

I had serious mommy issues as well. I was vindictive and always wanted revenge when you hurt me. I could charm my way back in, inflict pain and destruction, and leave again. Disappearing was my best course of action. I did it a lot. My priorities were out of order. Lust was my love; love was my loss. Being and feeling empty was fulfilling to me, as I didn't have to struggle with feelings—I had none. I was warm when things centered around me, but cold when you didn't center yourself around me. I was just afraid to hurt or allow you to see me hurting. I can't let you in, but you must let me in. I needed nurturing, I was a broken little boy and a confused grown man.

Hoovering

Because of my mindset, and the actions and mindset that I adopted, in the previous chapter, I developed a means to "hoover." This term is commonly spoken about because people without the personality disorder just don't understand it. I understood it quite well. It stems from many things: insecurities, jealousy, afraid of hurt, and others. I had to strike first when I left or when we broke up. To make the first move was crucial in my strategic mind game of hurting her or at least making her think that I really moved on. A simple text, maybe even a phone call to ask a question—normally a dumb one, to see if she would first, respond, and second, answer my question. It's a way of starting all over and wasn't meant to be healthy at all. I had to know if I was able to come back or reconnect, if I ever wanted to. Some times were scary, as she might have not answered, ignored me, or seriously moved on. My risk-taking was always at an all-time high and the thought of her answering or responding was always a good chance...in my mind. I would only let the phone ring maybe two or three times; after that, I had to hang up, not wanting to know if she was "really" ignoring me. I would tell myself maybe she was at work, or had the kids, was at the doctor, or something. Those excuses were good enough for my ego and if she called back, the deal was sealed, and I was highly motivated ready to start over.

Typical Immaturity, and Classic

As you continue to read my book, and learn about me and my loveless traits, you will see and notice an ugly pattern of self-loathing, low self-esteem, lack of confidence, addictions, fear of commitment, fear of love, and many more things. I blamed everyone except myself for all of them. In doing so, I kept a reprobate mind as well as a spirit of corruption. Oddly, when I joined the Navy, I became a navigator. I tell you this because as a navigator, I had to learn about the celestial bodies—the sun, moon, and stars—and their direction, guidance, planning, the ebb and flow of the tides, and speed of currents, in great detail. All of these relate to us as human beings and our alignment. Celestial bodies are things that affect our inner core. Although I read for thousands of hours about the celestial bodies, I never related it to my own mind and body, or relationships. Through the Navy, though, I had that capability. I used that opportunity for my service in the Navy, never for myself. I was even a weatherman for a bit, and this required me to look up in the direction of God, each and every day, nighttime and daytime, to see what nature had in store for me and the crew of many ships I served on. I was destined to get to God, one day, but I took him for granted and he showed me. I had to work with compasses also, understanding in great detail how they work and why we need them, for stabilization, course correction, guidance, and steering on a true, northern course. Yet again, I failed to relate it to my own inner and outer moral compasses. The best thing for me to do was to join the military, specifically, the Navy. Seeing as though it was predominantly white, I needed to be uncomfortable being away from my home and culture, to really see life for what it was, and not for what others said it was. My uncle told me to join the

Army because the black men would take care of me, and they did in the Navy, but there were more people that took care of me who were from other races than Black people. I had been comparing myself to people that looked like me all my life, and that wasn't a true measuring stick at all. I had demons, addictions, and evil thoughts, and for years, that felt good to me. There was more to me, I knew it—a lot more. I wanted to know if other races of people were like me or different. I needed to know, and I needed to grow. I knew this as a kid. In my parents' deaths, I studied them because even though they were gone, they were still in me and that was a major turning point in my life. I had been living through and for other people, and not true to my heritage. I wanted to make people laugh like my dad did, and I wanted to become a deep thinker just like my mom; however, year after year, I found myself forsaking their gifts.

Once you defeat a narcissistic person, it's best to leave them alone for months, maybe even years, or even forever because they'll consistently look for you, follow you, and try to pull you back in. Remember that trophy that I mentioned? They hate to be defeated. They are only safe after intense, inpatient therapy and counseling.

CHAPTER TWENTY-NINE

Signs of People
with Loveless Traits

Sign 1: *Being Closed-Off*

I wanted to be a person that was less in love. I felt weak being sub-missive and vulnerable. I wish that I had learned to cry more often, be open, transparent, and vulnerable. Instead, I chose to be tough and strong, and hard like my father, thus avoiding the nurturing traits of my mother. My father was a very loving man; he taught me well, directly and indirectly, and because I was hard, I was hard to love. It was impossible for true love to penetrate my exterior because I wasn't open to blessings; my soul and spirit were also shut off. I was open to many things, yet due to my fear, I was closed to many other things, including genuine people. They couldn't help me because I didn't want to help myself. Had I developed from a more passionate, empathetic, compassionate, and discerning core, my aura, presence, and truth would have attracted the same type of people. But I hadn't. I was rotten inside.

As a kid, I saw black women get beaten, disrespected, and cheated on. I also saw them perform as prostitutes. I saw them recover in spite of all the things they were going through. I thought their abuse was temporary, but I was wrong; it wasn't, and neither was mine. Later in life, I would see Latinas, Asians, Whites, Arabs, Indians, Canadians, and Native American women treated the same way, depending on what country I was in.

There was an evil storm going on inside of me, a tornado just whirring around causing internal bleeding and destruction. The first organ to go was my heart. It turned from red to blue, from warm to ice cold. This is where my lack of respect for women grew. I enjoyed seeing them cry, sadly. Still, I wasn't powerful; I felt powerless.

Sign 2: *Comfort in Drama*

The only way to calm my inner demons was to hang around demonic human beings, like-minded people, and settle in what they were involved in, in an effort to get rid of my temptations but still keep them close. So, I thought to myself, this does work, but please remember, it works in the opposite manner as well. Of course, it works for the betterment and good of the real seekers, but it also works for those that are fake and unsure. If you are not ready to change, you'll wind up the same person, fearful of letting go of addictions or vices, and this practice will backfire. You will make promises to others about your new journey, but you will also begin to hide your failures. Only put yourself in compromising situations if you are healed, covered, and confident. For those that are looking to be healed, you must face yours and others' demons and be comfortable with that, but not so comfortable that you accept their ways as yours and not become quick to forgive, or forget why you are facing them in the first place.

Sign 3: *Attracted to Subtraction*

If you know this person's track record, or the type of people that they are involved with or always with, then leave them alone. It is clear they are not being serious at that moment. They are relationship minimalists, and you'll get the bare minimum, with everything.

Narcissistic people who are not ready to move up in a relationship usually go after victims that are just like them. Subtractors believe that less is better. We're called, "UNEXSEX," which stands for Always UNavailable, Always having EXcuses, only wants SEX! The only place you're going with a person like that is down, not up.

CHAPTER THIRTY

Dangerous Mindset

*Narcissistic people are uncouth. We live life on the edge
in almost all areas. We are serious risk takers.*

The Street Walker

She was the evil that I encountered when I was only fifteen. We
matched each other's energy and neither one of us had time to like
or love each other; it was about business or pleasure only. She was
five feet tall, 145 pounds, and had a curvy body, full and plump lips,
nice buttocks, nice, firm D-cups, and thick thighs.

Her name was Cheryl, "the Street Walker!" She was twice my
age and demonic. Just what I was looking for. I bought my first prostitute at age fifteen, and it wasn't hard. There's an almost direct line
from being molested to being addicted to porn and eventually seeking
the services of a prostitute. What's in your partner's past? Do you
know who you're living and sleeping with?

Cheryl was just as "loveless" as I was. I gave her money, and
she gave me pleasure; we were both happy with the barest minimum.
Why should I ever want anything else from a woman? I saw her happy
about money and not love. I was wrong, of course, but when you're
with a mirrored person, this will be the yardstick for how you see other
women, until you find a real woman, that is, and realize that who she

was, was not my fault. I knew that I had more, could offer more, but I forgot that later in life. Repent and find yourself now.

From the tenth grade until my early senior year, I sought her services on a regular basis.

CHAPTER THIRTY-ONE

Path to Recovery/Awareness of the Narcissist

Not everyone will enter therapy, nor will they enter and come out and start working on themselves. I had to! Your personality is permanent!

Even without therapy, I learned what my traits were. Men avoid therapy far too often, and this causes a strain on the relationship, marriage, and family. Men would rather tough it out, but women make use of therapy to save or resurrect their relationship.

- You have to want to actually recover, heal, and not feel as if you're weak by wanting or asking for help.
- Identify your traits and be honest about them.
- Avoid the fighting and constant going back and forth.
- Accept being wrong when you are, and don't hold onto your anger.
- Take the time to see it from the other person's perspective.

Falling in lust with older women meant my vision had been sealed at the ripe period of seven to twelve. The glory-hole drilled in my parents' bedroom wall, a wall that was adjacent to the bathroom, allowed me to see well-developed women, and hear their drunken and horny conversations amongst one another while re-doing their makeup, adjusting their bras, and sharing who they liked at my mom's party. That turned me on. It also made me want to have traits or characteristics the men had.

Girrrrrrl, Greg smells good, you hear me?'

"Yes, and James is always well groomed, he always looks in my eyes when he talks to me, whew!"

"Darryl has a stern look, but he's kind and gentle."

"I'm enjoying Mark's conversation. It's pretty deep!"

I distinctly remember their conversations. I was hearing great qualities about men. Knowing this, there was always a path of recovery for me, I just had to want to do it. It would take years, though. I was nine when the glory hole became my friend!

This happened every Friday night when my parents threw great parties. I had now become even more sexually driven. I believe my first child-like narcissistic traits were living in a fantasy world and exploitation. I masturbated to the older women I saw through that hole.

As I became older, I got more engulfed in my narcissistic traits but I still knew deep down that I wanted to love one day. I knew what to look for, who to look for, her traits, a desired chemistry, a connection, and because of the conversations I'd heard between grownups, I had a vision. I could actually feel the pulling force of someone that I was deeply and spiritually attracted to, and it wasn't a form of sex. However, being emotionally detached, I fought it, constantly pulling away. Attraction must mean more than just sex. I knew that I had to reach and see her mind before her body, I had to enter her hurt and pain and submit along with her. I needed to have a resolution, a solution, honesty, evidence of my devotion, and perform above reproach. You gain this by first being exclusive and surrendering by showing your white flags, and then also presenting your red flags before she asks. Most of the time your partner already knows, so it's best to fess up before you go far.

That woman is living, walking, working, hurting, and desiring. She's waiting to fall into the right person's arms, life, and ingredients for a well prepared, and seasoned, relationship. Holding her walls up takes time and energy, but most importantly, it takes strength. It becomes very draining. And even though she deeply desires and needs affection and intimacy, she waits, and in a lot of cases and situations, she waits for a long time, only to be let down and disappointed. Women fear the rug being removed right from under their feet when they have been mentally abused for so many years. Be patient.

Being let down and disappointed, she gives up, and when you give up, you miss out on those that are honest and special to and for you.

It's because she's hurt, withdrawn, has her guard up, doesn't believe you, doesn't trust easily, or is apprehensive that you must give her a chance to accept herself by you being genuine, nurturing, trusting, and honest. It's in the little things like eye-to-eye contact, various levels of chemistry before sex, reciprocity, ambition, synchronization, confidence, unfolding right before her eyes, and touch-less intimacy, reserved for her alone.

In my recovery, I began to study women. I turned away from porn to understand and see them and not their bodies. I wanted to meet her before I teased her or physically pleased her. It's all different, means different, and feels different. Once I began to respect myself, I knew what it was like to be desired about mature and real things.

Leon's Assessment Recovery and Healing Grade Sheet

Grade yourself on your ability to do the following or plan to do them. Grade on a scale from 0 to 5. You must be honest, and this can be done either with your partner or alone. Fill in the appropriate circle next to the number.

Start or renew your relationship with God. (1.O) (2.O) (3.O) (4.O) (5.O)

Do you know why you are narcissistic? Don't be afraid to call yourself out. Identify your selfish and needy ways. (1.O) (2.O) (3.O) (4.O) (5.O)

Identify the negative traits that may have been passed down from your parents. (1.O) (2.O) (3.O) (4.O) (5.O)

Have you thought about your narcissistic traits? (1.O) (2.O) (3.O) (4.O) (5.O)

Are you; mean? (1.O) evil (2.O) jealous (3.O) weak (4.O) vindictive (5.O)

What is your EMIQ? low (1.O) high (2.O) unsure (3.O)

Have you repented and stayed the course? Yes (1.O) no (2.O)

Have you attended therapy with an open mind and with your partner if you are with someone? Yes (1.O) no (2.O)

Do you know how to apologize, with intent, purpose, and some added affection? Yes (1.O) no (2.O)

Have you identified your mommy or daddy issues? Yes (1.O) no (2.O)

Do you listen to manipulate? Yes (1.O) no (1.O)

Do you listen to receive? Yes (1.0) no (1.0)

Are you loveable or easy to dislike and why? Yes (1.O) no (1.O)

Are you selfless or selfish? Yes (1.O) no (1.O)

Describe what makes you feel better? An agenda, a plan, or a motive?

Will your change be for growth or revenge? Yes (1.O) no (1.O)

Please write all of your answers here, in the same order that they have been asked. Explain your answers to yourself and your spouse. Make sure to add in a plan of attack to correct all deficiencies after your answers.

Example:

Yes, I have a low EMIQ, or I don't know what my EMIQ is.

Yes, I have unresolved issues with my mom, dad, or both parents Answers:

1.

2.

3.

4.

5.

6.

7.

8.

9.

10.

The Woman's Reality Check

Ladies, your own assessment is crucial in your growth with your man.

As a woman, if you have unresolved issues with your dad, you may begin to see your dad in your partner. If he is absent or not as understanding as you wish he would be, this may cause you to take your anger out on him. It stems from him not giving you what you were missing as a little girl: a sense of protection and security. This is why when you are comfortable, you should express this to him so that he would know. You may also feel that your spouse does not possess the required male traits or skills you desire because your dad was not around. You may feel that he's not masculine enough, or even too masculine; you might think he is insensitive and doesn't deserve any rights to you or your heart. Again, this will be due to your dad not being around, and not because your husband or boyfriend is lacking in any category. Women begin to feel this way when they think that they have to play the role of a man. Open and trustful dialogue is key here, because you'll never be a man.

If your mom was a woman that felt resentment towards you in any way, you may feel fear of loving or knowing a man. This is what happened to my mother and her mother, which was then passed down to my sister. My sister was raised with four men around her for many years. This caused her to become extremely tough, wanting love but hardly ever expressing it in what she wanted or needed. Masculinity was indirectly forced upon her by me, my dad, and my brothers. She's very kind, understanding, and loving, but has a tough exterior. Having a tough exterior is good, but women that are missing their mom, and raised by men, have a hard time letting go, opening up, or trusting others.

The Man's Reality Check

Our assessment is just as crucial as the woman's. If our mom was dominated or absent in any way, we tend to take on a role of hyper-masculinity. Hugging, holding hands, or even crying with our woman are not things we do. My mother was there and at times, she wasn't true to her life's course. My dad gave me what he could but only what his dad gave him. This was in the late 1970s and 1980s, up until I joined the Navy. It was too late then. By that time, what resonated with me was how I had observed women being treated when I was a child and then what I was taught in the Navy, by broken, chauvinistic, or domineering men. The whole time, I knew to treat women as women, but I was highly influenced by players.

Before we go any further, I would like for you to know and understand certain assessments when learning of, and becoming aware of, your possible narcissistic child and what to do about it. From my experience, reading, researching, and learning of certain behaviors, I lay out in the next chapter, ways that parents can remain abreast of their children's activities and signs of those possible narcissistic traits.

CHAPTER THIRTY-TWO

Assessment and Prevention for Youth

I should have been in therapy from the first grade forward. When my parents divorced in 1976, my siblings and I were caught off guard. My dad being forced to leave our home shifted the dynamics of our household. Finances were reduced, leadership was non-existent, and discipline wasn't present. At that time, I was eleven years old and started doing what the hell I wanted to do. I was reckless, misguided, lost, hurt, and extremely angry at everything and everyone, angry at the world.

When conducting the below assessment, use a scale from 0 to 5 and write down your answers.

- Have you spoken about divorce, and was it explained during the process?
- Look for any signs of your child watching porn.
- Are you loving your kids equally?
- How and when do you praise your kids?
- Tell them you love them.
- Show them you love them.
- Be present, always.
- Treat all kids as equals.
- Before you scold your children, or even talk to them, practice with yourself as the child first and put yourself in receiving

mode, asking yourself the question that you would ask your own child. Make sure you do your best in seeing the question as you think your child would.

- Look for kids that seem withdrawn.
- Watch for kids that are happy to be away from you.
- Pay attention to their lack of hygiene.

I handled my divorce wrong, on all levels. To this day, I have deep regrets for both the divorce and how I did not convey it to my children. I was a coward!

CHAPTER THIRTY-THREE

Agenda and Motives

When we fail to do our own "self-due-diligence" prior to meeting someone for the first time, the stages of "agenda mismatch leading to agenda benders" begins.

Our love languages come from deep within; a desire to be happy, respected, respectful, welcomed, appreciated, caring, passionate, genuine, compassionate, and celebrated. We were born this way; however, over time, the places we've lived, how we were treated, mistreated, the high or even low expectations that were placed on us, and people we are attracted to, formed who we ultimately become and how we act and react. Again, even more traits to know, be aware of, and familiar with are right here in this book, *The 7 Loveless Traits.*

These traits are passed down from genuine men and women, just like the opposing traits which are passed down by unethical, unhealthy, untrained, and un-nurtured people. Ill-fated people possess violence, temper tantrums, bad habits, character flaws, greed, envy, and lust. They harbor them as well, leading to:

- Bad breath
- Dirty eyes
- Body odor
- Poor posture
- A lack of understanding people
- Filthy appearance

- Bad eating habits
- Excessive smokers and drinkers
- Nervousness
- Lies
- Poor planning
- No planning
- Large bank accounts
- Depleted bank accounts
- Nasty sperm
- A lack of love-making skills
- High body count
- Unreliable
- Low credit scores
- Extra hustles that benefit them only
- Avoidance of many things

All of this can result in an early death for them and could possibly leave you with excessive bills, sorrow, neglect, low self-esteem, reduced confidence, depression, or in some cases, happiness.

People that age gracefully embody a healthy spirit; those that don't neglect that route. They come with a dark presence, cold heart, and an uneasy feeling in their aura and presence.

What to Do

If you have plans to be with this person and they have the same feelings and plans for you, you must study and get to know each other with an open heart, clear mind, honesty, and forgiving soul. This is your time to formulate a precise and well-thought-out plan for a few things such as counseling and therapy and trying to attend sessions with your partner. If that doesn't work, share your discussions with your partner upon completion of therapy.

- Discussing each other's past

- Discuss likes
- Discuss dislikes
- Discuss young children and adult siblings
- Discuss flaws
- Character
- Sharing your past, including your parents positive and negative traits
- Integrity
- Spiritual beliefs
- Components of a relationship

When you all share such deep and profound events, thoughts, and tragedies, do your best to not have any regrets if it doesn't work out. There's nothing to be ashamed of. People knowing things about you should not make you feel like you're their prisoner. If you feel like that anyway, this is where God comes in; amongst many other things, he'll remove them, but you have to believe this and be willing to let go so you can "let grow." Also, keep in mind, this process can make people uncomfortable. Sharing family secrets and issues could scare people away; those people are the ones that don't plan to connect with you on a deeper level or just aren't ready for a real connection yet. Seeing as though it might push people away, you must take precautionary measures in observing that, so as to not push too hard or become overbearing or overcompensating. Sometimes, it's just your duty to point these people in the right direction; you do not have to settle down with them. You might only be a conduit to better health and a better life for them. Your opportunity for that purpose, is for your life, too, with them or alone, if they so choose to walk away. And this is why I am so happy, excited, and inspired to share my story in such a raw and transparent way. It has been truly liberating for me.

In moving forward, you'll become familiar with certain traits after a few dates or over time spent together. Proceed into a friendship/relationship not expecting anyone to save you, but as a way to gauge who you are, who they are, and if you all are meant for each other. We are all different and we want and need different things, but sometimes our desires are the same and this creates intense chemistry. Sometimes, other people can teach you how to let go, let your guard down, love, and forgive yourself with confidence and a feeling of safety again.

How Not to Waste Time

Don't ever go on your first date horny. If you are horny that evening, before you leave home, take the edge off and gain control of your hormones. If you don't seem so sexual on the first few dates, you'll gain knowledge and learn a lot about the person you're dating. You won't be distracted. Your head will be clear. The conversation will move in many directions, either towards you and your desires, or away from you, if it's not a sexual conversation.

Pay attention and remain focused. Never get caught up in "attraction shock." Attraction shock occurs when you place emphasis on looks, body, penis size, and what you hear about the quality of a woman's vagina or her ability to perform oral sex. These attractions will cause clouded judgment, drifting off, and the "Eyes-wide-shut" syndrome.

As a genuine and helpful person, "a giver," you will always immediately want to extend an olive branch, but you must take note of each encounter. The "agenda bender" doesn't understand the olive branch, nor do they care and will only take the olive, leaving you with just a branch. The next time you extend to them, leave your heart and emotions out of it and extend the branch only—but while extending this time, do so with a longer branch and without the olive. Take care of yourself.

Always expect them to let you down or ask for a favor. If they don't, this could be a good start. Lots of women are done with dating, so this expectation of being "let down" remains in the forefront of their thinking and expectations.

Learn how to say no, but make sure you mean it and that it feels good to your soul, because it will. Especially if you've been desperate for so long. This also goes for scorned spouses and fiancés. Scorned people will look for revenge over and over, and see the last man in the next man. Try not to make a hasty decision based on your anger or disbeliefs. Take deep breaths, and wait a moment or two before you react.

If you continue to go back and give to these people, you must realize that you are and have been addicted to neglect, abuse, and low self-esteem. This is also a trait that was passed down to you, possibly from the early slave days. You are involved in, and have a Modern slavery trait/Bonded slavery.

Be careful with exposing your titles, finances, and status. Keep the date professional, to keep the door open for another date. If a man is interested in you, *truly*, he'll let you know, if he's not, he'll ghost you, plain and simple. He won't *truly* inform you.

Refrain from self-pity, the "what's wrong with me?" syndrome. Instead, give yourself credit for managing a crisis or dodging a serious bullet, regardless of whether you're sexually starved or not. Your health is just as important as your wealth.

A quick note about slavery, as I mentioned it previously. Slavery isn't just for black people' believe that. With modern slavery and bonded slavery, you have now become their property. We associate bonded slavery with finances, but it's not only finances because, employment in a relationship is work as well. If you think about it, for some people, their debt to others, in their mind, is a feeling of "owing" by way of extra love and attention through rehabilitation. This is commonly found in nurturing women; they become humble and helpful to a fault. Empaths.

What *to* Be Aware *of*

Self-traps: They occur in genuine, wholesome, people. Those that have parents that have reached their fifty-year anniversary or beyond. They grew up with great marriage morals and are forgiving, but get hurt easily. People raised with one parent can also suffer from self-traps, from not receiving the other parent's perspective.

Late bloomers: The ones that have been sheltered all of their life can be victims as well. It's crucial that you all seek relationship and marriage counseling before getting in any relationships, friendships included. I lacked marriage and relationship strengths and this took me to the dark side characterized by a lack of morals, integrity, and character. I did the trapping. Self-trappers find it hard to believe that people can act the way that I did. It seems outlandish to them, but to people like me, it's just our norm, and we really don't mean any harm. It's all we know.

Low street credit score: If you have a very low street credit score, you are an easy target and will get used and abused. Not always, though. There were plenty of women that I dated who had "low street credit scores"—let me be clear, they *were not* gullible, not at all, yet much better off than I was. People will smile in your face and screw your man or woman and you'll never know, in many cases. You are aloof and naive, thus making you very forgiving, and then you'll feel sorry for your potential partner. You'll be the only one to not know you're with a menace.

"What did I do wrong—where did I go wrong"

A syndrome—a pandemic that *paralyzes* men and women!

A clear lack of wherewithal comes from being too trusting. You give people too much credit too soon—you lose yourself so much that even though you're hurting yourself and possible your kids through neglect, you still try to give a Leon credit! Giving the benefit of the doubt is one of the most dangerous nurturing traits women and men have. Pay more attention to the *doubt* and not the *benefit*, it'll save you some heart ache. Also, men and women both experience the "empty nest" syndrome too. This happens when they start paying more attention to only their child's safety and neglect their own happiness. Be careful with the "empty nest" syndrome, as it will lead to looking for another chick-a-dee to bring back to the nest, a grown one this time.

At this point, all you are doing is repeating the process of "giving to a taker."

You don't owe anyone; in all actuality, they owe you for the labor you put into rebuilding them. Men do this for women they deeply love and admire regardless of the woman's reprobate mind and ways.

If you have done anything wrong, it is that you gave so much that you forgot about yourself.

Agenda benders are also grandiloquent, pompous or extravagant, looking to impress. They are always self-aggrandizing and self-promoting themselves as powerful or important.

These people are actually inferior and look for your weakness to gain a sense of control and confidence for themselves, in an effort to keep you blindsided, off balance, and to continue feeding their greed. Their approach is very powerful and consistent. The reason they look different when you catch them off guard is because they actually reside in self-loathing. These perpetrators know who they are but fail to do the self-work. Most of them have low energy and are lazy; however, they regain their energy and motivation when any opportunity arises. They can turn it on and off, depending on what their gain or chances are. They embody the WIIFM (What's in It for Me) attitude.

If there's nothing in it for them, their energy level becomes extremely low; they're not helpful and will show a deep lack of interest. They run away at the first sign of trouble.

You can call them out and they will acknowledge this, but they will speak and respond in third person, as a means to deflect and not feel the negative effects of your truth. They also feel strongly about disagreeing with you even though they're wrong and they know it. Their IQ can be high, but their EMIQ is extremely low. There are very few people in this world that have both a high IQ and EMIQ; those people are closer to God, and they know it. They will not abuse anyone; they'll show kindness while receiving more blessings in return. The ones that only possess a high IQ and are not concerned with having or working on their EMIQ, are closer to the devil. Their fall from grace is imminent. If during their fall from grace, they are in the mode of working on themselves, they'll recover; if not, their fall will continue to spiral right down into hell.

You may wonder why they don't have emotional languages. Well, it's because above everything else, they just don't care. They begin to care only when they fall sick and are about to lose their job, or die. That's when they call out for their mom, dad, or God! They won't call out for you because of shame.

Certain traits and loveless languages become either defense mechanisms or void-fillers, depending not only on how and why they use them but also on who they use them on. If the love languages don't match, aside from any other mismatches, what takes place then are developments of continuous depleting of a person's soul, spirits, bank accounts, and a declining health. This leads to many things: a distorted mindset, disenfranchisement, emotional detachments, and death.

Agenda Mismatch

This is when the right person is with the wrong person, who has the wrong agenda for the right person.

We don't inform people of who we really are in the beginning stages, thus removing their decision-making abilities. They will do this for a job interview, though, because there is something at stake. They know that they have to rely on an employer to afford them the opportunity to keep up an image, a fake one, one that allows them to be covert predators. This is where and how they manage their facade. It's the first sign of someone who practices and exercises the mindset of "take and give"—giving false dreams and taking only things that they've studied about you, things you were open about, just to use against you .

- Words that move you.
- Small gifts.
- Things that you've never gotten but wanted for a long time.

- Compliments about physical things she's said she wish she had.

Truths about things people have said about her that hurt her. Mostly about her physical attributes, and you turn it around by telling her it's not true.

The *SEDUCTIVE* narcissistic trait is in full motion during this time. What now transpires is the process of the genuine person *giving* and the "wrong person" *taking*. This brings me to discussing the third Loveless Trait.

CHAPTER THIRTY-FOUR

Where My Loveless Traits Began

Before we move on, I want to tell you a short story about Leon and when I realized I had "Loveless Traits."

Narcissism isn't just an act or a trait, it's a feeling. Narcissists enjoy intimidating people, hate being intimidated, are always looking for revenge, are vindictive, desire praise, have a hard time praising others, and are uncouth. They act and react based on their feelings more than anything; these are feelings of protection and they do not want to get caught. If you call them out, they'll leave, disappear, and then reappear for the next victim.

January 2015. **Naval Station, Great Lakes, North Chicago, Illinois**

I was the Command Master Chief of the Naval Station, Great Lakes. There, we employed over 10,000 military personnel and civilians. It was January 2015. I was in my office preparing for my retirement, finishing up the paperwork on the computer, when I heard a knock on my door.

"Who is it?"

"It's me, Master Chief, you got a moment?"

"Sure, come on in."

My administration leader walked into my office and informed me of a few things.

"Master Chief, good morning. So far so good, you finished most of your physical, so I'll start your paperwork so we can get you a retirement date. Do you have any dates in mind?"

"Okay, cool, great. Have a seat. I'm thinking of August so my family and kids can come."

She takes a seat while going over my paperwork.

"Okay. Uh, ohh! Well, hold on, I'm looking at your paperwork again, and it looks as if you've seen all of the doctors except the psychiatrists."

"I'm not going to see another damn psychiatrist. I went last year and walked out!"

"Master Chief Walker, you have to, so we can prepare for your retirement date and pick a date. Millington won't approve it until you finish your full-body physical, sorry."

"Ughhh, maaaan! Seriously?"

"Yes, this isn't my first rodeo, Master Chief Walker."

11:00 a.m. January 2015. **Veterans Administration Hospital, Great Lakes, Illinois**

I entered the Veterans Administration parking lot and sat in my car for about thirty minutes. I leaned forward, my hands gripping the steering wheel with my chest pressed firmly against it. My fingers grew numb. I leaned back, covered my face, talked to myself, and cried. It was time for me to release this pain, I've held it in for forty-five years.

I looked out both car door windows, and the one at the back too, as if someone could hear my cries. It started to feel good at this moment because it had been years since I cried.

As a kid, I was always told not to cry, that crying was for girls, sissies, and little punks. I never knew that crying could actually make me more manly in not being afraid to express myself. When you cry around others, you'll attract those that truly care and send away those that can't relate or do not care. You're not a sissy, weak, vulnerable or a punk if you cry!

It was time to face the inevitable. I started talking to myself.

"Okay, Leon, let's do this. You've been an advocate for everyone, except yourself."

You deserve this help and it's time to forgive yourself."

I got out of the car and walked into the VA. I was so embarrassed of what I was about to ask the front desk receptionists, I kept my cover on. That's a no-no for any military person whenever they're inside buildings, anywhere. "Remove your cover, Sailor!"

"My man, where's the psych ward?"

"Master Chief, we call it the In-Patient Ward; it's on the Fifth floor. Could you please remove your cover, Master Chief?"

I didn't want him to see my tears, but I knew it was wrong to wear my cover inside. In addition to that, as a senior leader, for years I would always talk to my sailors about doing the right thing, so I had no choice. "Remove your cover, Sailor!"

"Right on, my man, my bad. *Sheesh!*"

I walked into the elevator, and pushed the button marked "5." Then I leaned against the wall and looked at the flickering lights on the ceiling. The elevator didn't make any stops. It felt like the elevator knew that I needed help. *"Let's get this screwed-up dude some help fast."* I was on a rollercoaster ride to heaven, but it felt like hell. My nerves were shot and my stomach hurt. I exit the elevator, turn left, walk twenty paces, and then make another left. I enter the office.

"Hi, Master Chief, please fill out this paperwork, take a number, and have a seat. We'll call you shortly," the receptionist informed me.

"Okay, thank you."

The paperwork you're required to fill out requires that you add your numbers up. I had no clue what those numbers meant, but I would find out. Thirty minutes went by and I fell asleep in the soft lounge chair.

"NUMBER 401—NUMBER 401!"

I wiped my mouth as I came to. "Yea, yea, yeah that's my number." I raised my hand like a nervous kid going to see the principal.

"Right this way, Master Chief."

Walking towards the doctor's door, it was quiet, and I could hear my boots scruff the carpet and my heart beat really fast in my chest. The cold atmosphere caused my hands to go numb a little. I chewed the hell out of that "coffee stopper" that I had grabbed from Starbucks earlier that morning.

"Come in. Welcome, Mr. Walker, have a seat."

The furniture in her room just irritated me. She was a small, white lady. About four feet tall and about a hundred pounds. Her hair was coal black, and fell down into her face in little strings. She looked like your average librarian from back in the 1960s and 1970s when they were all about their business and books. It was as if she was hiding from me behind her black, stringy hair; she'd already seen my numbers from the paperwork, so maybe that scared her. She wore all black; all I thought about was "Goth! Damn, I am screwed!" Her little, black church shoes were clean with a little gold buckle on each side. She sat back and crossed her legs, and then looked straight through my soul. My emotions were all over: first I got angry, and then I started to weep. She just sat there. At that moment, all I wanted was a very close and strong hug. I was very vulnerable, but it felt so good. I felt safe, finally, and it had been over forty-five years since I was able to let my guard down. My tears just flowed, and I hadn't even started talking yet, so I knew what was coming. In the previous years, between 1999 and 2012, I had only cried five times. Those dates are when my parents died, and when my three kids were born.

As I sat there, this thirty-two-year veteran, overconfident Naval Command Master Chief, went back to that little, broken boy, the one that wet the bed, was molested, abused, bullied, felt dumb, stupid, lost, neglected, suicidal, and basic. I was two people at that moment. Everything was on my sleeve. I wanted her to take this pain away. I was really tired of my head running wild. I knew that wanting a hug was inappropriate, so I didn't even bother to ask her for one. Instead, I tried to ignore my need and deflect my pain as always.

"Why is it so dim here? This furniture is like super boring?"

She looked up, stared at me for a few seconds, put her head back down and continued to flip through my paperwork.

She cleared her throat.

"Yes, we try to make it as comfortable as possible. Let's talk."

Note to the reader: You should know that almost all loveless traits begin their course when we're children. I know exactly when Leon's loveless traits started. I learned about loss, early on.

"Okay, where should I start, Doc?"

"Just begin and we'll course-correct as needed."

Saying the words "Doc" immediately took me back in time as I sat there. I then continued to speak.

"Can I tell you something, Doc?"

"Yes, sure. Speak."

I started to cry again.

It was late summer, in Cleveland Ohio, on 1770 East 70th Street and Hough Avenue.

It was raining that day. My dad told me to take the day off from school.

"She'll be here shortly," my dad would say.

"Who—dad?"

"Da Social Worker—fool!"

I froze.

The "Social Worker" was coming to inspect our apartment and to look at me and my sister. I was fourteen and my sister was thirteen. We were up early. My father didn't play that "sleep in" time, hell naw! He spent a few years in the Army, playing football and boxing, but he never forgot the army's terms and cadences.

"Rise and shine. It's clean up time." I popped tall, but my sister pouted.

"Toni, let's go. We gotta clean."

"Boy, shut up!"

I was wondering if this was going to be our last time together as a family. My nerves were shot and my heart raced all morning. I walked to the front room, which was my uncle's apartment; our apartment was in the back of the house. We had one small bathroom, one small bedroom, a kitchen, and a very small dining room sized ten by ten, just like a jail cell. The apartment was for three of us and a dog. The dog was a gangster, mean, but cool. He had a carpet and a little light in his dog house. My father loved dogs, and to this day, I do too, because of him. Our dog, Blackie, ate steaks, burgers, pork chops, and sometimes turkey and dressing. He might have been here before. I saw my dad feed him "pig's feet" one time, ewww!

We made the small apartment work for over a year; it was tough, but we got used to it and never complained. This has a lot to do with why I am so humble today. We were done cleaning and now we had to prepare for the social worker's visit.

"Doubleo, get the heater ready just in case we need it."

That day, the heat was out. I didn't want to walk down into the cold, wet, clammy basement but I had to. My uncle "Scoe" saved us that day too.

"Okay, daddy!"

Willie Lee, the fifty-year-old alcoholic, little-girl lover, was always tinkering with the wires in the basement when our heat went out. He was about five feet, five inches tall, about a hundred and ten pounds. Long black hair, big white teeth with a huge gap in the front. He had purple and pink crusty lips, more than likely from smoking Kool cigarettes. He'd keep one hanging from his mouth and could hold a two-hour conversation without smoking it. He just ran his damn mouth all day. I did learn from him when he was working in the basement. One day he called me down there.

"Look here, boy, you twist these wires, clip this, connect that, blah, blah, blah."

"See dat, boy, I know what I'm talkin' bout. "Click" oh yea, you hear that furnace hummin, boy?'

Willie Lee thought he was hot shit. I was just glad we had heat again.

His reward for "jury rigging" the wires was a fifth of vodka, a pack of Kools, someone braiding his hair, and reduced rent. We were only paying $148 for that apartment. Willie Lee was probably paying less for a one bedroom. He was a freaky little old man and had gotten drunk earlier that day. We were in dire straits and my father wasn't playing, he loved kids, especially his own. This wasn't a time to play with him as the social worker was on her way and my father was in rare form.

"Yo, Willie Lee, I need you my man, the social worker is coming and the heat is off."

"Aww, man, Zeke, I ain't in no shape to tinker wit no damn wires."

I braced for shock, looking up at my father tower over the little, frail man. I didn't want my dad to hit him; he would have probably broken his neck.

"Muthafu...man, damn, okay. Doubleo, go ahead and get the heater!"

I walked down into the basement and stood there looking at this thing. I had never seen one before, but I didn't want to let my dad down.

Between our apartment and my uncle's apartment, there was an adjoining door. My father removed the door and asked my uncle to leave for the day. With my dad removing the door, it looked like we had a two-bedroom apartment with more room, instead of a one-bedroom apartment for three people. We borrowed a kerosene heater from my uncle Roscoe. My dad called him "Scoe." He was left-handed, could roller-skate really well, and served in the Army. My uncle built Go-karts, mini-bikes, and worked on cars and trucks as well. I loved him dearly.

I pulled the heater from the basement and filled the kerosene heater up. My butt puckered; I could feel the pee coming on. I didn't know what I was doing, but oh well, here goes.

"Vroooooom!"

"Boy...watch out, watch out"

I forgot to move the kerosene heater away from the wall, and it sizzled and scorched the wall. My dad rushed over and shut it off. He never got mad, though, because we didn't have time for anything apart from preparing the apartment for inspection. I damn near burned both apartments down, but it worked. We needed it badly, because at the time, our heat was off. I can remember it very clearly. As we talked and worked on the kerosene heater, before we lit it off, smoke puffed from out mouths.

As I peeped out the front window, a black woman walked up to our apartment. She had long, beautiful hair and a beige trench coat. Red high heels. She looks very majestic.

Had the inspection gone wrong, my sister and I would have been off to foster care. The Social Worker had no clue that I was sleeping on the couch and sometimes in the same bed as my sister, at opposite ends.

We passed the inspection and remained together.

"Are you okay, Master Chief?"—my therapist asked.

She paused after calling me Master Chief, while her mouth hung open. It was like she was saying "Big bad Master Chief doesn't mean anything in here. You need help, buddy."

I leaned forward, curled my bottom lip in, and then rubbed my hands forward and backwards on my thighs.

"Yes, yes, I'm good, ma'am. You know what, thinking back on this now, now I see why I refused to fail any inspection in the Navy. My dad prepared me for being able to thrive in the Navy. My mother did, too."

I swallowed slowly, took a sip of the water and got started again; my face was soaked.

"There's more."

"Please continue."

Cleveland, Ohio, late summer, close to fall 1979

It was cool, tough, and even scary when my dad was at home, but overall we loved and respected him. He was a really good man.

I was still peeing in the bed at eleven years old, chewing my shirt collars, and sucking my thumb. There wasn't a bed to look forward to for me, at our house, just a mat on the floor. I was coming home from the sixth grade one day leaving Chambers Elementary School when something weird happened. Leaving school that year was always depressing for me. I enjoyed the teachers, kids, the food, and recess, but at the end of the day, I had no clue what awaited me when I got home. The fear and bad thoughts arose from my father or if my parents were going to be in a violent fight each day. My nickname is Doubleo!

I can still hear it...

"Doubleo, you feed them damn dogs, you take out the garbage. Did you piss in the bed again, boy?"

I'd stand there, in the kitchen, front porch, basement, wherever my father asked me questions. I couldn't run; to do that was to act like a punk.

"Stay right here, Doubleo," I mumbled to myself. "Stay right here. Deal with it!" Clenching my jaws and flicking my fingers were my only outlet. My butt was puckered but the stress was looking for an outlet, so I peed my pants with no answers whatsoever. Once I wet my pants, my father would become quiet and walk away. I still love my dad to this day, though. He passed away in 1999. Even though I feared my dad, those questions were harsh but there was nothing I could do about that.

"Do your chores, impress your dad, forget love!"

The origin of the first "Loveless emotion."

School was just a few minutes behind me. As I got to the corner of Alder Avenue and 141st Street, I turned right and looked straight ahead. Our house was about a hundred yards down the street. That morning when I left for school, we didn't have any lights, water, or heat. Even our phone bill hadn't been paid. The water we did have was borrowed from our neighbors. My sister and I took turns filling jugs of water up to take a "pot bath" in the living room. No soap! At least for me. I had already stopped caring about being clean and also stopped brushing my teeth; at that point, I already had two broken root canals and my teeth had started to turn green. This is what can happen when your parents get a divorce.

I'll never get married, marriage is for broke people and broken kids.

The electric hot plates shone bright orange and warmed the pots full of water; we would huddle by the hot plates because the heat rising up felt pretty good. The water began to boil so we had to let it cool down before dipping our rags in it. The extension cord running from our neighbor's house kept the hot plates going. Same routine the next morning. I'd get dressed and head out the front door, jump off the three steps, and start a little jog across the lawn. I would think of many things on my way to school that morning. When would I see my father again? Would my parents fight today? Not sure of the answer because my parents' divorce was in full swing; the finances at home were cut in more than half. I knew my dad wasn't coming back; that was wishful thinking. Zeke, my dad, previously worked at Ford Motor Company and made good money. That too was gone now.

That afternoon after school let out, I walked through Chambers Elementary School grounds, pacing up and down the baseball field and again, I arrived at 143rd and Alder, turned right, and walked down Alder Avenue. Same routine. As I got closer to our home, there was a mountain of what looked like trash on our lawn. It wasn't garbage pickup day, so I knew something was wrong. Fear engulfed my entire mind and body and for a moment I thought that I had forgotten to take the garbage out. When I did forget to take it out, my dad lit me up.

I was now in front of 14408 Alder Avenue, East Cleveland, Ohio and our furniture was actually on the front lawn. My dad had already been told to leave the house because of my parents' divorce. Like I said earlier, even though I feared my dad, I loved him deeply, and would do anything to have him back in our house asking me those questions again. It just wasn't the same without him. A woman's discipline is much different from a man's and I needed it at that time in my life. Because of the divorce, not washing up had gotten worse for my little, thick body. I can remember an old trick my friend taught me.

"Hey, Doubleo, if you ever need to leave school early and you're not sick, just put a penny in under your tongue when the nurse puts the thermometer in your mouth and that will raise the numbers on the thermometer."

I did that and she sent me home. I was so dirty that my butt would not stop itching. I remember as a kid, saying to myself, "I don't want to be a husband, ever; the wife will make you leave the house and kids. I want my daddy back."

This was the origin of the second loveless trait: *Fatherless Emotion*

I was now standing in front of our empty home. And on the front door, there was a red letter, an eviction notice. I stared at it for a moment as my brother, sister, and mother walked out of the house. My father took our dog Duke, and our fish-frog, Freddie, had died. My mother strolled down the driveway with a metal, crate-like buggy. It had two wheels and was loaded down with our clothes.

"Here, Doubleo, you'll pull the buggy down the street."

"Aww, Ma—where's dad?"

My mother didn't say anything. I already knew he was gone. Wishful thinking.

I can remember, back in 2006, when I called my wife during our divorce proceedings to see what my oldest son said about our divorce.

"Awww, mom– dad's leaving?"

Those words took me back to when I was eleven years old!

We continued our walk down Alder Avenue, buggy in tow.

My eyes filled up with tears. I took a look down the street; my friends were out there playing tackle football. I loved boxing and football, and every day after school, we'd pick teams and play tackle outside. Not today, though. It wasn't enough that we lost our house, but now I was going to be embarrassed to walk past my friends playing outside. We reached the crowd of kids playing football.

"Yo, Doubleo, where y'all going, man?"

My mother, brother, and sister kept on walking with our clothes. This really hurt. My breathing got more labored so I paused to gather myself.

"We're moving, man," I responded.

"Huh, where to?"

"I don't know, I'm moving in with a lady named Irene."

"Aww, man! Hope to see you again, Dub!"

Rick and I hugged and the other fellas gave me high-fives. I did my best to hide my tears, but I couldn't. My heart beat rapidly as I stood there for a few minutes, not wanting to leave. I had to, though. With my hood covering my head and my hands in my coat pocket, I stalled, confused and embarrassed. No one had warned me that morning when I left for school. I should have known since the utilities were all shut off.

I ran to catch up with my family with my little buggy in tow. It was bouncing around from hitting the cracks in the sidewalk. I was out of breath, my mouth was dry, and I tried to speak with my mother as I caught up to them.

"Ma-ma-ma, what happened, why did they put that red letter on the front door?"

"Doubleo, we got evicted. Just grab the buggy and let's go."

I looked at my brother and sister, just staring at them knowing we were about to be split up. They had already started walking up the street.

It still hadn't dawned on me quite yet; I just could not believe this was happening.

"Ma, where are we going?"

"Me and Donnie are going to the *Townhouse Motel*. Toni is going to live with Lisa, and you'll be staying with Irene."

"Who is Irene?"

"You know, the lady that works at the bar with me."

"Shoot. Okay." I was attracted to Irene. Saw her in the glory-hole. I was replacing my pain of being discarded with a deep attraction to an older woman.

We continued to walk as a family together up to Coit Avenue, turned right, and walked some more. The entire walk was about a mile. As we get to Coit and Taylor Road, my mom, sister, and brother continued straight up Coit, and I turned right onto Taylor. There was no huddle for a plan, they just kept walking and so did I. I peeled off to my right and started walking up Taylor Road.

"Okay, I'll see you all later."

They all responded in unison. "Bye, Doubleo, see you later."

That wave to my family killed me!

I didn't realize it then, but my emotional detachment had started. I stood there for about twenty minutes and watched my family walk up Coit Avenue until they disappeared, and just like that, I was alone. This was the origin of the third loveless trait: *withdrawn and bondless emotion.*

"If you never get closure from trauma as a kid, you become afraid of loss, you let things go by without even caring. You can walk away from relationships and not even care, you forget how to cry, you don't want to cry, crying becomes so painful, you feel it throughout your entire body. That feeling is the opposite of that first hit of crack or your first shot of warm heroin in your favorite vein. You do feel it all over, and you forget about reality, just like dope fiends but it hurts, it's not euphoric. Loss is a big fear for men, which is why we act like we don't give a damn. We become emotionally detached and refuse to believe, in an effort to not go insane. We teach ourselves how to forget about pain as pain becomes a trigger for loss. It's too hard to bear without closure, but not with that hit of crack or that warm heroine dancing in your bloodstream. I wanted that hit so bad!" Later in life, I would meet a mentor of mine. Smokey! Smokey was a murderer and had just served twenty years in jail for killing a man. Smokey was about six feet tall, 190 pounds, solid. He had prison muscles everywhere, even in his square jawline. He had a long scar that ran down the right side of his face from a fight in Lucasville prison. Smokey, smoked Kool cigarettes and had black lips, lips that matched his coal, dark skin but women loved him. We were playing spades one day on his mothers porch, Mildred. Mildred loved Smokey, even though he was a killer and she didn't have not one tooth in her mouth. She calmly sat in her rocking chair smoking a non-filtered Lucky Strike cigarette and watched us play.

"Baby you hungry?"

Smokey acted like he was mad at my bad card playing, I was about fourteen.

"Man, damn, play the right card, boy"—nah, ma, I'm not hungry

Smokey stood up from his chair and burst through the front screen door. We waited for about thirty minutes for him to return. He never did. Tommy and I look at each other. We knew something was wrong. Mildred put her cigarette out and thumped it onto the front lawn.

"Can y'all go check on my baby?"

Tommy and I ran upstairs and found Smokey bent over the tub. It was full of water and he was submerge in it, up to his waist. His legs were bent at the knees on the floor and the needle with a residue of heroine just floated around in the tub. Tommy and I pulled Smokey from the tub and he was just stiff. I don't want a hit of heroine, ever. Smokey was dead! Pulling those bodies from water and peeling them from the deck onboard USS *Stark* FFG-31 wasn't a big deal. Pulling Smokey from the tub, had gotten me ready for that!

Back to losing our home…

I continued my walk up Taylor Road, not knowing when I would see my family again. My mother and brother lived in the motel on Euclid Avenue in East Cleveland, for years it seemed. Most times when I would walk from school during lunch to eat lunch, which was only about half of a mile, my friends would want to come but I'd lie to them because I didn't want them to know that my mother lived in a motel! My sister lived with Lisa, and her living with Lisa felt just as long. That killed me deep inside, I felt worthless. Living with Irene, I now had a nice bed, food, clothes, lights, gas, water, and electricity, pretty nice stuff. Irene and her son were my new family, just like that. I graduated from the sixth grade, lost our house, my family was broken up, and off I went to live with another lady.

I advanced into the seventh grade later that year and my mother would eventually get us all back together in an apartment that had a small kitchen, bathroom, and one bedroom. The small dining room was made into a bedroom, with one bed where my brother slept. My sister and I slept on the floor. That wasn't a big deal, seeing as though I was always sleeping on the floor from peeing in the bed so much. Aside from living with Irene, it had been years since I had a bed. That small apartment we moved into with my mother wasn't good enough for all of us, so my dad took my mom to court but she never showed up and so she lost custody of us.

In custody court, I stood in front a mean white man.

"Your mother is unfit!"

How do you look in the eyes of a thirteen year old kid and tell him that?

I felt like I was given up again, damn!

Late in the eighth grade, my sister and I moved in with my father, down on Hough. I wasn't ready for that environment and what it would bring, but I had no choice. This is really where my demons came out. The adults down there were very dysfunctional and so were the kids that I hung out with, but they were all so cool and strong both physically and mentally. Those were some harsh living conditions. From that experience, every city I lived in and every port we visited, while I was in the Navy, I would always look for the ghettos and the rough, hard, dysfunctional people. The norm just didn't sit well with me and neither did comfort. *Abnormal people, unfamiliar people, and cold, dark environments suited me quite well.*

I became grateful for the ghetto, you know? Most days, living down on Hough Avenue, you had to suppress your emotions, couldn't cry, better not run from terror or adversity. I don't think my mother ever got over my sister and I moving in with my dad, and from that point on, we started to drift apart, including from my brother. My mother and brother remained together for years after that, and the distance hurt like hell. The divorce wasn't all my mother's fault; she had done the best she could. She was very fit!

"Get out and don't come back."

This was the origin of the fourth loveless trait: *Homeless emotion, comfortable in just having a house!*

I had become used to having a house and not a home. That house on 14408 Alder Avenue did that to me. I was now conditioned to pick up and leave in a moment's notice, leaving behind memories, clothes, broken appliances, my heart, emotions and now, any relationship. As an eleven-year-old kid, no one gave me a chance to work things out, so running away from people and issues at that time felt good to me. Longevity and staying power were stripped from my soul and would not return for over thirty-five years, but not really. Running away and suppressing my pain was a way of avoiding hurt, embarrassment, and my desire to physically hurt someone that had refused to explain to me why I had to lose my father, and my floor (bed). I had to learn about loss the hard way. It just wasn't fair.

The Townhouse Motel is still there in East Cleveland. Each time I visit my hometown, I go by and see it. I still have bad memories of that place. I still feel vindicated, though, because when my mom and brother lived there, sometimes the clerk wouldn't let me in when I wanted to see my mom, so I'd break into their little candy machines and steal as much junk as I could.

1500 hours. Veterans Administration Hospital.
She sat back in her chair. It seemed like we were face to face for hours. My neck and shoulders were aching, but I was feeling better.

The empty box of tissue was on the small table to my right. The jug of water was empty, too.

"We need to get you some medicine, Mr. Walker. That was a very touching story. Please sit back. You've told me a lot, you've cried, sniffled, wiped your tears, and emptied your soul. When was the last time you did this?"

"Never."

"Okay, I understand. My thoughts are that you'll need intense therapy—talk therapy. I need to see you for six months first, and we'll see how well you do after that. There will be homework assignments and plenty of follow-ups. My notes are annotated in the computer so they can prescribe your medications—for your headaches annotated here. Is that okay?"

"Yes, Ma'am."

"As you walk out and into the lobby, make sure you schedule more appointments too"

"Yes, Ma'am!"

"And start your medication today!"

When you love right or are loved right, you attract the people that want the right love—if you are not loved or loved right, no one else in your path will receive love from you!

Closed-off men are nothing more than pissed off and deeply hurt little boys!

Respectfully inquire about his past if you want him to open up. If not, he'll live right past you!

When a person loses these three things—a parent, love, and their home—everything in their path will suffer. They'll develop abandonment issues and become very independent and despondent!

– Leon R. Walker, Jr.

My cheating mindset began as a child because of:

- Excessive porn viewing
- A clear lack of not knowing love
- Emptiness
- Discard
- Greed
- Lust
- Stupidity

I extended these characteristics with ease.

It happened mainly because I didn't understand the women that understood me, and I kept running away from them. Men are afraid to step into their feminine side. It's not gay for us to do that, but we fear letting go or losing something that we never even tried or worked on all the same. In all actuality, you'll learn more about your entire DNA and genetics instead of just one side of it."

CHAPTER THIRTY-FIVE

Why I Was Closed Off, Afraid, and Shallow

After my cousins taught me how to kiss, destroying all good order and discipline, all I knew and all that I was interested in were lips on a woman. The first thing that I lost, even though I was five, was my ability to touch, hold hands, and later, cuddle. Not wanting to or not being able to use my hands was as a result of my hands being pinned to the mattress that morning. From that point on, as a child, I had developed a bad habit of looking at the girls' body parts and not touching, I was too afraid to touch. Being afraid to touch came from my teachings too. Apart from what I mentioned in the previous chapters, I was always told to keep my hands to myself, which was the right way to teach me; however, peer pressure caused me to go against all rules, policies, and principles, but more importantly, morals. I was anxious to touch girls and women, and I would do so eventually, but at that point, I lacked tact and I paid dearly for it.

In the early 1990s my ship pulled into Mexico. We hit a nice club full of women. I had a really crazy friend who was very daring and would get drunk and then lose all control. I was with him one night.

"Yo walker, as soon as we get drunk, we're going to grope these sexy Latinas. You in?"

"Hell yeah."

That night, we got the hell slapped out of us. That sobered us up really quick.

I knew better but I allowed a bad influence to get the best of me. She was right to slap us.

The following is one thing that drew me to body parts. I spoke about it in my book, *Broken.*

I was shown how to drill a hole in my parents' bedroom, adjacent to the bathroom; both rooms shared the same wall. The peephole and "glory-hole," as we called it, would be used for years in that house. I was seven and eight years old. The visions were burned into my young mind. The sight of an older woman undressing in the bathroom drove me to only want older women, women that were well developed, and not girls my age that weren't. Seeing these older women caused me to later on only become interested in certain body parts. I lived this way for years, not knowing that I was neglecting everyone I was in a relationship with. I never took the time to explore her entire body, nor her brain. It was an "attraction shock" to me and I never got over that. I did start to learn more about women later on, more things that would make them feel important, attractive, wanted, and desired. But my childhood visions really stuck with me. I will always say and believe this, Loveless Traits start in our childhood, or at least it did for me.

From spending hours looking through the "glory-hole" in my parents' bedroom, I saw that black women never shaved down there. In the porn that I watched, this was true for white women, too. From that point on, I fell in love with women who had hair down there, which was natural for me up until I went to Australia in 1987 and met a white woman who shaved herself down there. I was spooked; it looked odd, and pushed me back on my heels. I had no clue what to do with it, her vagina looked strange. She had to rewire my brain from what I saw as a child.

One other thing that caused a derailment in my childhood was when women would grab my face to kiss me. Although I enjoyed being face to face with them, admiring their looks up close and looking into their eyes, feeling their emotions, smelling their sweet breath, and hearing their heartbeat, I felt trapped and forced to kiss them. As kissing progresses, and by human nature alone, women proceed and tend to feel and want to touch a person's face, neck, head, and hair. Touching is a means of connecting on a deeper level to gain a feeling of being received, and it was in that moment that I found myself feeling suffocated and pulling away. Both grabbing and or pulling away can be a natural reaction depending on what you want or what you have gone through and experienced.

Childhood trauma causes many things:

- Not wanting to undress in front of others.
- A lack of penis discipline.
- Being afraid to engage in any sexual activity.
- Being unsure of sexual abilities and capabilities.
- Bathing and showering alone.
- Fear of falling in love.
- Anger towards men.
- Anger towards women.
- Being overprotective of children.
- Having sex with your eyes open.
- Non-verbal expressions during sex.
- Refusal to get close to people.
- Emotional detachment.
- Emotional dysregulation.

Pulling away from the women became a shock to every woman I kissed. My reaction occurred in this manner because as a child, my cousins would also "grab" my face and force themselves on me. It felt like I was dying, being smothered. I couldn't breathe and they didn't care! Through therapy, I was able to process this nervous condition. They are both deceased now; one was murdered and the other died from alcohol addiction. Other than being forced to kiss them, they were good women, for the most part, so it was easy for me to forgive them. Rest in Peace!

In my book, *Loveship*, at Body Portions (page 228), I go into great detail about the woman's body having many parts, tender and sensual locations, erotic and erogenous zones, and nerve endings. Some women go years before a man wishes to discover and explore other parts of her body. Through the "gloryhole" I only noticed five things about a woman:

- Breasts
- Buttocks
- Lips
- Vulva
- Labia (outer and inner)

Because of my childhood anger issues and being misguided, connecting with a woman's intellect was the furthest thing from my mind. I was selfish and I know that I left many women unsatisfied. Being selfish will catch up to you in many ways, and in some ways, you can push a woman into the arms of another woman. When a man performs oral sex on a woman and doesn't do it right, her vaginal area shuts down, with respect to oral stimulation, and she'll crave it for the rest of her life. She won't go too long without it, either.

Recruiting duty, Cleveland, Ohio, 1993. Local barbershop.
I had just left Shaw High School, talking to the senior counselors about students taking the ASVAB. I pulled up to the barbershop and walked in.

"Sup, Jo-jo, Jo-jo, what's happening?"

"Not much Leon, what's up?'

She was cutting a man's hair and then a woman brought her lunch in. Her high heels gently clicked on the wooden floor in the barbershop. The beautiful woman was popping her gum as he slowly glided across the room. She was tantalizing. She had nice, plump lips;

smooth, brown skin; thick thighs; and layered, short, dark black hair. She looked very familiar. Jo-jo shut the clippers off and spoke.

"Hey, boo!"

"Hi, Jo, are you ready to eat?'

"Like a mutha!"

The lady casually walked up to Jo-jo, whispered in her ear and handed her the large bag filled with two corned-beef sandwiches and a soda. Her perfume smelled delicious, and her hair was amazing. She kissed Jo-Jo and walked away.

I leaned to my right in the chair next to Jo-jo, stroking my chin. Damn, I thought. Jo-jo was dark skinned, with a short haircut, and talked just like a man. She was about five feet nine inches tall, weighing about a hundred and fifty pounds. The clippers clicked back on.

"Okay, Jo-jo, I see you," I whispered.

"Man, you know how I do, Leon."

The woman walked back to her chair and sat quietly, crossed her legs and read a magazine. After a few minutes, she got up and walked over to Jo-jo, and I was able to get a closer look. The lady opened Jo-jo's grape pop for her and handed her some napkins. I raised my eyebrows and sucked my lips in, and then watched her buttocks sway from left to right as she walked away.

"Yea, I know, you got some bad ones, damn!"

"She ain't the only one."

The woman walks back up to us, and just stares, and then speaks.

"Sup, Leon, looking good in that uniform."

"Thank you."

I think to myself. "Oh, shit. Damn, I see her in the bars with her boyfriend, that's why she looked familiar."

Jo-jo casually smirks and keeps cutting. The man in her chair gets up and leaves. "Leon, look, you don't know nothing, you hear me?" She gives me a fist bump. "I got you, I don't know her boyfriend, anyway."

I would visit Jo-jo often to talk to her and get advice. As men, it will keep you stagnant with your woman if you only pay attention to the five body parts like I did. Knowing her body is very important and makes her feel comfortable and confident. As men, we have the capabilities to take women to higher heights of intense pleasure, in and out of bed, by seeing things in her that she or her last partner never noticed. Start with her mind! Sometimes women think about women and on occasion, take the leap and really enjoy it.

If you want to really learn how to perform oral sex on your woman, don't be afraid to speak with a gay woman, both the masculine and feminine ones; they know better than we do.

Don't ever think that your woman is happy with just sex. Their need to be exclusive, honored, and respected for her internal qualities is immense. When she is touched properly and in a respectful manner, as well as caressed and held with care, it connects to her heart and womanhood. What I mean by "respectful touching" is less the aggressive manner, making sure she's open to your touch, and doing it only when appropriate. In public, she may feel that it's inappropriate, so don't argue with her or snap back if she pushes you away; remain calm and bring her in for a warm hug and slight kiss on her forehead. This shows that you respect her character and integrity or even her pain. Women that have been raped and molested will have mental boundaries and blocks and may feel guarded. You might remind them of their perpetrators who were also men, so have patience, be gentle, caring, passionate, and compassionate about this.

CHAPTER THIRTY-SIX

7

I have been single for seven years. On my son's birthday back in 2014 (7), I made a sad decision to be single. A woman that I respected dearly, left because of me on May 2nd (7). The next month, June 1st (7) I decided to move in with a friend and that began my single life of seven years (7). I had no clue what this journey was about at the time, but for some reason, I knew that it would take me a long time to rid my soul of the devil, and in the seventh year, of my single life—2021—things began to become very clear to me.

I have a short story for you...

The fifth month (May) and on the (18th) day is a special day for someone that I haven't been with (while writing this book). On the 18th day and the 5th month (1 + 8 = 9, + 5 = 14 divided by 2 people = 7. She's a special woman, and I can call it this, because this is what truly transpired. She may just be someone that I am supposed to meet to make me see a lot about myself; I'm not quite sure yet, but I am paying close attention.

This chapter will stand alone. The symbolic number seven explains it all and that's the title of this chapter. For years, I had a problem with church and some of the people in it. There were times when the Word spoke to me. One time was at my uncle's funeral. As I sat there listening to the service, I had a colorful vision of each character in the Bible as the pastor spoke; that had never happened to me before. I couldn't do anything but stare at him, as he stood above my uncle's casket and spoke about his wonderful life. I asked my aunt for his name and number, and she gave it to me. I didn't call him but I never forgot who he was. I always thought about that pastor each time I went to Cleveland. He's deceased now. Another time was when I was in the Navy, a friend asked me to attend his services, which I did reluctantly. Again, the colors of the people in the Bible, as he spoke, came to me. I never went back but I should have. I was afraid of the Lord and his Word, but only because I wasn't done with the devil. I am ashamed to admit to this, but I have to. There's more.

Haifa, Israel, 1996

I was surprised to find out that they smoked weed in Israel!

This was the first time I had gelato and had to read something written on a piece of paper from right to left. My ship toured through the Mediterranean Sea, visiting various ports until it was time for us to transit the Suez Canal, on to the Red Sea, and then into the Persian Gulf. Before executing our orders to patrol the Persian Gulf, we were granted some rest and relaxation, so my ship pulled into Haifa, Israel. A great place and very Biblical, as we know. I took a few tours while I was there. That was odd for me, because normally when we pull into ports overseas, I would look for liquor and women. Not here in Haifa, Israel.

Although the first women we met sat outside of a club, happy and energetic, they were freelancers, like straight from Woodstock. These ladies were jumping around, hair flying all over, and I just stood there watching them. They were tall and thick, long blonde hair, red lipstick, blue wigs, very tight pants, pretty eye liner, and nice-smelling perfume. I got excited and fearful, all at the same time. I just knew God was testing me. One lady stood up right in front of me.

"Sup Sailors boy, you guys look sexy as hell."

I froze as she looked into my eyes. She was gorgeous!

"Uh, uh, what's up?"

She was carrying some CDs, and one was the new Biggie Smalls CD.

"Let's go inside, you guys wanna party?"

Before I could speak, my friends and I looked at each other and started smiling. This wasn't good for me, even though I still had my demon, we were close to the motherland of Africa, and in Haifa Israel. It just didn't sit well with me. I knew then that I wasn't as bad of a person as I felt on the inside.

We went inside to dance, party, and drink. They started smoking weed, too. I was in a serious struggle with God and the devil, only because I allowed it. I knew who ranked supreme, but my flesh was weak. Luckily, we didn't take them to the hotel, which, back in the day, was a normal ritual for sailors. I felt like I had accomplished something that night.

The next day we toured many places: the Sea of Galilee, the banks of the Jordan, the Wailing Wall, and the place Jesus was anointed. We all had cameras during the tour, and I was clicking away. The camel ride was fun, but what happened next would shock me to this day. As I spoke to the tour guide, she instructed us of each location and gave us a brief. I stepped out and raised my hand.

"Ma'am, are we allowed to take pictures?" I asked her politely.

"Yes, you can, but not of this right here."

"What is it?'

"This is where Jesus was anointed, so no pictures, please!" Hardheaded sailor that I was, I decided to do it anyway. "Click, click, click!"

The tour was soon over; we ate and I had to get my film developed. I rushed to the local store that developed the film, dropped them off, and came back a few hours later. As I flipped through my pictures, I noticed that three of them did not come out. They were totally dark, nothing showed in the picture. They were of Jesus's tomb!

I was supposed to listen and not take pictures. Listen, Leon—just listen.

According to the Bible, seven is the number of perfection and completeness. Then, after seven days, the whole world was completed and God had done his work, God rested on the seventh day.

Angel number 7 is related to inner wisdom, mysticism, intuition, and inner strength. We all have it, without any doubt! Some people don't agree with the numbering of angels, though.

My life path relationship started back in September of 2020. A path of intelligence, and a quest for knowledge. I, like you, have started this journey months ago, or maybe even years ago. It is now your duty to remain on this path, regardless of the hurt, pain, weariness, doubt, or fear that you will face. People and things will try to disrupt you, but you must stand firm and steady on your number, it's yours.

As I held onto my demons, I lived in the opposite of the biblical seven. All things, I believe, have an opposite, in and out, up and down, happy and sad, good and bad, right and wrong, positive and negative, day and night.

When two people meet and are both interested in the number seven, solitude, peacefulness, calm, tranquility, and serenity will become your core strengths.

As I titled my book *The 7 Loveless Traits*, maybe some of us with these traits can now see more of what you do not have or do have. Reading more will bring you closer to what you feel, who you are, who shall become, and those that you just might be living with, seeing, sleeping with, or even married to.

CHAPTER THIRTY-SEVEN

Loveless Trait #5:
Out of Time and Wasted Time

I had two relationships that lasted six years, and my marriage lasted for twelve years. Even with that, twenty-four years didn't mean anything to me, sadly!

If you think that I am "Love Bombing" you, then stop me, starve me! If I come back, starve me again. If I come back again, only give me a little bit of your time, a very, very small, disrespectful, amount of your time. If I am not sincere about what I am doing, it'll stop after about ninety days. If I am sincere, it'll remain intense but do not give in or offer to give me anything. If it's natural, I will not require any reciprocity. If I get upset, this means that I am starting to like you but I do not like the notion that you have more control than I do. At this point, I am showing you my red flags and you must begin your exit strategy! I am falling now and do not like it.

Visitation...

"I will only come by if you are giving up something. I know you've figured me out, so we'll just play each other. You're lonely, and me, well, I'm just adding my women up. You are needy and I'm bored. Old girl ghosted me, she went out with her boyfriend, but it's cool. I wasn't feeling her anyway. I'll hit you up after we finish our tenth game of Call of Duty, cool?"

This is a true scenario, and you'll fall for it every time. He will come over and you'll act upset until you start to think to yourself.

"Shit, I might as well get some now, who knows when I'll get some again?"

Lovers Lane and Duracell have to enjoy this disconnect between men and women these days, and I know the "bullet and bunny rabbit" vibrators are flying off the shelves. Women are walking horn-boxes. The "Rose" is the new satisfier!

When you begin to feel that time is against you, you lose yourself, you become uninhibited, you rely more on your weak flesh as opposed to your strong but struggling inner-being. You put your "withdrawal" energies into the atmosphere, and just wait. Then they come. The person that wants to and those who will use you, they just wait. Being strong and honest, telling people your all, isn't always a good thing, as it will make you fall prey to those that don't pray.

Young ladies and younger women, aged eighteen to mid-thirties, are in trouble with reference to relationships, concerning "quality time." They are looking at and for men in their mid-forties, even those in their sixties. Sugar-daddies are getting a lot of attention these days. Cougars have lowered their age group to the mid-twenties, too. The average woman hasn't had love made to her in over ten years or more. They've immersed themselves in their job, bank accounts, and grown son. Sometimes she'll let her mind slip down in between her legs.

Out of time affects children, too. This generation of young men are only predominantly interested in smoking weed and playing video games. They hardly have sex or spend quality time with each other. If there's sex involved, it's short, aggressive, jackrabbit style, and lacks passion. Girls look to other girls for attention, spending time together, building confidence, attaining answers, asking questions, and gaining insight. They've gotten over not being accepted, wanted, or paid attention to and have moved on. Young women find the "quality time" in people that pay them attention and because of social media, that outreach has been very far. Strangers now have more connections than familiar people.

Both parents are needed for the teaching of "quality time," regardless of whether both are in the home or not. Kids and all of us need the male and female perspective. When people feel like no one has time for them, neglect begins to grow deep, and feeling odd resonates with them. Accepting the notion of seeming like an outsider can lead to people searching for love in all the wrong places, being lost, and easily influenced or becoming suicidal.

We are who we are, and we like, love, and enjoy what makes us feel good and also what fills us up. It takes time to fall into deep depression and even more time to come out, but quality time can bring people out of that. Society has gotten very soft, and those that are making the rules against stern parenting, were either bullied, forgotten about, left out, or left behind, so they lack the ability to discipline anyone, including themselves. Discipline is looked down on, even in the classroom. It's rare to find people with self-discipline, even self-starters. As tough and as mentally strong as Navy SEALS are, our nation's toughest and strongest men have lost the "self-starter" mentality too. People want everything right now; time has gotten away from us as soon as we wake up unless there's something in it for that individual. Yet, "quality time" has been removed, we want the quick fix. Kids do what they want, say what they want, curse adults out, and barely come to school. If a kid goes to school three days a week, there's a super, great chance that they'll still graduate. Quality time isn't about growth and development, nowadays; it's about greed, comfort, and being lazy.

The "old school" way of raising kids does not work, but the old school way of listening and giving advice still works. It all depends on how approachable we are, and we must slow things down in our minds so we can relate to this generation and their minds. They have tons of information right at their fingertips but struggle to apply it. They always feel "out of time." When we shut them down and out, they resort to drugs, video games, and other like-minded people or weaker people that will take them in and coddle them, instead of telling them the truth and why things are the way they are. Old-soul kids get that and kids without an old soul need it. We've been forced to be afraid to yell and scream anymore. I'm not saying that yelling and screaming was the correct way to lead or parent, but it worked, it kept people aware and on their toes. Expectations were known and met. Up close and personal communication has now been replaced by texting, social media, and silence. This is their "quality time," which in most cases is filled with lies and deception. Who actually does the "LOL and ROTFL"? When people text you that, they're lying most times.

The "click" of a button, "deleting", "swiping" left or right, "read" receipts, and "blocking" have become a way of telling people certain things instead of spending "quality time" discussing our differences and explaining what we really mean. Following and unfollowing now makes people feel important or hurts people's feelings. Quality time is now spent on drama and negativity on all social media, for reviews, views, and numbers. Our heads, hands, and minds are buried in apps, phones, tablets, computers, emails, text messages, and iPads but not in a lover's chest and arms. Reading everything on devices makes people think that it's all true. Our senses have been removed, we cry in closets, hold things in, and are not expressive. People spend more time thinking about negative things instead of opening up. We have a very hard time expressing ourselves, and are quick to consult a physician or psychologists for help or attention. Kids these days don't respect parents or proper parenting, they look for and desire the path of "least resistance" and for people that tell them what they want to hear, versus what they need to hear.

Hospitals have become pumps instead of filters; people have become drains instead of fountains; life has become lies instead of living. This mindset trickles down to people having the inability to face the truth and then grow, to get out of depression and build confidence.

Results of the "Out of Time" Loveless Language Person

- Poor selection of gifts.
- Time for holidays is short and non-adventurous.
- No time for you, but they make sure you have time for them.
- Short attention span. They forget the small things that are important to you.
- Spreading themselves thin trying to please many partners.
- Missing out on many things about you.
- Not learning or studying their partner.
- Poor planning.
- Rushed intimacy, if any.
- Horrible sex.
- Ghosting.
- High divorce rate due to not taking the time to know your partner.
- Mostly unavailable.
- High attrition in the relationship, losing continuity.
- Feeling unwanted.
- Feeling unimportant.
- Short and boring phone calls.
- If they're a good chef but possess horrible "Quality Time" skills, it'll almost always be netfuck and Scram!

Jealous Exes

They will sacrifice time with the kids because they don't want you and your new boo to enjoy time together or go on trips. They'll try to get out of child support so you can't give him or her money. These people will do and try everything to affect your new relationship and the quality time they want to spend with you. They are in deep denial about their jealousy or intimidation.

Ghosting

They "ghost" you after you get off the phone with them and they realize that you don't have any plans to sleep with them or aren't willing to spend money. Ghosters are really "Out of time." They are heartless and spiritless.

As men, we can be alone a lot longer than women. Quality time isn't as important to us, as it is for women. Women will do it but after a while, they'll cave in and settle, most likely for stingy and selfish people, known as:

- Misers
- Penny-pinchers
- Scrooges
- Hoarders
- Skinflints
- Meanies
- Money-grubbers
- Cheapskates

Every time I left women, I made sure to take a part of them with me, something only her and I shared, something that no one else could duplicate, man or woman. I wanted to always keep her open for me, regardless of who she was with. When you do things with a woman for the first time, it's usually special to her, and once you leave, she'll keep that with her for the rest of her life. I knew this, and if she didn't believe it, I did and that was all that mattered. My return was inevitable, in any form. There was no one like me. She'd wait for sure.

This thought process began when I started to become afraid of meeting my karma, a woman just like myself. I've seen women settle for these types of men and women, just to get some "quality time" from them. Settling and lowering your standards for a piece of a person, you'll wind up doing all sorts of things, like:

- Renting cars for them.

- Maxing out your credit cards
- Neglecting real friends and real people that respect you.
- Arguing with family about them.
- Distancing yourself from family.
- Being fooled and tricked.
- Being misled.
- Being kept in suspense.

When I was growing up and probably into the late 1990s, men were the money spenders. Now it's the women. Women offer money and many other things upfront. Lots of people are fine with being taken care of while giving back the bare minimum. Women will complain about this, but continue to give. Women are suffering because of this, and men are suffering because of a woman's past relationship with her lackluster partner. More people are into scams as well, in and out of relationships. OnlyFans has given people temporary satisfaction, both the performer and payee. People don't care about quality anymore; they are selling their souls to the devil daily.

Ghosting also happens when he/she feels like you are too much and are not feeding into their own agenda. They didn't have proper intentions in the first place. These people aren't on your level but will never tell you that.

When your partner doesn't have time for you, you'll begin to feel worthless and then seek help from someone, give in to them, and become weaker and weaker until you do what most women are doing now, giving up and quitting on relationships. I hear it all the time. I have talked to women in their twenties that are even considering polygamy.

Quality Time

I was horrible at spending quality time with a woman. I could plan a nice and beautiful weekend, but never considered what she wanted to do regardless of how nice it was. It was all about me, and what I wanted at the end of the night. I bet ninety-five percent of women want "QT"!

For Her

Listen to her and what she likes; it's usually the small things. Quality comes in many forms: quality listening, quality planning, quality spending, and high-quality sex. I discuss this towards the end of my book, *Loveship*, called "Body Portions."

She's Not a Secret

Quality time is also making sure that she trusts you. It's a peaceful time for her mind!

One key thing is to always introduce her to your female friends. Keep her involved and don't have any secrets. If you have a woman that's been hurt, you must be gentle with her. It doesn't matter how tough she is, she still wants to one day, rest and be a lady for you, not a punching bag. She wants to be desired, not run over, disrespected, and cheated on. I broke many women because of my ways, and while I was good in bed as an entertainer, I wasn't interested in the quality in her mind. Allow her to be your consultant, confidant, and cheerleader.

For Him

Men are really simple. Be fair and give him his space. Giving him his "Alone" time should happen every week, but only two days a week or so. As a couple, it's important to discuss the time he needs; please do not take his time from him. We don't ask for much. We look at "quality time" differently from how women look at it. We just want to be left alone for a short period of time—that's our quality time, and no disrespect in saying that. After that, his thoughts of "quality time" with you will come with more energy and thought. Spread the days out.

Leadership in the Home

Try not to step in the way or on his toes when it comes to the kids. If he has to discipline your kids or his, try your best to not take sides and let him do what he needs to do. This is also part of acknowledging his "quality time" in exercising his leadership skills. Leadership is extremely important to men. We like to be out front and make things happen, and then be celebrated afterwards. Celebrating with you makes it more special. We're both a part of it.

What Constitutes "Quality Time"?

- Walks in the park, talking.
- Learning together.
- Peaceful times.
- Learning different cultures.
- Enjoying nature.
- Discussing trauma and rebuilding from it.
- Sharing each other's passion.
- Being away from others, just the two of you.

CHAPTER THIRTY-EIGHT

Lost Time

You have to determine a time where you'll stop mistreating him because of your past, and stick to it—he must do the same.

Ladies, I applaud your strength, but please stop shielding your heart from a good man! I know all too well what a player is all about, because I used to be that man. When you come off as angry, overbearing, sour, bitchy, or nasty, that's the old you that we meet, but I know better and I must be patient, and at the same time, remain who I am, a strong and understanding man. We know there's a test; just remember that we show up healed and ready with our testimony.

You want to be happy; you yearn for love, respect, and a wholesome life with the man of your dreams. People grow and change, and men also unearth new soil while you remain in the old soil of unhappiness, distrust, and hurt. Women have been forced into a masculine role so much that they have become so strong. They handle hurt well, too well in fact, and it has become a badge of courage and honor for them. As if having to fight constantly is looked upon highly; it's not. This is how you lose good men, or men that are truly and genuinely interested in you. You have become so angry from dating and meeting men that don't measure up or men that have unpacked and sorted out baggage, that you have put them all in the same category.

Your mind is sharp, wicked, calculating, resolute, resolved, sure, and purposeful. You have a lot going on in your head, but give yourself time, vision, and a chance. You have allowed your body to remain starved, which is where the battle and conflict grows and grows.

I know women that have been engaged for ten years and some, separated for even longer. They are afraid to let go, not wanting to give up his benefits, but they still want a man to like or love you? How could he, or why should he, if you're still attached to your ex?

Until you let go of your last man, the next man will not take you seriously about anything. You are losing yourself every second that you hold onto nothing, or things that you can attain for yourself. We look at women in that way, as people that want to use someone else while pursuing someone else. It's not a good look, seriously. If I were dating a woman like that, I would not expect anything from her apart from sex and a good, home-cooked meal. You will not be special to me, and I will not do special things for you. I will be truly "out of time" for you. Women like this are easy to move on from as they're just placeholders. Very harsh, but true! If this is you and you keep asking yourself, "What's wrong with me?" Well, I just told you.

CHAPTER THIRTY NINE

Loveless Trait #6:
Words of Condemnation

As a leader, parent, or spouse, remember how powerful words are.

Norfolk, Virginia, October 2004

We were pierside and preparing to get underway. I was a Senior Chief in the Navy, I had ten quartermasters to lead. My divorce was on the horizon, probably two years away and my stress levels were extremely high. I used very inappropriate words towards two females for not being able to go out to sea. I wasn't very considerate of their families, probably because I was losing mine. I did get into trouble that day, but my career was saved. I was verbally abusing women and those were my charges.

Like I spoke about in my book, *Loveship*, white women hate being called "cunt," and black women hate being called "bitch." Although both names are disrespectful, it was odd to me how those words could be switched up and neither woman would get angry.

Women have a few words that can bring a man to his knees:

Little dick
Trash sex
You can't even find my clit
I played after we had sex

These words are reserved for when you really piss her off. We really don't have a comeback from that, but we try during an argument. It never works.

Yo head game is trash.

Uhh, your boy didn't think so!—she might respond.

Although most times this isn't true after she says it, we never look at our boy the same.

Ruling with an iron fist you will push your partner away. You can't break people down like this and then expect them to want or love or like you; they won't!

Back in 2005, I was written up again for abusive language to other Sailors. I almost lost my career. Had I done that a few years later, I would have been kicked out of the Navy.

Be careful with how you extend words to people. The effects can be permanent. "You remind me of your dad, just like your mom said you would."

Your mother was right, don't trust you.

The kids don't even listen to you.

You can stand to lose a few pounds.

You barely made my height cut-off, I don't usually date short men.

Baby, I blew your back out last night. ——silence from her.

I'on care what you say, none of my ex's said what you say.

Never get family involved if you're a verbal abuser. Most people hurt others with negative words that are related to our physical body and body parts. Definitely, never use the pastor or first lady against your man or woman and please do not berate each other in public.

The Pastor said...

The First Lady said...

If your man or woman goes to church with you and you mention a church member's negative comments, don't expect him or her to ever want to go to church with you again.

Please, at all costs, keep the kids out of your disputes.

Daddy doesn't love you, his friends are more important to him. Mommy left you all here with me, I don't know where she went.

CHAPTER FORTY

Loveless Trait #7:
Addicted to Lesser

People are chasing you, but you are chasing your addiction, the lesser person, the one that gives you the minimum!

This has kept men and women in therapy for years, mainly women!

If this person hasn't gotten over their ex, or has low self-esteem, they will always be damaged goods and hard to date and love. They could have a good man or woman, and still think about the person that treated them like crap. Only one thing keeps their mind and heart at bay, and they are not available for anyone. "Addicted to Lesser" people are attracted to and addicted to narcissistic people. They are accustomed to the "going back and forth with the pain" syndrome, and have a "lonely bonding" spirit causing them to wait for months, or even years, for that certain person to return. Some of these people have everything most people dream of, except their perceived soulmate. Things are important to them, but their lust drives them; they get run through until they become exhausted.

They constantly think of themselves as not being good enough for the person that left them.

I think that everyone has that one person that they genuinely connect with, that "someone" that knows and understands them, but they only come once or twice in a lifetime. Women receive this more and better than anyone. It's really heartbreaking when the opportunity passes them by, and it shows in their face and body weight. Their regret can and will last for years.

These people are hard to pay and pour into, because they are so broken, they fear a healthy spirit because of the paralysis that they've allowed the fear to manifest within them. They are simply not ready to heal. Goodness drowns them. They will run back to the lesser man or woman to fill the void that's most important to them and most of the time it's rooted in trauma. These people are numb, and isolation makes them comfortable.

A lot of times they haven't had either a short-term or long-term relationship, so they don't know or understand why people act the way that they act. They continue to get abused on many levels, creating an abundance of self-doubt. They are slow to act or react, and are very cautious and reserved. They make for boring partners until they get their life in order; that's when you'll discover that they actually have a heart of gold. Recognize this, it will help them. But once they find the right one, they become very trustworthy, honest, real, fun, and loving. Only boring because they allow themselves to take a back seat in the relationship and are apprehensive about leading, yet they know people very well. "Addicted to lesser" types of people have a huge heart, love deeply, and are usually committed and don't cheat. They may seem very distant at first, due to fear and lack of experience; however, you need to take time out to listen to them, let them talk, and then provide proper guidance. They are not shy about learning and have awesome qualities, but no one has been able to bring that out of them. You must be patient with these types of people, as they are wholesome individuals. They take notice of everything, and are very reluctant to hurt others because they've also been hurt. Lesser is a good thing for you and them; they are minimalists with the exception of giving you themselves, totally. They enjoy being exclusive but just weren't shown and didn't know how to because of their insecurities and their need to forgive everyone.

They make up situations in their own mind because of their need. They even shy away from God occasionally. They are without a doubt good people, though.

You're grown and you won't let anyone abuse your kids, but you'll let another grown person abuse you.

CHAPTER FORTY-ONE

Summary

We've talked about a lot, and so I waited until the end to close out some very important things, aside from others.

> The Friend Zone gives you time to develop your own play, to find yourself, regroup, and gather your feelings and emotions, so stop looking at it as a bad thing. It's your time to plan and get into the *end zone*.

Candy Store Friend Zone

It's really called the "Friends-with-Benefits" zone.

I wanted all of the candy. Sweet, sour, curly, curvy, creamy, soft, colorful, everything! Flavors I never had before, you name it. I wanted her. I had no respect for myself and she definitely wasn't going to get any respect from me. I didn't know how. I had it all twisted.

One, two, three women, whatever was possible. The Playboy mansion didn't have anything on the three-story tall buildings in the Philippines, Singapore, or the small, daring women in Thailand. All of those small women wanted their little bodies crushed, and they wanted to satisfy me and thousands of other men. I was treated like a king, a really nasty one, but that wasn't anywhere like being a king. I wasn't wearing a crown, yet; I was a clown.

Cater to my sins, right now. I needed that drug running through my body. That was my unspoken rule.

The euphoria was damning, devastating, deadly, draining, and dysfunctional and it connected to Doubleo, the little boy in me that craved to be desired and loved even if it was for three minutes. You tell me that you love me and I start to hate you. Don't lie to me. You don't know love in the heat of passion. That's my lust you're getting; because I didn't know love while I was falling down, it didn't feel the same for both of us. It couldn't have. You knew my weakness, so don't lie to me. Love doesn't exist for people like me. I knew the truth but couldn't live it.

I was quick to put women in the Friend Zone because I had insecurities, flaws, and many more things. I simply wasn't ready for her. When people put you in the Friend Zone, don't let it hurt you for too long. Yes, it does hurt, but they do it because they are not genuinely ready for you or are not the person that was sent to you, period. But we tend to look directly past this and just reside in our hurt feelings.

The "Candy Store Friend Zone" opens and closes, has discounts, new items, all of that. What if you were with mommy, wanting and desiring the best candy in the store, and all you could do was watch from the outside, see people coming out with big bags of candy, not sharing and poking fun at you because you couldn't have any? Now you're quiet and humble, your head is down, you might even shed a tear. It doesn't feel good to have to just window shop because you're broke and broken.

Your soul is tied for a reason. You're prepared but not ready to go into that store and pick anything or anyone. It's your time to be put in the Candy Store Friend Zone!

Men that put women in the Friend Zone don't know or understand how that feels. It crushes people, especially when you do it without reservation or not knowing how they really feel about you and being put in the Friend Zone. It's a blow to a person's ego.

I was never careful with dating women that were just as toxic as I was, because they were comfortable for me and could not do many things: challenge me, lead me, teach me, hurt me, or damage my ego.

They were just like me, so putting them down, being disrespectful, or anything nasty, egregious or malicious, actions and words, wouldn't work on them. I knew this well. I remained this person for many years, but it set me up for failure when I did meet a wholesome woman and was then put in the Friend Zone. Now that I look at it, and am able to accept that God was showing me the way the whole time, wrath included. It wasn't failure but mercy. I had to learn how to handle that, and then extend it. Be fair, Leon.

Since I was still growing and learning to forgive myself and others, it took around seven years before I became truly, honestly, and genuinely available. Once you meet someone that has been on the same journey as yourself—one of healing, openness, and transparency—the Friend Zone will expose itself. Pay attention to this, as this is where the best relationships and marriages start. Your "energy zones" could mesh.

The best people are sent to us; we don't need to look for them, we feel their presence. When they arrive, that's real beauty and love, and no one can entice you away from that person.

Mating Souls

Some women orgasm through deep kissing and touching,
and not from being penetrated.

We've been taught about soulmates for years without ever discussing how our souls actually mate. It comes from being patient and being honest about not only who you want, but knowing and understanding who wants you, who's sent your way, and how you receive them. We must stop being superficial, stop allowing our greed and lust to lead us, stop thinking with your clitoris and penis; those body parts only carry deep sexual desires, and in some cases, are only interested in a three-minute orgasm. In those three minutes, the rest of your body is still trying to catch up with your soul and spirit, but you don't give it time by repeating and chasing a sexual desire alone. Like I mentioned early in my story, I was just chasing a childhood feeling of a sexual desire, and there was no way that the devil would introduce me to the right person, no way in heaven, because he was sent away and knew nothing about clarity, humbleness, discovery, bigger relationship scales, best friends, and unfolding. In being sent away, the devil took people with him and some of us took that ride through hell. I, like others, was able to get off that ride, walk away, disembark, and exit.

A woman can whip out her vibrator and satisfy herself; a man can masturbate and feel relieved; but their souls and bodies will still crave intimacy, caressing, love, and attention.

When you are with your soulmate and the souls are mating, the orgasms will last much longer, you'll become more verbal. You'll find yourself going the distance, doing things that you don't normally do; you might even cry during intercourse.

Stop Repeating Yourself

I went into every relationship as the same person but expected a different person to see me differently!

Although you've been through a lot in life, it happens when we take on, attract, and engulf ourselves with and in other people's negative energies. This happens through drugs, shared addictions, trauma bonding; through their hurt, pain, disappointments, and letdowns, which are also included in "intergenerational transmission of family violence."

Sometimes you think you're just you and no one else, but you are also your toxic parents and "mirrored hell associates," too. You become addicted to matching their negative energy in an effort to win the war of attrition. Two things happen during this process: turn-ons and turn-aways.

Turn-ons and Turn-aways

You have to stop residing in your old pain and with people from the past and your connection to them. Toxins take time to rid from your body and mind, and just like your visits to the doctor for healing of any type of illness, you must be your own patient by providing yourself with serenity, tranquility, care, clean water, and herbal treatments while in the struggle. We must also pay close attention to our "four hills." More importantly, never be offended when someone tells you that they are "studying you." These are the people who are truly trying to get to know you and appreciate you; they are not trying to find out your triggers to use against you.

Earlier in the book, I mentioned just two hills: uphill and back on your heels. Here are the remaining hills.

Your Four Hills

1. Uphill
2. Back on your heels
3. Downhill
4. Healing

Upon managing your "hills," you must then begin to practice the art of "knowing." You will begin to now start "sowing." It's a new field, playing ground, new soil, and much less turmoil, if any. Knowing and sowing is a part of your healing in an effort to seek, attract, and select better people in your life. In your "four hills." there's a second phase that happens simultaneously, something that I learned in the Navy in 2000 when I was selected to Chief Petty Officer. It works for large groups of people, so I know it will work for you.

Your SFNM has to be solid, legit, and well-thought-out, with intentional meaning.

Storming - Gathering your thoughts, plans, and ways of executing them. In this process, you will cry, doubt yourself, have many fears, and start to grow

Forming - Coming together with yourself, less the brain wrestling. Writing things down, believing in them, envisioning where you want to be, and even the type of man or woman you desire to have.

Norming - Understanding all, your past, current you, and continued success. Being present in your "season" and all "reasons" for your season. This is the time to bring it all together, now that you are equipped with not only your season, but being aware of others'–seasons as well.

Mourning - The person you once were, is now gone. But always keep that person close. It's ok to go out and celebrate the person you left, both the old you and someone that caused you to find your SFNM!

You don't have to hold onto the 7 Loveless Traits. Your "four hills" and the SFNM alone, or with your current or next partner, works, and this is what will transpire.

Two-Sided Love Affair

- Clear and understood intentions
- No fear
- Discovery
- Intense love, loving, and love-making
- Proper presentation
- Quantum leaps
- White flags appear, instead of red flags
- Gaining things in common
- Proper alignment
- Energy shifts
- Mind shifts

Triggers

Know what triggers your partner. Past triggers do not have to be current triggers. Different people understand you in different ways.

Lonely Bonding

This keeps people in the same everything for many years. You remain in each other's misery, afraid to let go, not wanting to see someone else make them happy when you couldn't. Afraid to go into an uncomfortable zone and start over. Being each other's mental slave, pain slave. Immersing yourselves in the battle of the sexes, combating each other, continually seeking revenge, sleeping with your backs facing each other, fantasizing about someone else, turning yourself on, turning them off. You now enjoy killing someone's spirit and soul while keeping them alive. You never thought that you could just watch someone die from holding them back, huh?

I am now free, for the flowing and glowing of me and my woman. We'll fall for each other, safely, tenderly, without any reservations, declinations, hesitations; we know each other well. Rise in grace, share our mercy. Now it feels so good to exude the ultimate form and display of respect, being, and living exclusively, and receiving what you feel, giving back reciprocity on all levels. Once you are in alignment, you understand your past, the hurt, pain, your destruction, and everything that comes with being a Don Juan, like I was. You attract people that want what you want, like what you like, see what you see, and know what you know. You'll be surprised at who you'll meet when you free yourself from all judging, fears, and your negative soul ties.

And in the end, "ugly" is just a word; fear is what you make it, doubt is what you accept during weak times. People are who you encounter in a certain season, know what their season is. Beauty is a way of life: how you live, how you treat people, how you show up. Beauty starts from birth, from the core of who we were born to be. It will not forsake you; you forsake it by listening to bad influences and residing in sin.

This book was inspired by a beautiful presence that remained with me my whole life, GOD, who gave me the strength to tell the truth and not feel ashamed.

CHAPTER FORTY-TWO

Healing of a Narcissist

Narcissism is defined as having an excessive interest in or admiration for oneself and in one's physical appearance. Many more traits these days. The word "narcissism" has been around for many years. Narcissus, in Greek mythology, was known for his beauty and fixation on himself and outer appearance. From my research, the word "narcissism" has been used in many instances dating back to not only ancient Greek times but also as recently as 1897, 1899, and even in 1914. They say that narcissists cannot change, but I know for sure that if you want to, you can manage your traits and illness, but first through talk therapy. Understanding them and managing them will go a great way in helping you control the urge. Wanting, knowing how you are hurting, desiring clarity as to why, and acute awareness...is an exchange. It's your choice. I started my research, which I immediately followed up with management, back in 2015. But before that, there was first a shock and an awakening, as far back as 1991.

In 2015, seven months before my retirement, after I had completed my physical, I bumped into one of the physicians while walking down the hallway in the hospital. She was a heavy-set white woman with short, blonde hair. Her cheeks were rosy-red, and she had scars on both of them. She had really thick hands and wore square glasses with black frames down to the tip of her nose. The doctor was about five- feet-six-inches tall, and she had a husky frame and also rather large breasts. She was slightly hunched over with a slow walk. We chatted for a while, during which she took out her pen and scratched her scalp. There was a clipboard in her right hand.

"Hi, Doc, I guess I'll be seeing you shortly."

"So tired of this place. I see you're retiring. Good luck. You know, I really hate being a doctor!"

I took a couple of gulps and just stared at her. "Really?" I said finally.

"Yes, can't wait to get the hell out of here."

We sat in her office after her assistant took my vitals. I was very uncomfortable. She was by far the roughest, most callous person I had ever met in the medical field, and I couldn't wait to leave. I found what she said extremely odd. Moments later, I had a visit with another psychiatrist. I felt rushed out of there.

I headed home and decided to call a friend.

"Mike, something is wrong, man."

"Huh, whusup, my man?"

"I don't know, my head isn't right."

That day I was driving in an area that I had lived in for six years. I came to a light and just stopped. All of a sudden, the area didn't look familiar to me. I became delusional, and really frightened. My memory was leaving me. It did for twenty to thirty minutes. I called my buddy back and he recommended that I go to the hospital, but I couldn't. I didn't even know where the Veterans Administration Hospital was, and I had lived in the Great Lakes area on and off for the last twenty-one years. My mind managed to slowly come back to me, and I drove through the green light and headed home. I didn't think it was that serious.

In 2018, three years later, a friend called to check on me

"Leon, what's up my man, how you doing? Haven't heard from you."

"I'm good, my man. What's the deal?"

"Naw, cuz, you don't sound good, bruh!"

"Honestly, I'm fine."

"Go back to the hospital, go and get checked out by my boy, let him put your paperwork in again and wait for them to call you."

"Okay, I will, man, I will, I need it."

A month or so later, I went back to the hospital. After hours of brain scans and discussions with the psychiatrists, she informed me that they had misdiagnosed me back in 2015 and that I had been taking the wrong medicine for three years.

"I'm sorry, Mr. Walker, this should have been caught back in 1987!" She just stared at me, and after I looked through all of her degrees displayed on the wall, I stared back and dropped my head in my hands.

"I see you were aboard the USS *Stark* back in 1987. You should have been on medication back then."

I tell you this story because the medical professionals that misdiagnosed me had been in the medical field for over thirty years and had seen, diagnosed, and treated thousands of Soldiers, Sailors, Marines, Airmen, and the Coast Guard. Why is it that people believe that medical professionals can do no wrong? Well, as you have seen, they did not properly diagnose me. I have to take some of the blame as well, as I probably didn't tell them everything. Was I an experiment? It was easy for me to ask myself that question, as many veterans that I had come across were either mistreated or not treated at all. They were told to wait and come back, were disrespected or abandoned, and either died miserably or committed suicide. My suicidal thoughts from childhood hadn't come back, but there were hints of them here and there, and I was scared. It's better to do your own research and call yourself out; then you can begin your healing process by praying with your friends and asking God for help. There are some great and caring medical professionals out there, lots of them. You are not alone!

With my NPD, I was also dealing with the five stages of PTSD.

The Five Stages of PTSD

- Impact or Emergency Stage
- Denial/Numbing Stage
- Rescue Stage
- Long-Term Reconstruction Stage
- Short-Term Recovery Stage

My additional diagnoses

- Severe PTSD
- Acute Stress Disorder
- Sympathetic Trauma

God had my back. Visit your doctor. Listen to what they say, but more importantly, do your own research, study your parents, know your genetics, your DNA, family history, and why things are the way that they are. Don't be afraid to call yourself out. Ensure that you read, pray, and ask others to pray for you. Repent and stay the course. Be grateful, forgive your perpetrators, love and respect yourself, find a new journey, and stay on it. Then help people, give back, be truthful, honest, serve all who you come across, and love God.

CHAPTER FORTY-THREE

Evolution of a Narcissist
and the Collateral Damage

- Molested at age five
- Started chewing my shirt collars at age five
- Started wetting the bed at age five
- Stared sleeping on the floor at age six
- Started sucking my thumb at age six
- Addicted to older women by age seven
- Addicted to porn by age seven
- Lost my virginity by age eight
- Started sleep-walking at age eight
- Started working with my mother at the bar that she managed at ages eight to ten
- Saw God's eyes in the sky at age eight
- Started working out to make myself bigger and stronger at age nine
- Made my mind up to join the military at age nine
- Fondled by male family member by ages eleven and twelve
- Bullied at age eleven
- Started bullying my sister and other kids at age eleven
- Stopped taking showers by age eleven

- Stopped brushing my teeth at age eleven
- Developed anger issues by age eleven
- Suicide ideations at age eleven and twelve
- Lost confidence and self-esteem at age twelve
- Started stealing at age eleven
- Started smoking cigarettes at age eleven
- Parents divorce proceedings started during age eleven
- Family broken up at ages eleven and twelve
- Stopped wetting the bed at age twelve, in the seventh grade
- I stopped crying around 1977
- Sent to live with another family at ages eleven and twelve, and received a bed
- Moved back with my mother at age twelve, and went back to sleeping on the floor from ages twelve to thirteen
- Started stealing again at age twelve
- Attended court for possible transition into the foster-care system at age twelve
- My father received custody of my sister and me at age twelve
- Felt disowned by my mother at age twelve. She didn't show up for court
- Moved to the inner city of Cleveland at age twelve /thirteen
- Learned how to shoot pool and make money at age thirteen
- Hired for my second job at Angela Mia pizza at age fourteen
- Started sleeping on the couch until age fifteen
- Lost my first job due to being underage. I was fourteen
- Got my third job at an after-hour house on Hough Avenue at age fourteen
- Started paying bills at my dad's house at age fourteen
- Bought my first prostitute at age fifteen
- Failed the ASVAB four times ages fifteen to seventeen
- Turned out by my first girlfriend at age fifteen

- Finally got another bed at age fifteen
- Contracted gonorrhea at age sixteen
- Started stealing even more at age sixteen
- Started smoking weed at age sixteen
- Passed the ASVAB on my fifth try and joined the Navy at age seventeen
- Got my fourth job at General Electric at age sixteen
- Bought prostitutes in Milwaukee at age eighteen after boot camp graduation
- Started stealing in the Navy at age nineteen
- 1987 sent to see my first psychiatrists at age twenty-one
- Moved my girlfriend from Cleveland to San Diego at age twenty-one in 1986 to 1987
- Developed PTSD at age twenty-one when deployed to the Persian Gulf
- Entered treatment for mental health and learned about my narcissism at age twenty-one in June/July and October/December of 1987
- Discharged from the Navy in December of 1987
- Re-entered the Navy in March of 1988
- Started cheating in my relationship at age twenty-three
- Met my first "perceived" narcissistic leader, who put seven people in the psych ward
- Won Sailor of the Quarter and Sailor of the Year Awards in 1989
- My driver's license was suspended in San Diego from excessive, unpaid tickets at age twenty-four
- Deployed to the Persian Gulf in February of 1991 and told my girlfriend that I didn't love her, and that that morning I was going to cheat

- Called back home from Japan to San Diego to hear my girl-friend tell me that she had a boyfriend. It was 5:00 a.m.!
- Arrived back to San Diego from deployment in May of 1991
- Started stalking my girlfriend throughout the year of 1991
- Asked her to marry me and she told me no in 1991
- Got her back late in 1991
- Asked her to marry me in again 1991, and she said yes
- Called off the wedding in June of 1992
- 1992, Screened for recruiting duty and needed a score waiver, ASVAB scores were too low
- 1992, Attended Navy recruiting school in Pensacola Florida. Set back two weeks after failing tests and coming to class under the influence
- Left my girlfriend in our apartment in 1992 and moved back to Cleveland. I just walked away
- Slept with many women from 1992 to 1994 in Cleveland Ohio
- 1992 to 1994 started drinking excessively
- 1994 a drunk driver totaled my new car
- 1994 signed up to become a stem cell donor
- 1994 selected Recruiter of the Quarter
- 1994 selected Recruiter of the Year and ranked #3 of 144
- Got engaged in 1995, and then cheated
- Got married at age thirty, and my wife and the woman I cheated with were both pregnant at the same time
- May 1995, my first daughter was still-born
- September 1995, second daughter was born out of my infidelity
- Both daughters would have been born in September
- Both daughters had the same first name
- Within one year, 1995-1996, I went from 190 pounds to 245 pounds

- 1995 ordered to seek medical attention and psychiatric help for induced stress which caused depression and excessive weight gain
- 1995 and 1996, failed miserably at recruiting and was ranked #144 of 144 recruiters
- 1996, ordered to attend court for paternity, denied my daughter
- 1996, received paternity test and ordered to pay $361 per month in child support
- 1996, denied and neglected my daughter for six to seven years
- Started running and went back down to 190 pounds
- 1998 selected Sailor of the Quarter
- 1999 selected Sailor of the Quarter
- 1999 my wife made me pay off the tickets I had in San Diego. I paid $1400.00, and got my driver's license back. They had been suspended since 1989
- December 1999 to April 2000, I was selected Sailor of the Year on five different levels and ranked #1 of 25,000 candidates
- April 2000, Selected Sailor of the Year. Ranked in the top 4 of 90,000 Sailors on the East Coast
- May 2000 Screened for instructor duty and needed a score waiver, ASVAB scores were too low
- August 2000 Selected for promotion to Chief Petty Officer
- 2003 Selected for promotion to Senior Chief Petty Officer
- January 2004 selected to attend the Air Force Academy Leadership school
- January 2004 set back for one week in leadership class. Attended class hung over and failed the first test
- February 2004 selected Vice President of leadership class for 400 students
- 2004 received Letter of Instruction for abusive language to my Sailors

- 2004 to 2005 received my second Letter of Instruction for abusive language and poor leadership
- September 2004 ranked #1 Senior Chief onboard USS *Kearsarge*
- September 2005 dropped in ranking because of my poor leadership and abusive language
- Promoted to Master Chief in April of 2006
- Received divorce papers in April of 2006 on the pier in Norfolk
- 2006 Screened for Recruit Division Commander duty and needed a score waiver, ASVAB scores were too low
- 2007 Set back in Recruit Division Commander school for five weeks due to failing tests and missing class
- Summer of 2007 ordered to pay $2400 per month in child support
- December 2007 my divorce was final
- February 2008 ordered to pay $1200 a month for my two sons for child support
- 2007 Child support went up for my daughter to $741
- 2007 selected for the Command Master Chief program
- 2007 to 2009 selected orders to my first ship as a Command Master Chief. I was responsible for 300 Sailors
- 2009 to 2012 received orders to Great Lakes Naval Base as the Command Master Chief; we employed 10,000 people
- 2011 I became a match to donate stem cells for a woman in need
- 2011 Started a mentorship program in an elementary school in Great Lakes for fifth graders
- January 2012 donated stem cells to a woman in need
- August 2013, I had a heart attack and received a stent in my artery
- September 2013 entered rehab for five months for my heart attack

- 2012 to 2015 Received orders as the Command Master Chief for Naval Service Training Command; we employed 42,000 employees
- March 2014, I told my girlfriend of six years I wasn't going to marry her. She left
- May 2014, she moved out
- August 2014, started mental health therapy with psychotherapist and walked out
- December 2014, Re-entered psychotherapy treatment.
- December 2014, I walked out of psychotherapy and psychiatric treatment
- January 2015, I started intense inpatient therapy for seven to eight months
- 2015 Diagnosed with mood disorder, nightmares, anxiety, and oral fixation from my childhood. I was misdiagnosed also.
- 2015, I retired from the Navy
- 2016, became a teacher in a military academy, high school
- 2018 re-diagnosed for severe PTSD, sleep apnea, arthritis, migraines, and a host of other things
- In 2014 total paid child support for three kids was $323K
- 2018 published my first book, *Broken*
- 2019 published my second book, *Keeping Kids Safe from Porn*
- January 2019 received back pay from my misdiagnosis, $9.5K
- February 2021 published my third book, *Loveship*
- March 2021 started writing my fourth book on narcissism

Fail Familiar

> *I have failed many times in my life. Often, I would let the failure bully me until I realized that the failure didn't have a mind until I gave it a mind and energy, which then gave it legs and life. I figured out then that I wasn't a failure but I was failing at being familiar with the failure. It wasn't*

failure, it was a clear lack of proper preparation and giving up on the first try. Failure can happen a hundred or even a thousand times; it's how many times we allow the failure to bully and defeat us and then give up or give in, that is the issue. It does not have a mind of its own. The more you prepare, the less you are bullied by something, or anything that does not have a mind, feelings, or any kind of direction of its own. This also applies to people.
– Leon R. Walker, Jr.

God Will Welcome You Back

God created us to be kind, loving, beautiful, happy, caring, intelligent, seekers, visionaries, leaders, followers, growers, developers, passionate, to have self-worth, confidence, self-validation and many more things. God did not create us to be narcissistic.

We become narcissists because we are a product of our environment, which includes unhealthy people with unresolved issues and unhealthy living habits, such as rapists, murderers, child molesters, and so on. I truly believe that we can go back to how God created us even though it might be tough, because ***God will welcome us back*** with open arms and guide us to how we are supposed to be. Outside of God's creation, nothing is permanent; those things are merely shadows, addictions, comfort zones, or even hard-to-live-with traits. You can exchange!

My First Psychiatric Visit

During my first psychiatric visit in 1987, all I heard in the psychiatrist's office was, "disorder—disorder—disorder!" I didn't know what "personality disorder" or "narcissism" meant. I didn't even want to talk about it. The psychiatrists looked at me as if I knew. I didn't. The USS *Stark* FFG-31 was the same class of ship that I was on with USS *Reid* FFG-30, at the time, during our escort services of the battle group in the Persian Gulf, so the compartments and sleeping arrangements that I walked through, onboard the USS *Stark*, with the dead and burned men, had become a very dark and scary contrast for me. From the time my ship left Hawaii, en route to our homeport of San Diego, for about one week, I tossed, turned, cried, had many sleepless nights, and a lack of appetite. I could not tell my friends onboard what had just happened to me, the news that the psychiatrist gave me; they would not understand. My nightmares were intense; the dead bodies just would not leave my mind. The smell of burned flesh seemed like it was rotting my nostrils away.

The crew that I hung out with were all aged twenty-one and over. Our crew was tough, strong, funny, and we supported each other. But after leaving the psychiatrist's office, I felt weird, even crazy, and not a part of them anymore. I felt aloof and disoriented.

I did my best to hold it in but I couldn't. I was once a very outgoing, young Sailor, trying my best to be happy, to love the Navy, but not my girlfriend or anyone that I was dating or would encounter. She and they had to save me from me. My girlfriend back then was really good for me, my heart, soul, and my spirit. I wasn't good for her and could not give her what she needed. I struggled with love and care but enjoyed hanging out, drinking, partying, flirting and even cheating. It was like something was feeding my soul and it didn't feel good at all, but I made it feel good.

I wonder how many of my friends onboard the USS *Reid* FFG-30, had personality disorders too. As odd as it may sound, I wanted some sort of company. That thought made me comfortable, but I just could not say anything to them. I'm sure my fire team all had PTSD, but the psychiatrist barely spoke about my PTSD, so I didn't think I had it. Did he not speak about it on purpose? I don't know. I do know that I suppressed it along with those excessive feelings for the next twenty-eight years. Had I become too strong mentally, too uncaring, weak, but felt good about those lesser than I was? I believe so. I was ashamed, embarrassed, and had to hide it, for sure.

I was due to re-enlist on December 20,1987. I had just spent six months on a deployment, four months in the Persian Gulf, and they wanted to send me right back to the Persian Gulf for another four months, onboard the USS *Harlan County*. This ship was an LST (Landing Ship, Tank) and carried Marines. Whenever the Marines were deployed back then, they were most definitely going to get blood on their hands and even die; I could not handle that. As much as I loved the Navy, and knew that I would miss my friends, I told the CC (Career Counselor) that I was getting out of the Navy. He was pissed, but I was sick. When you plan to stay in the Navy and then prepare to re-enlist, there's lots of paperwork involved along with re-enlistment bonuses, gifts, praise, and so on, but I didn't want any of it. I just wanted to go, walk away, or what they call it now—just *ghost* the Navy, and I did. After going through my parents' divorce, losing our home, being molested, and feeling dumb, stupid, and lost, I had to create a whole new person. I couldn't let anyone know this. No one! I was sick and crazy and no one loved me, so I had to love myself at any cost. What did my childhood give me and who injected these demons in me?

I separated from the Navy on December 21, 1987 and went back to Cleveland. I told my then-girlfriend that I would return. I lied. I didn't have any plans to return to San Diego!

The career counselor gave me my paperwork along with my Honorable Discharge and gave me a few choice words:

You motherf&*ker, Walker, don't ever come back!

I lied to my friends and family as to why I got out. Don't admit any weakness, I thought. *Just lie, Leon, just lie.*

I left the Navy and my girlfriend right there in San Diego. My running away had begun, and oddly, it felt good to me. I was showing my weakness anyway, but never admitted it. I stayed home for seventy-seven days and came back into the Navy in March of 1988. With the psychiatrist not speaking about my PTSD and just concentrating on my personality disorder, he allowed me to act as if I didn't have PTSD. One thing was for sure: by avoiding and not deeply educating me about my personality disorder, PTSD, and childhood trauma, and other areas where he thought I needed help, I was forced to learn and research my parents and what they might have possibly passed down to me.

Neither of my parents were ever diagnosed with anything, but from my observations, research, reading, asking questions, and studying their past ways, I knew that something was wrong with me, because of them. I noticed one major thing during my study of them.

Both of them didn't or couldn't process the pain that they imposed on others. Events during my childhood were repetitive: spankings, drugs, shunning, divorce, ghosting, and in some cases, dissociation, whether directly or indirectly. It seemed like they felt good about seeing others hurt, and then seeing others happy. I never understood that. I was a kid then, so my understanding was not fully formed. Then, for many years, I was the same way. They were both also very mentally strong, overbearing, and even extreme. For some reason, I was extreme and overbearing too, but my happiness was always short lived in whatever I did or attained.

My parents were awesome people, though. I miss them both dearly and would not have it any other way if I were able to do it all over again.

I am not clinically qualified, nor am I a psychiatrist, psycho-therapist, or social worker, but my parents may have had a PTSD trait passed down to them from slavery, along with some sort of personality disorder as well. One of my family members, who is a social worker (not performing), seems to think that my mother could have been a narcissist. I still love her, though, and she was a great woman and mother.

Thank you, mommy and daddy. I am you and proud of it!

CHAPTER FORTY FOUR

Mental Health Record

MENTAL HEALTH RECORD
CHRONOLOGICAL RECORD OF MEDICAL CARE

Location: Psychiatric clinic, Great Lakes, Illinois. VA hospital. Date: December 2014 @1000

Current Meds: None.

Psychotherapist notes and Iraq and Afghan post-deployment screening: PTSD is possibly positive. Pt states that he served almost 32 years at this point and doesn't feel like he has any issues. Watching television reminds him of his past experiences in the Persian Gulf. He feels emotionally numb often and is afraid of bad things happening to him or people close to him. Pt seemed restless and didn't want to remain in the session.

He also stated that his girlfriend told him a few times that they had sex and he doesn't remember the next morning. He feels like she's lying to him.

He asked to leave and then walked out after 18 minutes. Pt should have been treated for PTSD at age 21, but the psychiatrist back then only spoke about his personality disorder.

Pt seems to suffer from avoidance. Follow-up session scheduled for next week. We'll further discuss PTSD as well.

Session concluded @1018.
Anticipated length of treatment: INDEFINITE.
Psychotherapist, Jane Doe, M.D.

MENTAL HEALTH RECORD

CHRONOLOGICAL RECORD OF MEDICAL CARE

Location: Psychiatric clinic Great Lakes, Illinois. VA hospital. Date: December 2014 @1000

Current Meds: None

Past Psych meds: None

Session focused on a lack of relationship with family in Ohio and past negative relationships. It also included speaking about his lack of emotions, ability to care, and avoidance. In addition, we spoke about the Pt knowing when relationships are becoming unhealthy.

Right now, I recommend that Pt refrain from being in relationships and to track his anger.

Pt stated that he enjoys women very much but has a hard time being committed and faithful.

Pt stated that he feels ok with being vindictive, unapologetic, and not trying to better his relationships with certain family members. He has a bad habit of holding on to anger. He admitted that it feels good to do that. Pt also stated that he feels like he's wasting his current girlfriend's time. Doesn't want to get married but doesn't know why not; he says it could be from his childhood. They've been together since 2008.

Pt was a no-show for numerous appointments during the month of December. Session concluded @1130.

Anticipated length of treatment: INDEFINITE

Psychotherapist, Jane Doe, M.D.

MENTAL HEALTH RECORD
CHRONOLOGICAL RECORD OF MEDICAL CARE

Location: Psychiatric clinic Great Lakes, Illinois. VA Hospital. Date: January 2015 @0830

Current meds: None

Past Psych meds: None

Subjective: Mr. Walker is a 49-year-old AA. Our first session started with me asking service member why he missed appointments last month and walked out of the psychotherapist's office last month as well, December 2014. His response:

"Doc, with all due respect, I was irritated and it's hard for me to know and feel that I have mental issues. I've hidden it for years and I can continue, so I felt like she (the psychotherapist) was a waste of my time."

Objective: Service member began talking and looking around. His mood seemed good. We began with how he was doing. He seems to be doing okay. Pt seems to be better at remaining in the present and letting things go. Pt seems clearer about past behaviors but doesn't have plan in place. He shows fears about being in a relationship. He stated that he still doesn't trust himself. Pt sees the importance of being in a healthy relationship with himself, prior to beginning one with someone else.

Neurological:

Cognition: Alert

Anticipated length of treatment: INDEFINITE.
Psychotherapist,Jane Doe, M.D.

MENTAL HEALTH RECORD

CHRONOLOGICAL RECORD OF MEDICAL CARE

Location: Psychiatric clinic, Great Lakes, Illinois. VA Hospital. Date: January 2015 @0830

Current meds: None

Date: January 2015.

Objective: Pt attended appointments for anger management, personality disorder, and PTSD. Pt walked out after 50 minutes.

Intense talk therapy highly recommended, with medication for other issues.

Aside from other mental disorders, Pt suffers from severe PTSD, which has been untreated since 1987. Meds prescribed.

Pt doesn't make therapy a priority. He became agitated when I mentioned this, but also seemed unbothered by missing appointments.

Subjective: Nothing to report.

Session ended @0920

Current Meds: Sertraline, Prazosin

Zoloft, Wellbutrin.

Anticipated length of treatment: INDEFINITE

Psychiatrist, Jane Doe, M.D.

MENTAL HEALTH RECORD

CHRONOLOGICAL RECORD OF MEDICAL CARE

Location: Psychiatric clinic Great Lakes, Illinois. VA Hospital Date: January 2015 @0930

Current meds: Sertraline, Prazosin, Wellbutrin, Zoloft

Objective: Pt showed up on time but was smelling of smoke again.

I informed him, "Before you come in here, can you not come in smelling like smoke?"

Pt looked at me for a few seconds, became quiet, looked down, and then obliged. "Sorry about that, Doc."

"Doc, you know what, when I say "sorry about that," it doesn't seem sincere, so, I'll say..."I'm sorry!"

"In the past, I would never say...I'm sorry, to say that, was very, very hard for me. Now, it feels kind of good to hear that come from my mouth...thank you, Doc!"

"I think it's how you responded when I said...I'm sorry." You were gentle in your response, like...you really believed me. That helped me."

Pt has regrets about spanking his kids and not talking to them more. He stated that his kids told him, "Once you get angry, dad, about something we just did, you bring up old things and the punishment gets worse for us."

He admits to passing down trauma and how he was verbally abusive. Today, Pt came in, in a much better mood. He smiles when we talk about his upcoming retirement. He also informed me that his ex-wife didn't like him smoking. When she would ask him, he'd lie about it. At first, lying about smoking cigarettes bothered him, but after a while, he liked lying to her!

Pt admitted that he was wrong in smoking since she didn't like it, and then lying about both. He also stated that she didn't deserve that.

Subjective: Pt speaks highly of his mother but goes deep into a depressed mood when speaking of how his mother left him, how they lost their house, and her drug addiction. He seems to praise his father more than his mother, so I asked him why?

"Doc, my father saved us, me and my sister. It just seemed like he cared more."

Pt was agitated today after we spoke for about an hour or so.

We spoke further and in great detail. Pt understands more of why he was angry with his mother and stated that, in the past, he looked to his many girlfriends' mothers, as a mother for him. He mentioned that when he hurt women, he now realized that he hurt their mom first, and then possibly other family members. After further discussion, about Pt's mom, it seemed like a light bulb went off. Pt sat up straight and thanked me. He never blamed the drugs that his mom did, her trauma and lack of love from her own mother (his grandmother). Pt stated that his mom and grandmother had a very toxic relationship, which in turn hurt his sister's growth and development. The men in his family were treated like royalty and not the women! Pt stated that he saw this often. His grandfather was verbally abusive to his grandmother, and his uncle was, too, her only son. Pt mentioned that not only was he still upset with his cousins, and babysitter, but an uncle that touched and bullied him as a kid. We then spoke about forgiveness, Pt stated that he didn't know how to forgive them, or anyone, and he held onto anger for many years. We also discussed forgiveness!

Pt wanted to find the good person within himself, and said he was tired of living the way that he was living. Pt mentioned that his promiscuity was a learned trait from childhood and the Navy. After further discussion, Pt realized that he was using others and his childhood as an excuse to continue living a life of toxic behavior. Pt struggled with taking responsibility and stated that certain vices helped him cope.

Session concluded @11:30

Current Meds: Sertraline, Prazosin, Wellbutrin, Zoloft

Anticipated length of treatment: INDEFINITE

MENTAL HEALTH RECORD

CHRONOLOGICAL RECORD OF MEDICAL CARE

Location: Psychiatric clinic, Great Lakes, Illinois. VA Hospital. Date: January 2015 @0830

Current meds: Sertraline, Prazosin,Wellbutrin, Zoloft

Objective: Pt came into the session antsy. He stated that he felt ok from the last session and had a lot on his mind. He thought a lot about what we talked about in the last session and was finally able to forgive his perpetrators, the uncle, his cousins, and his babysitter.

"Doc, when my cousins would kiss me, they'd grab my face. It hurt and I didn't like it. Now, when a woman wants to kiss me, some of them grab my face and I pull back."

"Remember, forgiveness. Not just forgiving them, but in forgiving, you must also let go of the pain that's associated with it, too. New girlfriends are not the cousins that hurt you."

Subjective: Pt informed me that he was tired of having to be so strong for everyone and felt like no one was there for him. He also stated that sometimes being there for others, made him feel a sense of power and entitlement. One of his commanding officers told him that he wants to, or needs to be, liked, and that he was humble to a fault. Pt didn't like hearing this. He stated that he uses his heart and toughness for gain and not love and that it's been a long time since he cried.

I informed Pt that he doesn't always have to walk around like the "Big, Bad, Master Chief."

Pt sat back when I told him this. Pt laughed, and smiled, and opened up even more. Pt became more comfortable when he realized that it was ok to not be so tough or strong all the time. Pt informed me that he was always walking around guarded and that he never told anyone. That drained him, but he didn't know why he was afraid to let go.

Pt eagerly wanted to tell me more about his mother and how I helped him forgive her. He stated that, over the weekend, he went into deep thought about his childhood and could vividly remember how loving, caring, and strong his mother was. Pt stated that his mother did a lot for the family, the kids in the neighborhood, and would always take him to football, baseball, and karate practice. She was the one planning the birthday parties, Halloween parties, and the Friday night parties that his mom and dad had. Pt became very emotional, and broke down and cried! His mom put him in the Cub Scouts and she was his first Den Mother.

Session ended @1030

MSE: Pt came in casually dressed with good hygiene. Thought content: No suicidal or homicidal thoughts

Anticipated length of treatment: INDEFINITE

MENTAL HEALTH RECORD

CHRONOLOGICAL RECORD OF MEDICAL CARE

Location: Psychiatric clinic Great Lakes, Illinois. VA Hospital. Date: February 2015 @0900

Current meds: Sertraline, Prazosin, Wellbutrin, Zoloft

Objective: Pt walked into the office, stating that he felt ready to change. He immediately told me his dad's name was Zeke. He smiled while speaking of his dad, like he had now smiled about his mom. His dad was an alcoholic and that in the past, he drank often. Pt mentioned that, as a kid when his dad drank, he became fearful of his dad.

Relationships: Pt mentioned that it felt good to have women depending on him, but when they did depend on him, he became upset.

Pt didn't always compliment his girlfriend, hardly ever, but would get upset when other men would compliment her. He mentioned that he was afraid to admit that he was jealous, instead of admitting that he would do something to make her or any of his girlfriends mad about other men making them feel good.

Pt stated that his parents' divorce made him fearful of marriage. He also stated that his divorce was filed 31 years after his parents, but in the same month, December of 2007.

Pt admitted that he found it easy to walk away from all of his relationships. He did it numerous times. His last girlfriend, they broke up in March of 2014, and she left in May of 2014. They were together for six years. I asked him how he felt about it, and he stated: "Nothing at all"— then he just stared into space.

After a few moments, he stated that he felt bad because she was good to and for him. He was cool with her mother, sister, aunts, and her son, and he still has a good relationship with all of them, especially her son.

Pt admitted that in the past, walking away felt good and it didn't bother him at all. He could easily walk away and then start over, without a problem. Pt also stated that he felt like he could come back to anyone, at any time. Not once did he ever process their hurt.

Session ended @1100

Anticipated length of treatment: INDEFINITE

MENTAL HEALTH RECORD

CHRONOLOGICAL RECORD OF MEDICAL CARE

Location: Psychiatric clinic Great Lakes, Illinois. VA Hospital Date: February 2015 @0900

Current meds: Sertraline, Prazosin, Wellbutrin, Zoloft

Objective: Pt walked into the session with a straw in his mouth. We discussed his oral fixation again. He stated: "I know, I know, Doc. I'm dealing with a lot."

Pt removed the straw but had a hard time throwing it away or letting go of it. I asked him why, he stated: "Since you're a doctor, it's easy to listen to you, kind of hard, but easy since I think you're helping me. It's hard for me to listen to women, outside of here, but I am working on it. I realized that all my ex's were just trying to help me and not control me. One thing for sure that I struggled with, is that I had to win all of the arguments. It hurt like hell to admit that I was wrong, or to even feel like I lost an argument, that was really hard. Pt immediately went into discussing his ex-wife.

I noticed the oral fixation comments earlier in his record, dating back to 1987.

Pt states that he feels detached.

Subjective: "Speaking of controlling, my ex-wife was very controlling. The word and act of controlling is a huge trigger for me, Doc. Now, while going through therapy, I realize that she too, was just trying to help me."

"I can start to see how I was hurtful to women."

I asked why they divorced, and he stated:

"It started with me cheating while we were engaged. How sick and stupid is that?" Pt sat back on the couch and laughed.

"I laugh now to keep from crying. Maybe I just need to cry and let the emotions out, right? I...I...laugh at my stupidity, it doesn't hurt as much when I laugh. I do know the deal. My cheating became very embarrassing. I hurt an entire family, my wife's family, and some of mine. You know what was odd to me, Doc— is that some of my family members, when I told them that I cheated and the woman that I cheated with, got pregnant, they said...well, you weren't married!

Doc, along with my own issues, I have family moral issues, too! My ex-wife had great morals, and I wasn't used to that. Trauma in the Walker family is accepted and just dealt with, we need family therapy."

"Have you heard of 'Trauma bonding,' Mr. Walker? We'll talk about that in our next session.

Pt was given homework. To write down his issues, how he plans to deal with them. Pt stated that he hates homework and wasn't sure if he could complete it.

Session ended @1100

Anticipated length of treatment: INDEFINITE

MENTAL HEALTH RECORD

CHRONOLOGICAL RECORD OF MEDICAL CARE

Location: Psychiatric clinic Great Lakes, Illinois. VA Hospital. Date: February 2015 @1000

Current meds: Sertraline, Prazosin, Wellbutrin, Zoloft

Objective: Pt walked in, in a very good mood and without a straw in his mouth. I informed him that he's doing better with his oral fixation, and his therapy. Pt smiled and laughed.

We began our discussion about trauma bonding.

"Doc, I should have attended therapy a long time ago, but I was afraid to hear the truth, and also, I was in denial that there was anything wrong with me, and my family even though the signs were there. My sister and I are very close and my older brother, over the years, he and I drifted apart. I gave him money while I was in the Navy and he never gave it back. For some reason, that made me extremely upset. At the time, he told me "the check's in the mail" and it never came. I felt like he just took me as a fool and used me. I met my other brother in 1978 or 1979 and we became very close, we're still close now. I needed that male figure in my life at that time, and he was there. He gave me money instead of taking money from me."

Subjective: "I might be the only one in my family that is going through any kind of therapy. Neither of my parents did, and as far as I know, their parents didn't either. Someone has to make a change. My family is strong, most times, too strong, both the men and women, but that has become our weakness. As kids we went to church but not that much. I was never forced to go, and when I did go, it was for the little girls, milk, and cookies. I remember that, but nothing about the Bible. One of my girlfriends knew the Bible well, but her actions didn't match how we were living. I was the common denominator of that, but I blamed her. That was just my excuse to stay out of church and she allowed me to. As far as my family, I think we bonded on not bending, mainly not submitting to anything, but definitely not submitting to and for each other. The older siblings still argue, fight, and probably even hate each other. If my dad and uncles were still around, this kind of crap would not happen. They held us together. My cousins living now, we don't talk, we don't go out, we don't eat together, nothing. We don't even talk on the phone. The Walker family used to be pretty large in Cleveland, and even in other states. Since my family roots are from the south, Alabama, North Caroline, South Carolina, Mississippi, I feel like we are suffering from an untreated trait or condition, called slavery PTSD!"

The next session, we will talk about the components of a relationship.

Session ended @1130

Anticipated length of treatment: INDEFINITE

MENTAL HEALTH RECORD

CHRONOLOGICAL RECORD OF MEDICAL CARE

Location: Psychiatric clinic Great Lakes, Illinois. VA Hospital. Date: March 2015 @1000

Current meds: Sertraline, Prazosin, Wellbutrin, Zoloft

Objective: Pt came in ready to go. He stated that he looked up the components of a relationship and has never used them. I asked Pt if he is still single and he stated:

"Yep, and you know what Doc? It feels good to be alone. I realize, since you told me that I should not be dating, that I had been in relationships for almost 32 years and I was carrying all of my hurt and anger forward. I never knew that."

Subjective: "It hit me that since I was a cheater, that my ex-wife would not allow me to hold her accountable. I get it now. It was like 'pay the bills and shut up.' I was unfair in the marriage so my word wasn't any good. I hated that but didn't have the strength to fight back or even say anything. She didn't say those words, but it was the way it was."

"Doc, reading about the components of a relationship and learning about them, I realize that my relationship and marriage were off balance. There wasn't any kind of structure. I wasn't disciplined at all. I was only disciplined at work but not home. I held my kids accountable but not myself. I expected certain things of my ex-wife but why? I was the one that destroyed my marriage. Her and I never had intimate discussions, and that was my fault. I wasn't a man at all. I was a little boy, acted like a little boy but didn't want to be called a little boy. One day I told her 'you're not going to keep treating me like a little boy'—and she said, 'yes I am.' I wanted to drive somewhere and cheat right there! Thinking back on it, she knew that I wasn't the way a man should have been, a man like her father but I saw it as an attack. It hurt to hear her say that and to be treated like that but she was right because my actions proved her right. I felt like I was just a bill payer around the house. We weren't very loving to each other. I know she tried, but I just wasn't loveable, not on *any* level. I was just acting like a husband and I wasn't performing as one. There weren't any components in our marriage, at least from my side of it. She kind of told me what to do when things needed to be done, and I did them, knowing that I would later drink or smoke because I was angry about feeling like I was being controlled and I even lied about the smoking. I would do sneaky things to satisfy my cravings, but I really did them to hurt her, not knowing that I was hurting myself. It was like my little payback to her. I even began to enjoy lying to her. Looking back on it all now, because of my infidelity, I was being stripped of my power because I didn't deserve to be the head of the household. I truly believe that God shifts power to the one that can save a family and keep it together. I wasn't selected for that role and I didn't deserve to be, so I was forced to take a lesser role because I was already taking my family down the wrong path with my leadership, or lack of it. I can thank God for that role now, but before, I fought it and relied on my addictions to make myself happy."

"As far as my ex-girlfriend, I see now that I was very selfish towards her. She told me that I was controlling and that she was scared of me. At first, I became upset, because I do not like being called names and if it's true, I shut down instead of accepting it and working on it. But now with therapy, I see that she was right and I may have been projecting my anger from my marriage onto her. I did take pride in helping take care of her son, and I enjoyed that but felt like his dad was allowed to not do his part. We never really discussed how I felt, and that was my fault. I should have realized that she enjoyed seeing me as a father figure for him. That would have been a compliment, one that I needed, compliments motivated me, I was foolish with that! I should have cleared things up instead of holding them in. Also, what I am learning is that I constantly needed my ego stroked and didn't allow her to ever question me or ask where I am or where I am going! It was like since I'm doing this for you and your son, then I can do whatever I want, and that was wrong, especially since she didn't know how I was feeling. She was a good woman, a really good woman! She left in May of 2014. When a woman knows that she deserves better and has wasted her time with me, she says little things, off and on, she'll mention marriage, ask me what's wrong with her, why we haven't gotten married, etc., trying to let me know. I was really good at avoiding questions and not caring about the impending doom. I know now that when they ask those questions, it's because they feel unimportant, they feel lonely, like they aren't worthy. I know now that I made her feel empty and unwanted. My actions showed that. She's happily married to someone else now."

Session ended @1130

I let the Pt talk the whole time since he seems to be getting much better. He does want to date but needs therapy much more. He listens more now.

Current meds: Sertraline, Prazosin, Wellbutrin, Zoloft

Anticipated length of treatment: INDEFINITE

CHAPTER FORTY FIVE

The Narcissist's Recovery Plan

- *YOU*...need to read *The Four Agreements*!
- Believe in God and let the devil go.
- Admit to who you are.
- You shouldn't just go into therapy, you must connect with that therapist.
- Fear the old you.
- Practice what you learn in therapy and implement it.
- Believe that therapy works.
- Pay attention to the pain that others receive from you, and know why.
- Learn and practice forgiveness.
- Stop using your dysfunctional past as a reason for your future gains.
- Stop running away from responsibility.
- Learn how to take blame.
- Learn how to apologize because you're wrong most of the time.
- Realize that the people in your life deserve better.
- Realize that you will always be in some sort of therapy and be okay with it.
- Realize that you are addicted to hurting others and stop doing it.
- Fill yourself with what you expect from others.

- Learn what humility is.
- Admit that you are needy and greedy.
- Be alone so you can truly and honestly find yourself.
- You're not smart.
- Realize that someone might harm or try to kill you.
- Acknowledge that you are no match for a real and strong person and don't get upset, get better.
- Understand that no one is lower than you, but you are lower than them, currently.
- Be mindful.
- Stop dating.
- Learn humanity.
- Go no-contact with others so that they don't have to see, hear, or smell you.
- As weird as this may sound, ask people to ghost you, to bread-crumb you, gaslight you, gray rock you, shun you. Either way, if you do it or not, it's going to happen. This will be a part of your karma, so you might as well try to get used to it, because it's coming.
- Apologize and mean it.
- Your issues aren't personal to them. We do not get a certificate. Our job, after therapy and rehab, is to make sure those we hurt, get their certificate. Below are some things for both men and women to incorporate into their life and relationships. These are the thoughts of two great men, but women can use these as well.

CHAPTER FORTY-SIX

Rolemate to Soulmate

I learned the following twelve pieces of knowledge from my brothers, Gerald Thompson and David Noble, whom I met in 2021. I love these two men, unconditionally, and have only known them for just a few months. These men are sincere, genuine, real, honest, and upright! Strong and powerful—pillars in their home, community, and in the minds of many. I needed to at least hear these thoughts and idealism, as a child, but I didn't pay attention, nor did I take heed. I have always had great examples in my life, as a kid; my parents, my brothers, sister, uncles, grandparents, and cousins, so the teachings were there, I just allowed myself to be lured into hell.

THE SEVEN L'S

Like

This is the beginning of the creation of connecting, as I sat and listened to Mr. Gerald Thompson speak. He stated that "liking" is basically the visual of love. The one thing that begins the process of creating love. We have all been at a point in our lives when we like someone, and where we feel like they're a great person in what they bring to the table. We make that known and so it begins. You have two people that generally like each other and they hopefully begin down a path to a long-lasting connection. Which brings us to the next part, when they find out that the person they like has something they can teach them, and each other. I think people can and will, climb in love with the "likeness!"

Lessons

The person that you like, now you are learning that this person has something you can benefit from. They have something they can teach you, as you start a deep, desired connection. On the flip side, there's the lesson part that they can teach you and also the part where you are willing to learn from that person. This is invaluable, cherished, and adored.

Leverage

This is taking that lesson that you have learned from that person and using it as a benefit for you in that relationship. It's the balancing sequence and synchronization that both are not only aware of, but look forward taking heed to. Equality, understanding feminism, and proper submission for dual compatibility, cohesion, and comprehension.

Example: If I know a person is more emotionally stable than you are, then you can use that lesson as a part of leveraging what they have to offer. I now know what they bring to the table and I also like what they bring. I am now able to leverage and utilize this in the relationship.

Listen

Being intent, having standards, and being able to respond accordingly and intelligently, with results. Do they genuinely listen to you? Do you feel as if this person has the best interest at heart? Do they take time to make sure that you are in a good and solid emotional state? Is there reciprocation in that connection in which you are able to listen to them and you want to learn in those conversations?

Lean

In your time of need, your time of distress, can you and do you feel supported by the person you are building a connection with? Is there reciprocity in which both of you feel in tune with one another? Listen and lean is where most relationships falter. Ready and approachable, being above reproach without judgement in your time of need, your time of distress. Can you and do you feel supported by the person you are building a connection with? Is there reciprocity in which both of you feel in tune with one another? Listen and lean is where most relationships falter without these two.

Love

Should never be under certain conditions. At this stage you have established a strong connection. You feel in tune with your partner. You feel supported in the relationship and it allows you to not fall, but grow in love. During the creation of this connection, your feelings may lead you to believe that it is love. And it very well could be. However, it is important to access the creation of the connection and be self-aware enough to know where the two of you stand in the partnership.

Longevity

Now that you have created a viable holistic partnership, it is important to do and recycle each step as you move throughout your love.

THE DIVINE FIVE

Faith

Mr. David Noble knew that he needed to be more of a complete, well-rounded man. Developing a relationship with his heavenly father was crucial, and when meeting his wife, David knew that she was further along than he was on a few levels. Before marriage he needed to be completely in tune with her. He needed to be equally yoked with his future wife to start their union and countenance. He could not put it off any longer, so David started getting into the teachings of the Bible. Once he did that, he felt more freedom. That caused him to reverse engineer his thoughts and pour in more faith into his world. Putting God first as his guide to cherish, protect, adore, admire, appreciate, and love his rib!

Family

How David wanted his family to look. From traditions and a mental wellness standpoint, him being the head and his wife being the neck. To be the best possible father and husband, a better steward and better protector. If he got his faith right and kept the lord first and built that into his life, now what does it look like for his life insurance/ensuring?

Fitness

Extremely important. We only get this one vessel. In order to be operational for his family, physically, he needed to be operational for himself. Visiting the doctor often, desiring a head to toe physical, with his wife present, or if she wasn't, immediately informing her of his diagnosis, both good and bad, as a means to always be prepared for any uncertain occurrences. He knew that longevity would be crucial. In 2013, David stopped drinking alcohol. He wanted to be sober minded and sober bodied. In order to protect his family and his vessel, substances could not go into his body. Eating better as he got older, with a history of diabetes and hypertension, he had to be very careful to have longevity to be the best version of himself and family.

Finances

We live in a capitalistic society, so David needed to be more disciplined to acquire the things needed to provide for his family. Whether it be owning a home, being a great steward of his finances, teaching his children about how to handle finances, what it looks like for their legacy when he's no longer here and his wife. Having the opportunity to do the right thing and to be a philanthropist, helping those in need also.

Freedom

To do what you want to do with intention. The freedom of peace and holistic thought as he moves on to provide for family and others who share like minds. This can look different for anyone, but for David, it's freedom of mind to operate with the best version of himself in all previous four. Without the freedom of the mind, the previous practices of the divine five, David found that he wouldn't be operational or maintain peace within his family. These are all interconnected. Without a strong family, there's no strong union, nor good faith, mind, or finances.

CHAPTER FORTY-SEVEN

Gateway to Safety

I would like to thank the reader for going on this journey with me. I know, for some of you, my medical records made your stomach curl, or even triggered some of you. That wasn't and isn't my intent. If that did happen, I am sorry! I had to face and release my demons!

Strong and aware people are created through the strong storms created by weak and unaware people!
– Leon R. Walker, Jr.

I concluded my twelve months of therapy sessions in August of 2015, three to four days before I retired from the Navy. I retired on August 7th, 2015. I am now equipped and over the months, I could feel myself unwind, like loosen up. I have a very loving relationship with God, through conversations, understanding, and believing. There was a time when I didn't believe in God and I finally realized that it was because I didn't want to get myself together, to be pure and cleansed. I had resided for so long in negative vibrations, that the negativity became my norm. I was a "functioning dysfunctional." All of my life, I actually held onto anger, my past, my evil ways, and sickness. I was killing myself without it being suicide.

If you're still waiting on someone, you're being ignored!

I am extremely aware now, and I choose now, not to be the way that I was. God is the most forgiving and only creator, and he will always receive us back. He created us to be nice, caring, loving, passionate, compassionate, understanding, courageous people, and many more things. We weren't created to be evil; we weren't created to be narcissists, murderers, thieves, abusers, bullies, etc. Our environment and others created who we are, and who we became, in the ill-mannered sense. So, you can exchange and if you choose to exchange, you will be welcomed back to the way that you were created. It's tough to do, and hard at times, very hard; just stay the course when you decide. The temptations will always be there, and so will the devil! It takes each and every awakening hour; it takes days, months, and even years of practice, implementing what you've learned in therapy, and then implementing those changes. You cannot go back to those old ways, places, and people, or you'll never change. You can put yourself around those people, go to those places and ways of misery to test your mettle, and if you can do that and come back out successful, that will show your growth. You must not avoid that!

> *If I tell you about my past, it's not to give me a pass, but to show you my strength so that you can see what I can get past.*

Work on the hard things that were toxic but felt good to you: gas-lighting, bread- crumbing, gray-rocking, love-bombing, the silent treatment—you know, those things that made you feel good and powerful when you hurt someone; and then sit in the temptation, don't act on the urge, and defy it. When you sit with it, you'll experience what you have been putting others through and it will not feel good; it's not supposed to. Normally when you hurt others, it's a release for you. I know this all too well. Try holding that in and not being able to release it. Most narcissists are only courageous to those that they think are less than themselves, those with low self-esteem and those that lack confidence. Women that are vulnerable, on the cusp of giving up, letting go, those that have had enough but deep down inside, want just "one more chance"; women who yearn for their dad, men that yearn for their mother, people that search for love and understanding, women that were abused by their mother, whether it was passive abuse or not, men that had fathers who called them weak, and other names. Those people become pin-cushions, targets, and they empower the narcissists by accepting fear, fear of losing them, fear of letting them down, fear of not being good enough. Narcissists become abusive parents to their partners!

Find the courage to inflict change on yourself, by way of honestly wanting to be better and by parting ways with the devil. Doing so, just fighting the temptation, you will feel your body catch on fire, you'll feel those demons in an uproar—let them extinguish themselves—hell, they extinguished the good in you, find the time and ways to pay them back. That's why I called it "inflicting change"—because it does hurt. If it's anger, manipulation, seduction, needing your ego stroked, whatever it is, know that it's there but do not act on it. This comes with exercising positive thoughts when the negative thoughts come to you, the ones that ruled you, the ones that destroyed your family, the ones that broke up friendships and relationships. I think it's great to go to and through therapy with the partner that you are abusing and disrespecting. I don't know of anyone that's done this. People go through marriage counseling, family counseling and while doing so, some even sit in counseling as a possible narcissist, but no one says anything or that person hasn't been diagnosed. I walked out of marriage counseling and never went back. I felt like my wife (at the time) and the counselor were against me. Thinking back on it now, they should have been.

In attending counseling and while issues, addictions, truths, and secrets are being divulged, make sure to not hold that over their head. This is a time to apologize to each other and mean it, to understand them, their past, and their attempts to change. This goes for both partners, because each has had their times of hurting the other person. This is not a time to go back and forth, yet to communicate and while doing so, look in each other's eyes. Enter your partner's soul through their eyes. For some, this will be the first time of genuine eye contact. I didn't do this in marriage counseling, hell—I looked at the ceiling most of the time. Highly disrespectful and disconnected. I was dead wrong!

I'll be honest. Words touch me, they bring me back to normality; words ease my soul. I knew this but was afraid of sharing it with the women that I dated because I was still in the mindset of not wanting to change. It's not just the words that work for some men, but *the delivery*. This may sound childish, but I know it has worked on me, many times. Although I didn't totally come back around, my response and actions were much different and so was my demeanor at that moment. I knew what I needed to change and to grow, but I fought it. She knew what to do, and when she did it, it was hard to be a bad person or resort to being a mean person.

"Leon, we're not doing this, okay?"

Her voice had to be very soothing and not in a condescending way. Such as:

"Leon, I'll let you cool down, and then we'll fix it, okay?"

"Cool down" and not "calm down"—there's a difference.

Calm down can be interpreted as the aggressor having anger issues. Even though I did have anger issues, the difference in words really helped me bring it back to normal.

The aggressor or abuser has to learn how to do this, too. Especially when they are in their character or when they feel *the rage coming on*. I needed to practice quite often.

> *If you have a partner and you feel alone, you have a roommate. Break the lease or charge them rent. At that point, two things will happen. They'll really leave or agree with the fact that you suggest that you all are better off, being roommates.* That's the answer to your question about— *What are we doing here, Leon?*

I'll end with this. Therapy is very important. It is, and it's a must so that you can heal and gain clarity and awareness. There are two parts to therapy, and this is where most people fail or remain in therapy, still having tons of questions and feeling the same, even after years of therapy.

Part 1 - Initial therapy

The first part. You must realize that while in therapy, your time spent there has been spent talking about your partner, your mother, father, kids, or their parents. You spend hours on that couch. Then you leave, go home, to work, or back to the same person you just spent hours talking about, and then re-living your triggers all over again. You remain in the spin cycle. You've lost your sanctuary! Being home with that person, the negative vibrations consume you, the reminders attack you as soon as you walk into the house, whether they are home or not.

Part 2 - Rehabilitation

Rehabilitation is an extremely crucial pivot-point and mind-shift. Rehabilitation isn't just for drug addicts. Rehabilitation is for people that are addicted to others, addicted to someone's trauma, addicted to time spent with someone, regardless of how broken they are, addicted to their smell, the way they walk, the old times, addicted to the time you all first met—addicted to the memories. That person is now deeply embedded in your DNA, your bloodstream; they have become a part of you. You've left and forgotten about friends and family for them; you've simply become them. They are a part of your daily routine of thinking, and even planning. If you find yourself as the type of person that I mentioned above (man or woman), what you are experiencing is your most dominant Love Language, "Acts of Service," and you have ignored their most dominant Loveless Language, "Acts of Disservice." Your rehab is for your compulsive behavior, tied into your impulsive behavior and a need to satisfy, impress, or draw people back to you.

For some people that are in therapy (and this isn't always, and not true for all), I think you develop a means of remaining close to the person that has you in therapy. The conversation is usually consumed (and based on) them since they are the root cause of your problems (addictions), and it becomes a comfort zone. The mere fact that you can or have confided in the counselor—that you still love him or her, makes it seem like it's an okay little secret. Their office has become a place where you can cry freely, or even with a counselor that may make you think about good things about that person, even though you know it's over! Either way, if you are there alone, and your partner knows, then you were alone before you arrived. Be careful as to not allow the office where you are supposed to grow and get over someone—become a dwelling for your little love which will keep you holding on! Go into therapy strong and come out with your crown on straight, and then start your 12 Affirmations and Promises to Self and Loved Ones!

CHAPTER FORTY-EIGHT

12 Affirmations and Promises to Self and Loved Ones

1. *Promise. To* your friends and people you love, that you will make it through. This is not just for you, as the person that has hurt you or is hurting you, has hurt your family, too. Family and close friends have to realize that they are in rehab with you.

2. *Don't avoid any mirrors.* You need to see the scars and then see them disappear. It's important to notice your skin changing, eyes clearing up, etc, so that you realize that that person was killing you from the inside out.

3. *Find her/him again.* YOU left YOU for someone else. Start doing what makes you happy and attractive.

4. *Inventory.* Your lost items, to include family, friends, hair, weight, money, credit score.

5. *Count the amount of negative "Ings"* in your life and remove them. CryING, procrastinatING, waitING, stalkING, overeat-ING, complainING, smearING, damagING, hurtING, shakING, wonderING, wanderING, hyperventilatING, lurkING, sextING, textING, lying, etc.

6. *Take a picture.* At your worst, keep it, and do not look at it until you feel like you are really and truly changing. You should expect results if you are being true to the people you love.

7. *Write letters.* To God and instead of asking him to send you the right man or woman, ask him to send *you*, who he created *you* to be.

8. *Promise to stop doing self-harm.* We all know people that self-mutilate, and we can see their scars, but you must stop "self-mentally mutilating" your brain. Your scars are hidden.

9. *Ask powerful prayers, to pray for you.* I am not talking about putting this on Facebook, but the real people that know how to pray, with meaning and intent.

10. *Get yourself two jars.* Label them "Did" and "Didn't." Put money in the "Didn't" jar, every time you didn't think about that person, and put money in the "Did" jar, every time you did think about that person. You select the amount. It can be pennies or dollars. The more you become confident, change the amount that you put in each jar. Make this a month-to-month challenge for yourself and tell the people that you love, about this self-challenge. Ask them to donate as well. After you are done with the first month, the money earned (because you should be in the plus now) can be used for a good cause, your own shopping spree, or anything to celebrate.

11. *Remain/Do/Don't.* Remain around people that want to see you recover, people that uplift you, people that celebrate you, people that tell you the truth, people that don't judge you, people that have high standards, morals, integrity. Join positive groups (Yoga, walking, bike riding, baking, the gym, painting, etc.).

Don't avoid triggers. If you do, you will think that every little thing is a trigger. If you encounter a trigger, laugh instead of being shocked and/or crying. Sanitize your closet, jewelry box, your car, anything that has a scent that reminds you of him or her. Stop hoping and wishing and asking everybody "What do you think about this, or that!" Do not masturbate and think/drink about them. When or if you drink, give your cell-phone to the people you love and trust so that you can't text that person. Drinkers are thinkers!

12. *Forgive them.* Remove your anger towards them and don't allow them to kill any more of your brain cells. Understand that you were too good or even too much for them, and that they reduced you to a shell of yourself. They were there to do damage to you, carnage, insult, assault, and for some, they've given you thoughts of suicide. Count their 8 ways of giving and see what you come up with. Lastly, turn your journal into a book and start helping other people. Don't just write a journal and hide it, make it public—some of it.

Below is a certificate of completion for those entering and completing their rehabilitation. We attend therapy, but after graduating, we stop right there. Rehab is crucial in total recovery—I truly believe this. You have to take your rehab seriously, and this certificate as well. After you have completed your 12 Affirmations and Promises, celebrate! Celebrate with those you love, and have them present the certificate to you. This is the trophy that you now take back from the person that took your time, your heart, your money, your mind, mental health, dignity, and pride!

CERTIFICATE OF COMPLETION
Rehabilitation and Recovery
For
The 12 Affirmations and Promises to Self

This award is to acknowledge that YOU have Thoroughly, Genuinely, and Honestly completed and implemented the *REQUIRED* 12 Affirmations and Promises to Self course. During the process of giving *YOURSELF* daily affirmations, you have also continued to be proud of yourself for instituting healing, perpetuating the act of forgiveness, self-love, self-respect, confidence, self-esteem, awareness, hindsight, understanding, wherewithal and foresight. Throughout the weeks, months- and years, you have endured many things: abuse, neglect, being ignored, doubted, misled, lied to, wronged, cheated on, walked away from, unappreciated, dismissed, and devalued. But through it all, the hellfire, the tears, hard times, and broken spirit, you were forged into a weapon of mass development! You will not be forgotten, yet esteemed, respected, and highly regarded. Those tragic events, although hurtful, painful, and at times devastating, have now been defeated and mastered, and now you must forgo the past, share your new gift, empower all, celebrate YOU, and NEVER turn back, yet run away as you successfully repent. It is now very important that you relish your newfound life, lifestyle, accomplishments with those that have been on this journey with you, as God has witnessed. ALL, CONGRATULATIONS NOW…tell your story, write a book, speak at events, give back, lose your shame, show up, show out, shine, be divine , fabulous, virtuous, hot, and beautiful—YOU'VE EARNED EVERY OUNCE OF IT!

THE BEGINNING

MEN SUBMIT TOO!

As a man, struggling with words, actions, fears, inabilities, and fear of submitting, I would like to ask that you try changing the wording. Change what you call it; *SURRENDER!*

SURRENDER—to give up completely.
To give (oneself) up into the power of another, especially as a prisoner. The power of greed, lust, drugs, anger, over us!

In my book *Broken*, "Survival Instincts of a Child"— Doubleo saw God and then hopped off of his little Huffy bicycle and ran away from God. I did so for many years. Little Doubleo and Leon are now back together again, as *ONE*—running towards God. He has welcomed me back, took away my fears of him, and will welcome you back as well, regardless of what disorder, addiction, or vice you have! We are *STILL HIS* creation, and no other!